HOW *to* USE

Microsoft®
Office 2000

Sherry Kinkoph

A Division of Macmillan Computer Publishing, USA
201 W. 103rd Street
Indianapolis, Indiana 46290

SAMS

Visually in **Full Color**

How to Use Microsoft® Office 2000

International Standard Book Number: 0-672-31522-X

Library of Congress Catalog Card Number: 98-86837

Printed in the United States of America

First Printing: May 1999

02   01   00   99   4   3   2   1

Executive Editor
Jim Minatel

Acquisitions Editors
Jill Byus
Don Essig

Development Editors
Kate Shoup Welsh
Susan Hobbs

Managing Editor
Thomas F. Hayes

Project Editor
Sossity Smith

Copy Editors
Malinda McCain
Hugh Vandivier

Indexer
Lisa Stumpf

Technical Editor
Don Roche

Proofreaders
Jeanne Clark
Sheri Replin

Layout Technician
Trina Wurst

Book Designers
Nathan Clement
Ruth Harvey

Cover Designers
Aren Howell
Gary Adair

Contents at a Glance

Contents

About the Author

Sherry Kinkoph has authored more than 30 computer books for Macmillan Publishing over the past five years, including books for both adults and children. Her recent publications include *Easy Office 97 Small Business Edition*, *Sams Teach Yourself Quicken Deluxe 99 in 10 Minutes*, and *Using Microsoft Works Suite 99*.

Sherry started exploring computers back in college, and claims that many a term paper was whipped out using a trusty 128K Macintosh. Today, Sherry's still churning out words, but now they're in the form of books. And instead of using a Mac, she's moved on to a trusty PC. A native of the Midwest, Sherry currently resides in Fishers, IN, and continues in her quest to help users of all levels master the ever-changing computer technologies. You can email Sherry at **skinkoph@inetdirect.net**.

Dedication

To all my old camping buddies of yesteryear: the Sechrests, the Farmers, the Lovings, the Howells, the Tolivers, the Janeses, the Crossons, and the Willards.

Acknowledgements

Special thanks to Jill Byus and Don Essig for their excellent acquisitions work; to Susan Hobbs and Kate Shoup Welsh for their fine development work; to Malinda McCain and Hugh Vandivier for dotting the Is and crossing the Ts; to Sossity Smith for shepherding this book every step of the way until its final form; and to Don Roche for checking the technical accuracy of the book. Finally, extra special thanks to the production team for assembling this visual masterpiece.

Tell Us What You Think!

As the reader of this book, you are our most important critic and commentator. We value your opinion and want to know what we're doing right, what we could do better, what areas you'd like to see us publish in, and any other words of wisdom you're willing to pass our way.

As the Executive Editor for the General Desktop Applications team at Sams Publishing, I welcome your comments. You can fax, email, or write me directly to let me know what you did or didn't like about this book—as well as what we can do to make our books stronger.

Please note that I cannot help you with technical problems related to the topic of this book, and that due to the high volume of mail I receive, I might not be able to reply to every message.

When you write, please be sure to include this book's title and author as well as your name and phone or fax number. I will carefully review your comments and share them with the author and editors who worked on the book.

Fax: 317-581-4770

Email: **office_sams@mcp.com**

Mail: Executive Editor
General Desktop Applications
Sams Publishing
201 West 103rd Street
Indianapolis, IN 46290 USA

How To Use This Book

The Complete Visual Reference

Each chapter of this book is made up of a series of short, instructional tasks, designed to help you understand all the information that you need to get the most out of your computer hardware and software.

Each task includes a series of easy-to-understand steps designed to guide you through the procedure.

Click: Click the left mouse button once.

Double-click: Click the left mouse button twice in rapid succession.

Right-click: Click the right mouse button once.

Pointer Arrow: Highlights an item on the screen you need to point to or focus on in the step or task.

Selection: Highlights the area onscreen discussed in the step or task.

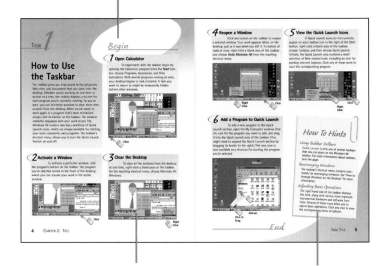

Each step is fully illustrated to show you how it looks onscreen.

Extra hints that tell you how to accomplish a goal are provided in most tasks.

Click and Type: Click once where indicated and begin typing to enter your text or data.

Menus and items you click are shown in **bold**. Words in *italic* are defined in more detail in the glossary. Information you type is in a **special font**.

Click & Drag

Release

How to Drag: Point to the starting place or object. Hold down the mouse button (right or left per instructions), move the mouse to the new location, and then release the button.

Continues

If you see this symbol, it means the task you're in continues on the next page.

Key icons: Clearly indicate which key combinations to use.

Introduction

*A*re you a visual learner? Do you like to see how to do things rather than read about them? Need to learn how to use Microsoft Office 2000 but don't have time to wade through an exhaustive tome to find out what you need to know? If you answered yes to one or all of these questions, *How to Use Microsoft Office 2000* is the book for you.

This book is written and assembled especially for visual learners and users who want to get up and running fast with new software. In the pages to follow, you will learn how to use the basic features and functions of the Office suite of programs in an easy to understand, straightforward manner. You will learn

- ✓ How to create and format Word documents
- ✓ How to work with Excel formulas and functions
- ✓ How to create slide show presentations with PowerPoint
- ✓ How to use Access to organize your data
- ✓ How to send and receive email with Outlook
- ✓ How to use Internet Explorer 5.0 to download files
- ✓ How to use the Office graphics tools to add pictures and shapes to your files
- ✓ How to integrate the Office programs to work together

Each topic is presented visually, step by step, so you can clearly see how to apply each feature and function to your own computer tasks. The illustrations show exactly what you will see on your own computer screen, making it easy to follow along.

You can choose to use the book as a tutorial, progressing through each section one task at a time, or as a reference, looking up specific features you want to learn about. There's no right or wrong way—use the method that best suits your own learning style.

In no time at all, you will have mastered all the basic tools needed to use the software for your own office or home needs. In addition, you will have gained the fundamental skills for working more productively on your computer. You can't find a more powerful set of computer applications than Microsoft Office 2000, and you can't learn them more easily than with *How to Use Microsoft Office 2000*.

Task

How to Use Common Office Features

*E*ach program in the Office 2000 suite has a common look and feel with plenty of shared features and procedures, such as saving and opening files.

In this chapter, you learn to use many of the shared features. Each program, for example, is opened and closed in the same way. As you use the programs, you will notice similar dialog boxes for common tasks, allowing you to apply the skills you learn in one program to another.

The Office programs share help features, including Office Assistant. You will also encounter smaller applications that are shared across the Office programs, such as WordArt—a program for creating text-based graphic effects. (You will learn more about the drawing and graphics tools in Chapter 16, "How to Work with Office Graphics Tools.")

How to Start and Exit Office Applications

You can start Office programs via the Windows Start menu. When you install the programs, each application's name is added to the Programs menu list. With Outlook, a shortcut icon is also added to the Windows desktop for quick access to your daily schedule and email. You can easily add shortcut icons for the other Office programs, but you can also access them quickly by using the Start menu. After you finish using an application, use one of several methods for closing the program window. Don't forget to save your work before exiting.

Begin

1 Open the Start Menu

Click the **Start** button on the Windows taskbar.

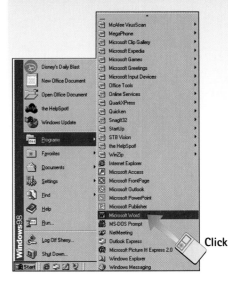

Click

2 Choose Programs

Click **Programs** to display the menu list.

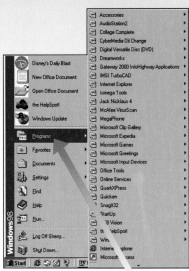

Click

3 Choose an Application

Click the name of the Microsoft Office program you want to open. To open Word, for example, select **Microsoft Word**.

Click

4 View the Program Window

Immediately, the program opens into its own window, with its name in the title bar. Depending on which program you open, you can begin working on a blank Word document, an Excel worksheet, a new PowerPoint presentation, or an Access database, or you can start using Outlook.

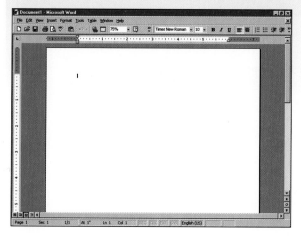

5 Quick Exit

The quickest way to close an Office program is to click the window's **Close** button, the button with an × in the upper-right corner of the window. You can also press **Alt+F4** on the keyboard.

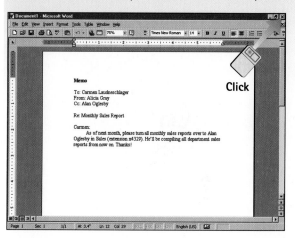

Click

6 Save It

If you haven't saved your work yet, the program prompts you to do so before exiting. Click **Yes** to save, **No** to exit without saving, or **Cancel** to cancel the exit procedure. (Outlook doesn't work with files like the other programs, so you won't see this prompt box when exiting Outlook.) To learn more about saving files, turn to Task 5, "How to Save Your Work."

Click

End

How-To Hints

Other Exit Routes

You can also close the program window by displaying the **File** menu and selecting **Exit**. Yet another way to exit is to click the **Control menu** icon and then select **Close**, or just double-click the icon itself.

Switch Between Open Programs

To switch between open program windows, use the Windows taskbar. Each open program is represented as an icon on the taskbar. Press **Ctrl+Esc** to display the taskbar and then click the program you want to see onscreen.

Create a Shortcut Icon

You can easily create a shortcut icon for any Office program you want to access from the Windows desktop. Display the **Programs** menu and drag the Office program name off of the menu and drop it onto the desktop. This creates an instant shortcut for the program. Next time you want to open the program, just double-click its shortcut icon.

How to Work with Menus

Microsoft has changed the way menus work in Office 2000. The new Office offers personalized menus that show only the controls you use the most. Simply put, this means a menu doesn't show every available command unless you tell it to; instead, it shows the commands with which you work most often. You can also customize how menus are displayed. In this task, you learn how to work with the new menus and customize them to suit your needs.

Begin

1 Display a Menu

To open a menu, click the menu name. If you're an avid keyboard user, press the **Alt** key and the underlined letter on the menu name.

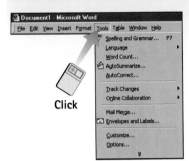
Click

2 Select a Command

To choose a command from the menu, simply click the command or press the command's selection letter (the underlined letter in the command name).

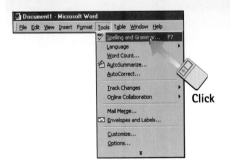
Click

3 View the Whole Menu

To view the entire menu with all of its commands, open the menu and wait a few seconds or click the double-arrow icon at the bottom of the menu.

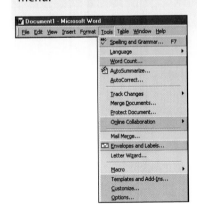

4 View Submenus

A right-pointing arrow next to a menu command indicates a submenu is available. Move your mouse pointer over the arrow to display the submenu. (Some submenus even have their own submenus.)

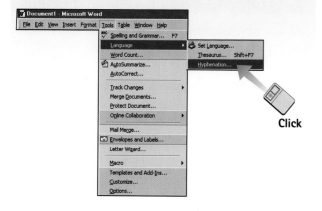

Click

5 Customize Your Menus

To customize your menus, open the **View** menu and select **Toolbars**, **Customize**. (Depending on which Office program you're using, the View menu might differ slightly.)

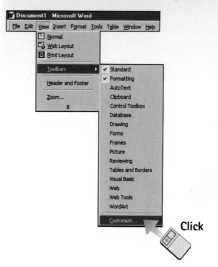

Click

6 Choose an Option

From the Customize dialog box, click the **Options** tab to view menu options. To turn off the personalized menu feature (which means the menus will no longer display just the commands you most recently used), deselect the **Menus Show Recently Used Commands First** check box. To reset the default set of visible commands, click the **Reset My Usage Data** button. Click **Close** to exit the dialog box and apply your changes.

 Click

End

How to Customize Toolbars

The default toolbars in Office 2000 look and work a little differently from the ones in previous versions of Office. For starters, they share space onscreen. Office programs that normally display two default toolbars now show them sharing the same toolbar space below the menu bar.

As you work with Office programs, the default toolbar buttons you use the most stay visible and buttons you use less often no longer appear on the toolbar. The buttons aren't gone—just not visible. As you work with the program, the toolbar buttons displayed vary based on how much you use them. You can also customize the toolbar to show only the buttons you want.

Begin

1 Display Nonvisible Toolbar Buttons

If the button you're looking for isn't onscreen, click one of the **More Buttons** icons on the toolbar to display a pop-up list.

Click

2 Select a Button

From the pop-up list, select the toolbar button you want to use. As soon as you make a selection, the command is activated and the button is added to the visible display of buttons on the toolbar.

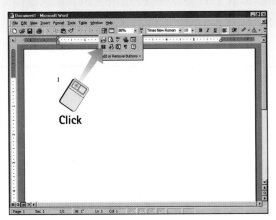

Click

3 Hide or Display Toolbars

To display or hide a toolbar, open the **View** menu and select **Toolbars**. This opens a submenu that lists every available toolbar for the program. A check mark next to the toolbar name indicates the toolbar is already displayed. To hide a toolbar, deselect its check mark.

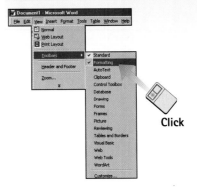

Click

4 Open the Customize Dialog Box

To customize a toolbar, open the **View** menu and select **Toolbars, Customize**. (Depending on which Office program you're using, the View menu might differ slightly.)

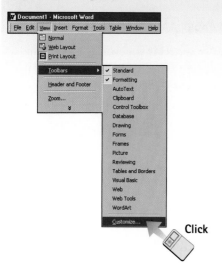

Click

5 Choose an Option

From the Customize dialog box, click the **Options** tab to view several toolbar options. To show each toolbar in full, click the **Standard and Formatting Toolbars Share One Row** check box to deselect that option. To switch to larger toolbar button icons, click the **Large Icons** check box.

Click

6 Customize the Toolbar

To customize which buttons appear on the toolbar, click the **Toolbars** tab and choose the toolbar you want to customize. This displays the toolbar onscreen. For example, to customize the Drawing toolbar, select **Drawing**.

Click

7 Change the Buttons

Click the **Commands** tab. To add a button to the toolbar, select a category. Scroll through the **Commands** list box to find the icon you want to use. Select it and drag it off of the list and onto the toolbar where you want it inserted. To remove a toolbar button, drag the button off of the toolbar. Click **Close** to exit.

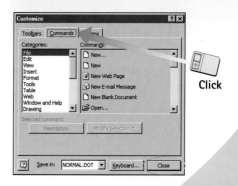

Click

End

How to Create a New File

When you installed Office, two new items were added to the top of the Start menu. One is the New Office Document command. This feature, when selected, opens the New Office Document dialog box, which enables you to select the type of file you want to create (a Word document, an Excel spreadsheet, a PowerPoint slide, an Access database, and so on). You can also open new files within each Office program (with the exception of Outlook). Use the program window's File menu to start a new file based on a template, or use the New button on the Standard toolbar.

Begin

1 Use the New Office Document

One way to create a new file is with the New Office Document command. Click the **Start** menu and choose **New Office Document**.

Click

2 Select a File Type

From the New Office Document dialog box, use the tabs to locate the type of template on which you want to base the new file (click a tab to display its templates). Then double-click to open both the program window and the new file. For example, to start a new Word file based on the Normal default template, click the **General** tab and then double-click the **Blank Document** icon.

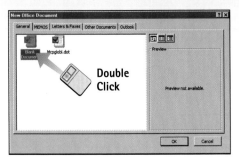

Double Click

3 A New File Opens

The file type you selected opens into the appropriate program window.

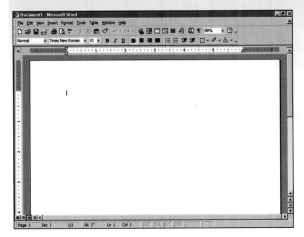

4 Open New Files Within Programs

You can also open new files within a program window. To open a file based on another template, display the **File** menu and select the **New** command.

Click

5 Use the New Dialog Box

When the New dialog box appears, double-click the template on which you want to base a new file. Here again, you can click the various tabs to view different categories of available templates.

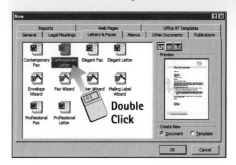

Double Click

6 Or Use the New Button

You can also click the **New** button on the Standard toolbar to open a new file. In the case of Word and Excel, a new file immediately opens, based on the default template. In PowerPoint, a dialog box appears for you to select a slide layout; choose a layout and click **OK**. In Access, the New dialog box opens (that is, clicking the **New** button in Access is the same as selecting **File**, **New**).

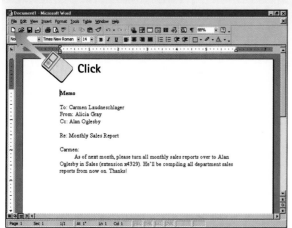

Click

End

How-To Hints

All Files Are Templates

Every file you open in Office starts from a *template*, a bare-bones, ready-made document, worksheet, presentation, or database. When you first open Word, for example, a blank document awaits you. The document is actually based on the Normal template—a no-frills template.

What's a Wizard?

Some of the file types listed in the New Office Document dialog box are *wizards*. Use wizards to help you create a new document, step by step, based on choices you make in the wizard dialog boxes. You can start a wizard just as you start any other file—by double-clicking the icon.

Macro Warning

Depending on the template you choose, a warning might appear to tell you the file you're about to open contains macros (stored automated commands for common tasks) that might have viruses. If you purchased your Office program from a reliable source, click the **Enable Macros** button and continue. If you're not sure, you can choose the **Disable Macros** button to disable any macros from running.

How to Save Your Work

After you start working in an Office file, you will want to save it so you can open it again later. A good idea is to save your work often in case of power failures or other computer glitches. When you save a file the first time, you must give the file a name. You can use up to 256 characters, upper- or lowercase letters, in a filename. You can also choose a specific folder or disk to save the file to, and choose to save the file under a specific file format. All of the Save options are found in the Save As dialog box, which looks pretty much the same for each Office program (with the exception of Outlook, which doesn't use a Save As dialog box). After you have saved a file, subsequent saves don't require renaming (unless you want to save a duplicate of the file under a different name), and you don't have to reopen the Save As dialog box. Instead, just click the **Save** button on the toolbar.

Begin

1 Save a New File

To save a file for the first time, open the **File** menu and select **Save** or **Save As** to display the Save As dialog box.

Click

2 Designate a Folder

In the Save As dialog box, choose a folder in which to save the file. Use the **Save In** drop-down list, if necessary, to locate the folder where you want to save your file. To open a folder, double-click the folder icon. You can also open any of the folders displayed in the left pane of the dialog box by clicking the folder icon.

Click

3 Enter a Filename

Type a name for the file in the **File Name** text box.

4 Click Save

Click the **Save** button and the file is saved.

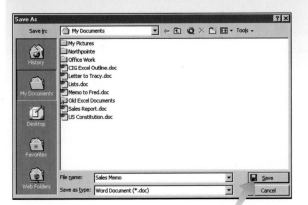

Click

5 Title Bar Name

Notice that the program's title bar now reflects the name you assigned in the Save As dialog box.

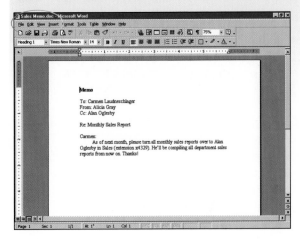

6 Use the Save Button

For subsequent saves of the same file, click the **Save** button on the Standard toolbar.

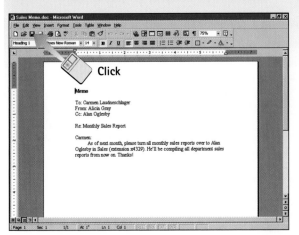

Click

End

How-To Hints

Changing the Format

To save a file in another format (for example, to save an Excel file as a Lotus 1-2-3 file), open the Save As dialog box. Then click the **Save as Type** drop-down arrow and choose a file type from the list.

Saving as a New File

To save an existing file under a new name, use the same steps shown in this task but enter a different filename. A duplicate of the original file is saved under the new filename, and the original file remains intact.

Saving to a New Folder

You can click the **Create New Folder** button in the Save As dialog box to create a new folder to save to; just enter a folder name and click **OK**.

How to Open and Close Files

If the program window is already open, you can use the Open dialog box to quickly open existing files you have previously saved. If you haven't started the program yet, you can use the **Open Office Document** command on the Start menu to open both the file you want and the program in which it was created. If you finish working with a file but want to keep the program window open, select the **Close** command. This closes only the file, leaving the program window open to work on other files or start new ones. If you haven't saved your work, you are prompted to do so before closing the file.

Begin

1 Use the Open Dialog Box

To open a file from within a program window, display the **File** menu and select **Open** (alternatively, you can click the **Open** button—the button that looks like an open file folder—on the Standard toolbar).

Click

2 Locate the File

Next, you must locate the file you want to open. The list box displays the files stored in the default folder. To open a different folder in the list box, double-click the folder icon to display the folder contents. You might need to use the **Look In** drop-down list to find the folder, or click a folder listed in the left pane of the dialog box.

Double Click

3 Select the File

When you find the file you want to open, double-click the desired filename, or select it and click the **Open** button.

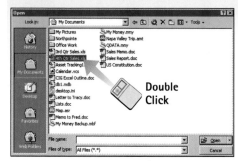

Double Click

4 Open Office Document

Another way to open files is with the Open Office Document command. This is a quick way to open both the file and the program window (if it's not already open). Click the **Start** button on the Windows taskbar and choose **Open Office Document** at the top of the menu.

Click

5 Choose a File

From the Open Office Document dialog box, locate the file you want to open. Double-click the filename to open both the file and the program, or select the file and click **Open**.

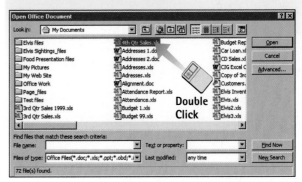

Double Click

6 Close a File

To close a file—but not the program window—open the **File** menu and choose **Close**.

Click

End

How-To Hints

Preview the File

If you're not sure about a file's contents, click the **View** button on the Open dialog box's toolbar and select the **Preview** command to peek at the file before opening it.

Open Options

Notice that the **Open** button in the Open dialog box has a drop-down arrow. Click the arrow to display a drop-down list of four Open commands: **Open, Open Read-Only, Open as Copy, Open in Browser**. If you select the **Open Read-Only** command, you can view the file but not make any changes to it. If you select **Open as Copy**, a copy of the file opens—not the original. If you select **Open in Browser**, the file opens in the Internet Explorer browser window.

How to Preview a File

Before you print out a file, whether it's a Word document or a note you've created in Outlook, a good idea is to preview how it looks by using the Preview window. Print Preview lets you examine exactly how your file will print and make any last-minute changes before printing. When you're working on the file, for example, you can't always see how all the page elements—such as page numbers or graphics—look or tell whether the page layout is pleasing to the eye. With the Preview feature, you can get an overall look at your file, page by page. The Preview window has a toolbar you can use to adjust your preview. Depending on the program, the Preview window might offer various tools for working with the file.

Begin

1 Open Print Preview

Open the **File** menu and select **Print Preview** (or click the **Print Preview** button—the button that looks like a sheet of paper under a magnifying glass—on the Standard toolbar).

Click

2 View the Preview Window

The file opens in a full-page preview. Use the toolbar buttons on the Preview toolbar to adjust your view of the page or pages. Click the **Magnifier** tool, for example, and then click anywhere on a page to zoom in for a closer look.

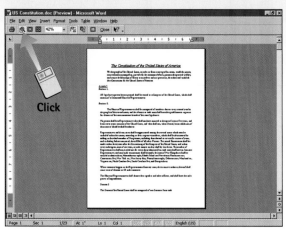

Click

3 Zoom In

Preview zooms in on the area you clicked. To return to the full-page preview, click again.

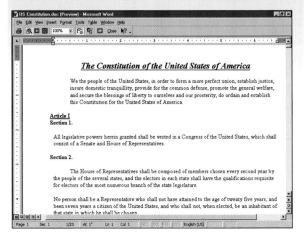

4 Make Changes

To edit while in the Preview window, use the Magnifier tool to zoom in on the area you want to edit. Then deselect the **Magnifier** button on the toolbar by clicking it a second time. The mouse pointer becomes a cursor you can click in the text to make changes to the data.

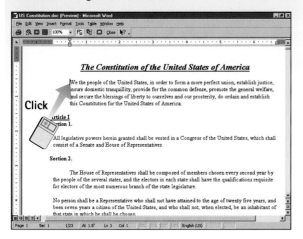

5 Print the File

If your file is exactly as you want it to print, click the **Print** button on the toolbar to send it immediately to your printer.

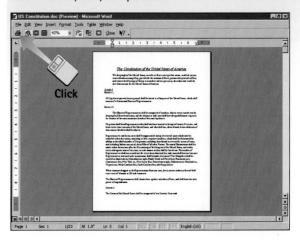

6 Close the Preview Window

To exit the Preview window, click the **Close** button.

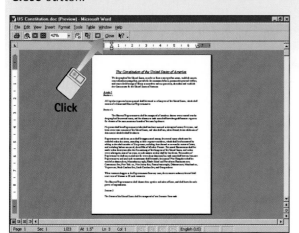

End

How to Print a File

Printing an Office file requires that you have a printer connected to your computer, the appropriate printer driver (printer software) installed, and the printer turned on and online (ready to print). When you're ready to print, you can send the file immediately to the printer, using the default printer settings, or set specific printing options first by using the Print dialog box. Depending on the program and your setup, the printer options you see might vary slightly. The figures in these steps show Print dialog boxes from Excel, Word, PowerPoint, and Access. Despite subtle differences, the Print dialog box works the same way for every Office file or Outlook item you print.

Begin

1 Open the Print Dialog Box

To set printing options, open the **File** menu and select **Print**.

Click

2 Choose a Printer

The Print dialog box reveals several options you can choose (the Print dialog box shown in this figure is for Excel). If you have access to more than one printer, use the **Name** drop-down list to choose another printer.

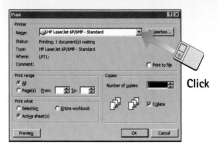

Click

3 Choose a Page Range

To designate specific pages or selected data to print (such as an Excel range or an Access record), use the options in the **Page Range** or **Print Range** areas (the precise name of this option depends on what type of file you're trying to print; the dialog box in this figure is for Word). To print every page, select **All**. Use the **Pages** option to indicate which pages to print (type in a single page number or a range, such as 2–4).

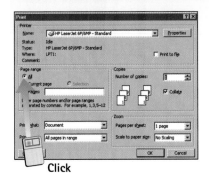

Click

4 Number of Copies

To print multiple copies of the file, indicate a number in the **Number of Copies** box. (The figure shown with this step is from PowerPoint—notice the numerous options for printing slides, which are more graphic in nature than other Office files.)

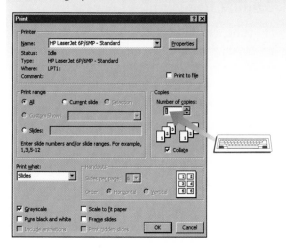

5 Print

Click **OK** to print the file. (The figure shown with this step is the Print dialog box that appears when printing from Access.)

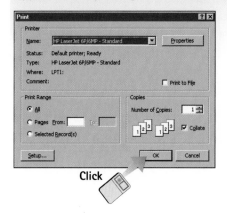

Click

6 Use the Print Toolbar Button

To print the file without selecting any new options, click the **Print** button on the Standard toolbar.

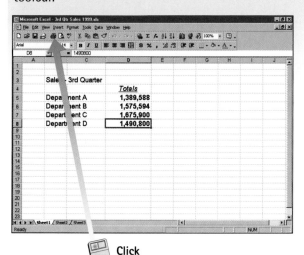

Click

How-To Hints

Printing in Outlook

Use the Print Style area in the Print dialog box to choose a print style for the Outlook item you're printing. You can also edit the style by clicking the **Define Styles** button, or change the page setup settings by clicking the **Page Setup** button.

End

TASK 9

How to Work with Multiple Files

You can have several files open at the same time while working with Word, Excel, Access, or PowerPoint. You can easily switch between them by using the Window menu or the taskbar, or you can choose to view multiple files onscreen at the same time. With multiple files open, you can copy and move data from one file to another. To try this task, you must first open two or more files. Use the Open dialog box to locate the files, if needed (click the **Open** button on the toolbar or select **File**, **Open**).

Begin

1 Display the Window Menu

One way to switch between open files is to use the Window menu. Click the **Window** menu; the bottom of the menu lists the names of the open files. The currently active file has a check mark next to its name. Click the file you want to view.

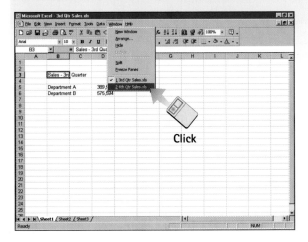

Click

2 View the Active File

The program window now displays the file you selected.

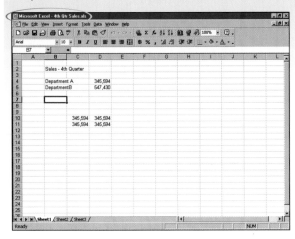

3 Or Use the Taskbar

Another way to switch between open files is to use the taskbar. Simply click the button representing the file you want to view. (Press **Ctrl+Esc** if your taskbar isn't onscreen.)

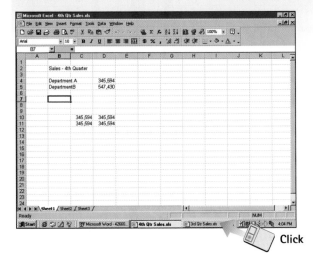

Click

4 View Multiple Files

To see all the open files onscreen at the same time, open the **Window** menu and select **Arrange**.

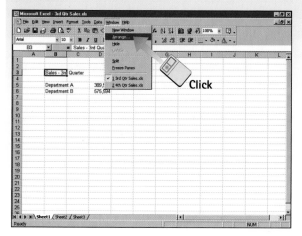

Click

5 Choose an Arrange Option

In the Arrange Windows dialog box, select an arrange option for viewing the open files and click **OK**.

Click

6 Maximize the File Window

The open files are displayed onscreen at the same time. To return a file window to its full size, click the **Maximize** button on the file's title bar.

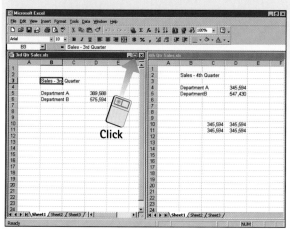

Click

End

How-To Hints

Copying and Moving Data

With two or more files open and viewable at the same time, you can drag data from one file to another by using the drag-and-drop method. Select the data, click and hold the left mouse button, and drag the data to a new location in the other file. To copy the data, hold down the **Shift** key while dragging.

How to Use the Office Assistant

Regardless of your level of computer experience, you might need help from time to time, especially when you're learning a new software program. By default, Microsoft's Office Assistant appears, ready to help you, as soon as you start a program. The Office Assistant is an animated feature you can use to help you navigate new tasks or find additional information about a feature. Use Office Assistant to look up specific instructions or topics with which you want help.

Begin

1 Open Office Assistant

By default, Office Assistant appears when you first use a program or tackle a new feature. To summon the assistant at any time, simply press **F1** or open the **Help** menu and select **Show the Office Assistant**.

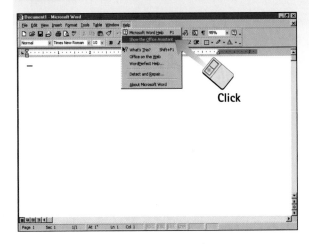

Click

2 Ask a Question

From the Office Assistant balloon, you can type a question or select from options the Assistant lists. To ask a question, click inside the text box and type your question. Then click **Search** or press **Enter**.

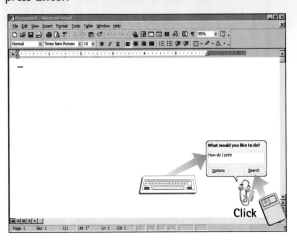

Click

3 Choose a Topic

Office Assistant produces a list of possible topics from which you can choose. Click the topic that most closely matches the information you desire. (If the question you typed didn't produce the results you expected, enter a new question and try again.)

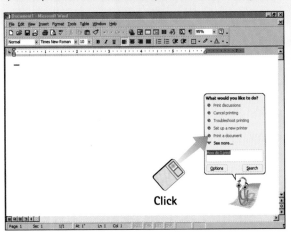

Click

4 Read the Help Window

A Help window appears with more information detailing the topic or showing additional topics you can choose. Underlined words are links to related topics; click the text to follow the link. Use the **Back** and **Forward** buttons at the top of the Help window to navigate between topics.

Links Back Forward

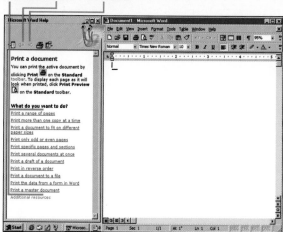

5 Close the Help Window

To close the Help window when you finish reading, click the window's **Close** (×) button.

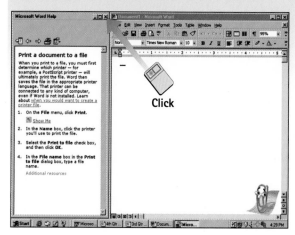

Click

6 Close the Office Assistant

To close the Office Assistant completely, open the **Help** menu and select **Hide the Office Assistant**, or right-click over the Office Assistant character and select **Hide**. You can also choose to leave the Office Assistant open onscreen in case you need more help. As you work with the file, the Office Assistant moves out of your way as needed.

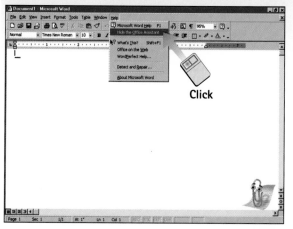

Click

How-To Hints

Customizing the Office Assistant

If you don't like the default Clippit character (the animated paper clip), you can change it. Click the **Options** button in the Office Assistant balloon to open the Office Assistant dialog box. Click the **Gallery** tab and choose another character by using the **Back** or **Next** buttons. Click **OK** after choosing another character.

Changing the Office Assistant Settings

Use the **Options** tab in the Office Assistant dialog box to change which options are turned on or off. Click **OK** to exit and apply any changes.

End

How to Use the Office Help System

If asking the animated Office Assistant a question isn't your cup of tea, you can tap into several other help features. You can use the Help window to access a list of help categories, as well as an index for looking up specific terms. You can also use the What's This? feature for help with onscreen elements.

Begin

1 Open the Full Help Window

From the Help window, click the **Show** button.

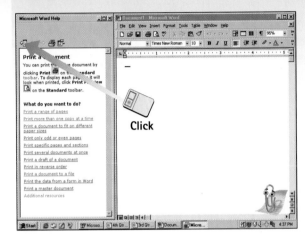

Click

2 The Answer Wizard Tab

The **Answer Wizard** tab works just like the animated Office Assistant balloon; click inside the text box and type in your question. Click **Search** or press **Enter** when you're ready to view the topic.

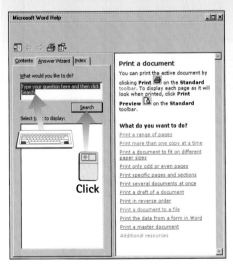

Click

3 The Contents Tab

Use the **Contents** tab as you would a book's table of contents (click the tab to bring it to the front of the window). Double-click a topic category to open a list of subtopics. Click one of the subtopics to display more information about the topic.

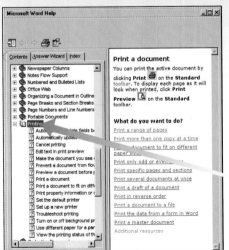

Double Click

4 The Index Tab

The **Index** tab (click to display) is an alphabetized list of help topics, much like a book's index. You can type the term (or phrase) you want to look up (for example, **print**), and the middle list box scrolls alphabetically to the term.

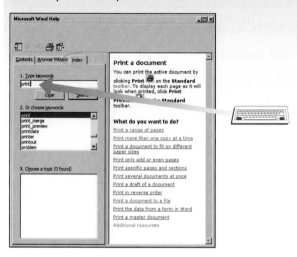

5 Look Up a Term

Click an entry in the bottom list of the Index tab to display detailed information about the word or phrase. To close the Help window when you finish reading, click the window's **Close** (×) button.

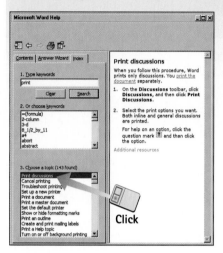

6 Use the What's This Feature

To find quick information about an onscreen element, use the What's This tool. Open the **Help** menu and choose **What's This?**. The mouse pointer takes the shape of a question mark. Click the onscreen element you want to know more about, such as a toolbar button or dialog box option, and an information box appears, as shown here. (Click anywhere onscreen or press **Esc** to close the help information.)

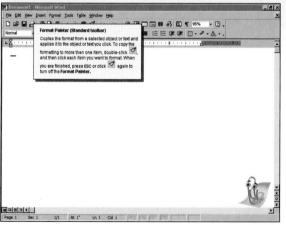

How-To Hints

Printing Help Topics

From the Help window, click the **Print** button and then click **OK**.

Finding Help on the Web

In addition to the help that appears when using the Office Assistant and the Help window features, you can log onto the Microsoft Web site to find more help with your program. Open the **Help** menu and choose **Office on the Web**. This opens your browser window and a connect box for you to log on to your Internet account. Click **Connect** and follow the Web page links to the information you're looking for (try starting from the Microsoft Home page).

End

Task

CHAPTER 2

How to Use Word

Microsoft Word is one of the most popular, best-selling word processing programs ever created. With it, you can create all manner of documents: letters, memos, reports, manuscripts, and newsletters. When it comes to working with text, Microsoft Word has no match. Out of all the programs that compose Office, Word will probably become your most-used application: It's so versatile that you will use it for just about anything involving text.

In this part of the book, you will learn how to get up and running with Word: acclimate yourself with the various elements in the program window, learn how to begin working with text, and understand how to assign templates to help you build better documents. The fundamental skills covered in this chapter will prepare you for working with Word's numerous formatting tools in the chapter that follows.

How to Get Around the Word Window

When you first open Word, a blank document opens onscreen. The document is surrounded by tools you can use to help you enter text and work with it. If you prefer, many of the elements can be hidden to free up window workspace. Use the View menu to turn the display of certain onscreen items on or off (such as toolbars or the ruler).

Each Office program uses similar onscreen elements, so if you learn how to use them in one program, you will be able to use these same elements in another. If you're new to Word, take a few moments to familiarize yourself with the window elements in this task.

Begin

1 View the Blank Document Window

The program window opens along with a blank document window. Usually, both windows are maximized: The program window fills the whole screen, and the document window fills the program window. (When both are maximized, two Restore buttons—one for each window—are displayed in the set of buttons in the upper-right corner of the window's screen.) If your program window isn't maximized, click its **Maximize** button. To minimize the program window to a button on the Windows taskbar, click the **Minimize** button.

Program window   Minimize   Restore   Close

Document window

2 View the Title Bar

The title bar tells you what is in the window. When the document window is maximized, it has to share the title bar with the program window, so the title bar contains the names of both the program (Microsoft Word) and the file. (Document1 is a temporary name for your document. When you save it for the first time, you will replace that name with a name you choose.)

Title bar

3 Use the Menu Bar

The Word menu bar contains menus, which in turn contain all the available Word commands. All the tasks you need to perform are available through menu commands. To use the menu commands, click the menu name to display the menu and click the command you want.

Menu bar

4 Use the Standard Toolbar

By default, Word displays the Standard and Formatting toolbars side-by-side onscreen. The Standard toolbar appears on the left, as shown in this figure. The Standard toolbar contains shortcuts for frequently used commands such as those to open, save, and print documents, and to undo mistakes. To activate a toolbar button, click it. To see a button name, hover the mouse pointer over the button for a moment; a ScreenTip appears with the button name. (Learn all about using and customizing toolbars in Chapter 1, "How to Use Common Office Features.")

Standard toolbar

ScreenTip

5 Use the Formatting Toolbar

The Formatting toolbar, located next to the Standard toolbar, contains shortcuts for commands that change the appearance of the document. To activate a toolbar button, click it; to view the name of the button, point at the button to reveal a ScreenTip.

Formatting toolbar

6 Use the Ruler

The ruler shows you where your margins are, and it lets you set tabs and indents. If you don't see the ruler, you can display it by opening the **View** menu and choosing **Ruler**.

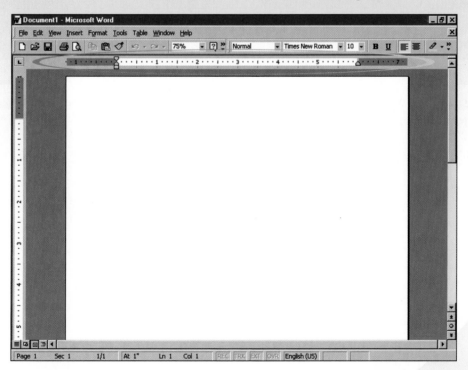

Continues

7 Use the Work Area

The typing area in a new document is the large blank space bordered by vertical and horizontal scrollbars. The *insertion point* (a vertical, blinking line, also known as the *cursor*) shows you where the next character you type will appear. When the mouse pointer is placed over the typing area, it resembles an I-beam.

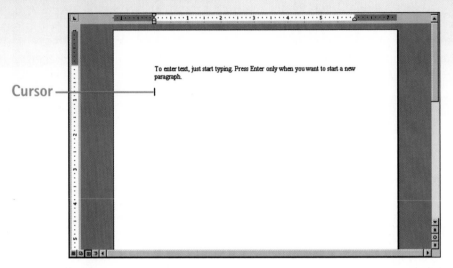

Cursor

8 Use the Scrollbars

The vertical and horizontal scrollbars allow you to view different portions of your document. Use the arrows on the scrollbars to scroll in the appropriate direction or drag the scroll box. Use the **Previous Page** and **Next Page** buttons (at the bottom of the vertical scrollbar) to jump quickly from one part of your document to the next.

Vertical scrollbar

Horizontal scrollbar

9 Viewing the Status Bar

The status bar indicates the current page, the total number of pages, and the location of your insertion point on the page. As you use Word, the status bar sometimes displays other information as well.

End

How-To Hints

What Toolbars?

If you don't see the Standard or Formatting toolbar or if you see other toolbars you would like to hide, open the **View** menu and choose **Toolbars**. Select the **Standard** or **Formatting** toolbar. A check mark next to the toolbar name means the toolbar is displayed. To display the default toolbars in full, select the **Customize** command on the **Toolbars** menu, click the **Options** tab, and deselect the **Standard and Formatting Toolbars Share One Row** check box. Click **Close**.

No Scrollbars?

If either of your scrollbars or your status bar isn't showing, choose **Tools, Options**. Click the **View** tab. Then, under the **Show** heading, click any check box that isn't already marked— **Status Bar**, **Horizontal Scroll Bar**, and/or **Vertical Scroll Bar**—and then choose **OK**.

Use the Shortcut Menu

To open a shortcut menu that contains often-used commands, click an object with the right mouse button (called a _right-click_). Next, use the left mouse button to click the command you want. Almost everything in the Word window has its own shortcut menu.

Keyboard Shortcuts

To choose menu commands with the keyboard, press the **Alt** key, press the underlined letter in the desired menu, and then press the underlined letter in the desired command. To display the Format menu, for example, press **Alt+O**. When the Format menu is displayed, press **P** to choose the Paragraph command.

How to Use Word's Views

Word offers you several ways to view your document. For starters, you can use the Zoom tool to view your document in detail, or zoom out to view your document from a "bird's-eye view." You can also change the way you view a document page using four main view options: Normal, Web Layout, Print Layout, and Outline.

Use Normal view to see only the text area of the page; no graphics or special elements appear. Switch to Print Layout view to see graphics, page margins, and elements such as headers and footers. Use Outline view to help you build and maintain outline levels in your document. Web Layout view takes its cue from Web pages, allowing you to take advantage of the full width of a Web page document.

Begin

1 Use the Zoom Tools

The quickest way to zoom your view of the document is to use the Zoom control on the Standard toolbar. Click the drop-down arrow to display the list of zoom percentages, and click a percentage (such as 200%) to zoom your view.

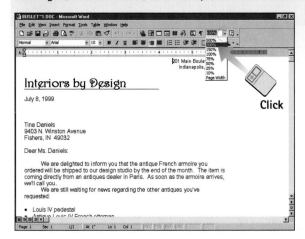

Click

2 Your View Is Zoomed

Word zooms your view of the document based on the selection you made in step 1 (in this case, 200%).

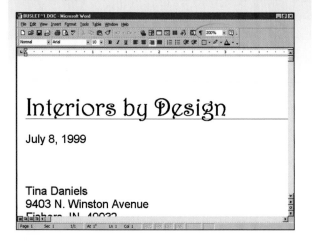

3 Open the Zoom Dialog Box

To specify an exact zoom percentage, open the **View** menu and select **Zoom**.

Click

4 Specify a Zoom Percentage

In the Zoom dialog box, you can enter an exact zoom percentage in the **Percent** box (such as **50%**). The **Preview** area gives you an idea of how the zoomed text will look. Click **OK** to apply the new view.

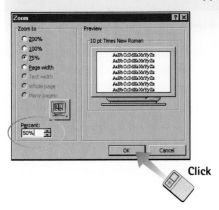

Click

5 Use the View Buttons

Use the View buttons in the lower-left corner of the Word window to switch between Normal, Web Layout, Print Layout, and Outline views. Click the view button you want to switch to; for example, click **Print Layout View**.

Click

6 Change the View

Word displays the document just as it will print. Most users stick with Normal and Print Layout views to work with and view document pages. To change your view again, click the View button you want to use.

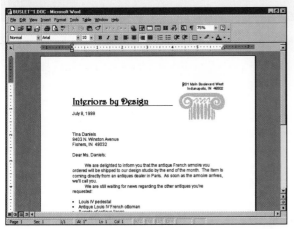

End

How-To Hints

Use the View Menu

You can also switch your document page views using the **View** menu.

Use Outline View

Outline view is intended to help you modify the structure of your outline. In Outline view, you can move headings—and any body text or subheadings they contain—by dragging and dropping them. You can hide and display heading levels by clicking toolbar buttons. You can also apply heading styles or outline levels to your headings while you're using Outline view.

How to Enter and Edit Text

Microsoft Word opens with a blank document window ready for you to begin typing text into, whether it's in the form of a bestselling novel, a personal letter, or an interoffice memo. The flashing insertion point indicates where the next character you type will appear. Simply start typing to enter text. If you make any mistakes, use the Backspace key to delete unwanted characters.

Begin

1 Start a New Paragraph

Each time you press **Enter**, you start a new paragraph. Press **Enter** to end short lines of text, to create blank lines, and to end paragraphs. Don't press **Enter** to start new lines within a paragraph: Word wraps the lines for you.

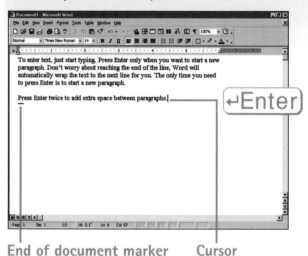

End of document marker   Cursor

2 Indent with the Tab Key

Press the **Tab** key to indent the first line of a paragraph. If you keep pressing **Tab**, you increase the indent one-half inch at a time. (To indent all the lines in the paragraph instead of just the first one, right-click in the paragraph and click **Paragraph** on the shortcut menu. Next, click the **Indents and Spacing** tab, reset the indentation settings, and click **OK** to apply them.)

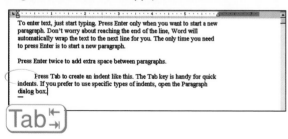

3 Type Repeating Characters

To type the same character repeatedly, hold the key down. Word automatically converts some repeated characters into different types of lines, as shown here. If you type three or more asterisks (*) and press **Enter**, for example, Word replaces them with a dotted line. Do the same with the equal sign (=) for a double line, the tilde (~)for a wavy line, the pound (#) symbol for a thick decorative line, or the underscore (_) for a thick single line.

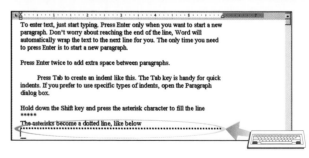

4 Type Uppercase Letters

To produce all uppercase letters without having to hold down the **Shift** key, press the **Caps Lock** key once before you begin typing. Press the **Caps Lock** key again when you're ready to switch caps off. Caps Lock affects only the letter keys, not the number and punctuation keys. Therefore, you always have to press **Shift** to type a character on the upper half of a number or punctuation key, such as @ or %.

To enter text, just start typing. Press Enter only when you want to start a new paragraph. Don't worry about reaching the end of the line, Word will automatically wrap the text to the next line for you. The only time you need to press Enter is to start a new paragraph.

Press Enter twice to add extra space between paragraphs.

Press Tab to create an indent like this. The Tab key is handy for quick indents. If you prefer to use specific types of indents, open the Paragraph dialog box.

Hold down the Shift key and press the asterisk character to fill the line
*****

The asterisks become a dotted line, like below

CLICK THE CAPS LOCK KEY TO TYPE ALL CAPS

Caps Lock

5 View Nonprinting Characters

Every time you press **Enter**, the **Spacebar**, or the **Tab** key, Word marks the spot in your document with a nonprinting character. You can't see these characters unless you click the **Show/Hide** button in the Standard toolbar. You can use this button to check whether you accidentally typed an extra space between two words or to see how many blank lines you have between paragraphs. To turn Show/Hide off, click the button again.

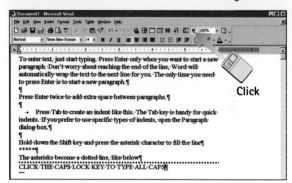

Click

6 Fix Mistakes

Press the **Backspace** key to delete characters to the left of the cursor. You can also click inside a word and press the **Delete** key to remove characters to the right of the cursor.

Hold down the Shift key and press the asterisk character to fill the line
*****

The asterisks become a dotted line, like below
CLICK THE CAPS LOCK KEY TO TYPE ALL C

Del ←Backspace

End

How-To Hints

Overtype and Insert Modes

By default, Word starts you in Insert mode: Any time you click the cursor in the document and start typing, any existing text moves to the right to make room for new text you type. If you prefer to replace the existing text entirely, use the Overtype mode. Press the **Insert** key to toggle Overtype mode on or off. You can also double-click the letters **OVR** on the status bar to toggle the feature on or off (the letters OVR appear in black when Overtype mode is on).

Need a New Page?

By default, Word starts a new page when the current page is filled with text. At times, you may want to start a new page without filling the current page (when you want a title page, for example). Press **Ctrl+Enter** to insert a manual page break. To remove a manual page break, click the page break line and press **Delete**.

How to Navigate a Document

As you begin filling a document with text, the view area will move down to show your current cursor location as you type. When your document becomes longer or wider than a full screen of text, use Word's navigation tools to view different parts of the document.

Begin

1 Use the Scrollbars

Depending on the size of your document, use the vertical or horizontal scrollbars to view different portions of the document. Click the scrollbar's arrow buttons to scroll in the appropriate direction.

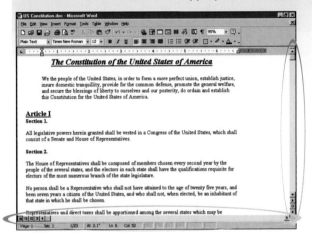

2 Drag the Scroll Box

You can also drag the scroll box to move your view. Drag the vertical scroll box up or down to move up or down or drag the horizontal scroll box to the left or right to move your view of the document page.

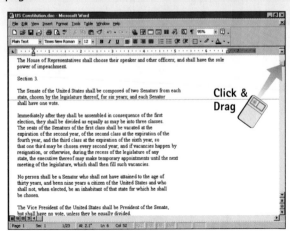

Click & Drag

3 Use the Page Buttons

If your document is longer than a page, click the **Next Page** button to immediately scroll to the next page. Click the **Previous Page** button to scroll back a page.

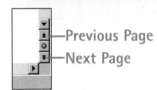

—Previous Page
—Next Page

4 Use the Mouse

Click the mouse anywhere in your document to move the insertion point to that spot.

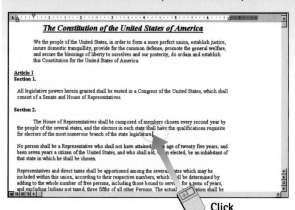

Click

5 Use the Arrow Keys

Use the arrow keys on the keyboard to move up, down, right, or left in the document. Press the right-arrow key, for example, to move right one character; hold the right-arrow key down to move across many characters quickly.

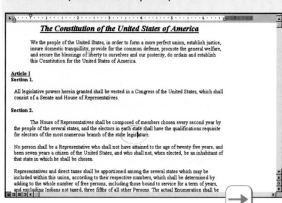

6 Use Keyboard Shortcuts

In addition to the navigational arrow keys, you can use numerous other keyboard shortcuts to navigate documents. Press **Ctrl+→** to move right one word, for example; press **Ctrl+←** to move left one word.

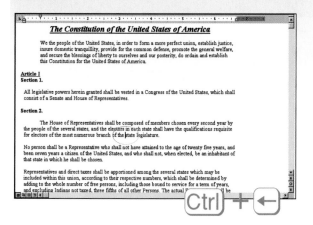

End

How-To Hints

Go To

If you know the page you want to view onscreen, use the Go To command to get there. Select **Edit**, **Go To**, or click the **Select Browse Object** button on the vertical scrollbar, then click the **Go To** icon. In the Go To tab, enter the page number and click the **Go To** button. (You can also locate specific document elements, such as footnotes or headings.)

More Keyboard Shortcuts

To learn more about Word's many shortcut keys, use the Help system. Open the **Help** menu and select **Contents and Index**. Click the **Index** tab and type in "shortcut keys" to look up the subject matter.

How to Select Text

After entering text, you can do a variety of things with it, such as applying formatting or moving and copying the text. Before you can do any of these things, though, you must first learn to select text. *Selecting text* means to highlight the specific text you want to change or apply commands to. Selected text, whether it's a single character, a word, a paragraph, or an entire document, always appears highlighted onscreen with a black bar.

Begin

1 Select Text with the Mouse

To select a character, word, or phrase, click at the beginning of the text you want to select, hold down the left mouse button, and drag to the end of the selection. Release the mouse button, and the text is selected.

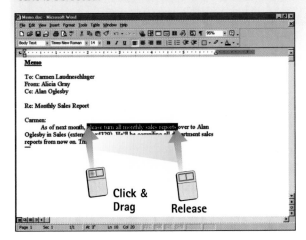

2 Select Text with the Keyboard

To select text using the keyboard, press the arrow keys to move the cursor to the beginning of the word or phrase you want to select. Hold down the **Shift** key and move the appropriate arrow key to select the desired text. To select a word, for example, move the cursor to the beginning of the word, hold down the **Shift** key, and press the right-arrow key until the text is selected.

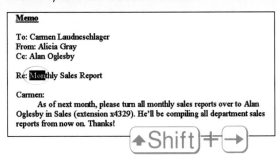

3 Mouse Shortcuts

To select a single word quickly, double-click inside the word. To select a paragraph, triple-click inside the paragraph.

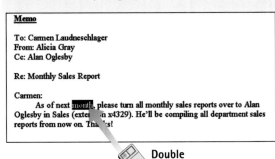

4 Click Inside the Left Margin

You can also click inside the left margin to select lines of text. Hover your mouse pointer to the left of the line you want to highlight until the mouse pointer takes the shape of a northeast-pointing arrow, and click once to select the line.

> **Memo**
>
> To: Carmen Laudneschlager
> From: Alicia Gray
> Cc: Alan Oglesby
>
> Re: Monthly Sales Report
>
> Carmen:
> As of next month, please turn all monthly sales reports over to Alan Oglesby in Sales (extension x4329). He'll be compiling all department sales reports from now on. Thanks!

 Click

5 Select a Paragraph

You can also use the left margin to select a paragraph: Simply double-click next to the paragraph you want to select.

> **Memo**
>
> To: Carmen Laudneschlager
> From: Alicia Gray
> Cc: Alan Oglesby
>
> Re: Monthly Sales Report
>
> Carmen:
> As of next month, please turn all monthly sales reports over to Alan Oglesby in Sales (extension x4329). He'll be compiling all department sales reports from now on. Thanks!

 Double Click

6 Select the Entire Document

Finally, you can use the left margin to select the entire document: Triple-click anywhere in the left margin to select the entire document.

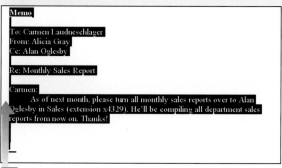

> **Memo**
>
> To: Carmen Laudneschlager
> From: Alicia Gray
> Cc: Alan Oglesby
>
> Re: Monthly Sales Report
>
> Carmen:
> As of next month, please turn all monthly sales reports over to Alan Oglesby in Sales (extension x4329). He'll be compiling all department sales reports from now on. Thanks!

 Triple Click

 End

How-To Hints

Unselect Text

To unselect text quickly, click anywhere outside the text or press any arrow key.

Edit Selected Text

You can easily replace selected text with new text. Just start typing, and the selected text is deleted and replaced with any new text you type. To delete selected text without typing new text, press the **Delete** key.

Keyboard Shortcuts

To select one word at a time using the keyboard keys, press **Ctrl+Shift+Right Arrow** or **Ctrl+Shift+Left Arrow**. To select one paragraph at a time, press **Ctrl+Shift+Up Arrow** or **Ctrl+Shift+Down Arrow**. To select all the text from the insertion point onward, press **Ctrl+Shift+End**. To select all text above the insertion point, press **Ctrl+Shift+Home**. To select the entire document, press **Ctrl+A**.

How to Move and Copy Text

Use Word's Cut, Copy, and Paste functions to move and copy text from one location to another. Word makes it easy to pick up characters, words, sentences, paragraphs, and more and to move or copy them to a new location. You can even move and copy them between files.

You can apply a variety of methods to move and copy text. You can use menu commands, shortcut menu commands, toolbar buttons, keyboard shortcuts, and drag-and-drop techniques. Everybody finds their favorite method. To move text, cut it from its position and paste it somewhere else; to copy text, make a copy of the text and paste it elsewhere.

Begin

1 Select the Text

Select the text you want to cut or copy.

2 Use Cut and Copy

An easy way to cut and copy is to use the toolbar buttons. To move the text, click the **Cut** button in the Standard toolbar. The text is deleted from your document, but it remains in a special Windows storage area called the *Clipboard*. To copy the text, click the **Copy** button in the Standard toolbar. When you copy text, nothing appears to happen because the text remains in its original location, but a copy of the selected text is sent to the Clipboard.

Cut Copy

3 Relocate the Cursor

Click to place the cursor in the document where you want to paste the cut or copied text. If necessary, you can open another document or switch to another already open document to paste text there.

Click

4 Use Paste

Click the **Paste** button in the Standard toolbar to paste the text. The text is pasted into the document beginning at the position of the insertion point.

Paste

5 Drag and Drop to Move Text

Another easy method to move or copy text is to drag and drop it. To move text, click in the selected text, hold the mouse button down, and *drag* the mouse where you want to paste the text. Release the mouse button to *drop*, or paste, the cut text.

Click & Drag   **Release**

6 Drag and Drop to Copy Text

To copy text by dragging and dropping it, select the text you want to copy. Click in the selected text and hold the mouse button down, hold down the **Ctrl** key, and *drag* the mouse to the new location. Release the mouse button to *drop*, or paste, the copied text.

Click & Drag   **Release**

End

How-To Hints

Keyboard Shortcuts

If you prefer using the keyboard, try these shortcut commands: Ctrl+X for Cut, Ctrl+C for Copy, and Ctrl+V for Paste. These keyboard shortcuts are standard for all Windows-based programs.

Use the Clipboard Toolbar

Office 2000 comes with a new feature, the Clipboard toolbar. This feature lets you cut or copy up to twelve items and paste them in any order you want. When you cut or copy two or more items, the toolbar appears onscreen. To paste an item, click in the document where you want the data to go, then from the Clipboard toolbar, choose the item you want to paste. If you're not too sure which item is which, hover your mouse pointer over an icon and a ScreenTip appears describing the cut or copied data. Click the icon representing the item you want to paste and immediately paste it into your document. To paste another Clipboard item, use the same steps. To close the Clipboard toolbar when you're finished pasting, click the **Close** button.

How to Use Templates

Use Word's templates to create documents quickly when you don't have time to format and design them yourself. A template is a ready-made document. Just fill in your own text. Word comes with numerous templates you can use. If you don't see a template that meets your specific needs, you can choose a template that is close, add your own design and formatting elements, and save the document as a new template. Next time you need the template, it's ready to go.

Begin

1 Open the New Dialog Box

Open the **File** menu and select **New** to display the New dialog box. (You can't use the New button on the Standard toolbar as a shortcut. If you click the **New** button, Word assumes you want to start a new document based on the Normal template; it doesn't give you the chance to choose a different template.)

Click

2 Choose a Tab Category

The New dialog box has several tab categories to choose from, such as **Letters & Faxes**. Depending on the type of document you want to create, click each tab and see what is available. (Depending on how Word was installed and whether anyone has created new templates, the tabs and templates you see may differ from those shown here.)

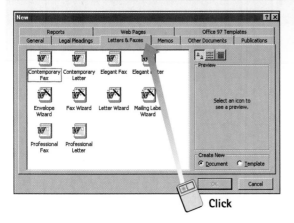

Click

3 Preview a Template

When you locate a template you want to use, select it (by clicking just once on the icon); the **Preview** area lets you see what the design looks like.

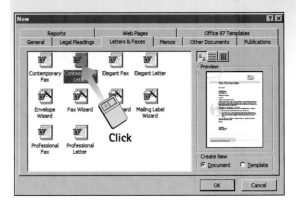

Click

4 Open the Template

If you decide you like the template, double-click its name or select it and choose **OK**.

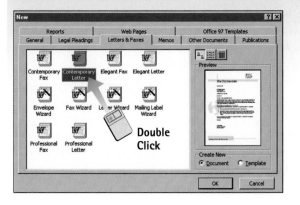

5 Fill It In

Word creates a new document based on the template you chose. Many templates, such as the one shown here, include placeholder text with instructions to "Click here and type" to help you fill in your text. You may also see some cross-hatched boxes. Word uses these for formatting purposes only: they won't print. Click the placeholder text and type your own text.

6 Save, Print, and Close

The text you typed replaces the "click here" text. Continue replacing all the "click here" instructions with the text you want in the document. When you have completed the document, use the regular methods to save, print, and close it.

End

_How-To Hints

Use Wizards

You may notice that some templates in the New dialog box are called *wizards*. Wizards are specialized templates that let you customize the document you create by walking you through each step necessary to build the document. To start a wizard, double-click its name.

Create a Custom Template

You can save a Word template as your own personalized template without changing the built-in template. In the New dialog box, click the **Template** option in the lower-right corner before you open the template. This opens a copy of the built-in template that you can save as your own template with a different name. You can personalize the text and formatting in this template. After you save this template, its icon appears on the **General** tab the next time you choose **File**, **New**.

Delete Templates

To delete a custom template, open the New dialog box, right-click the icon for the template you want to delete, and click **Delete**. Choose **OK** to close the dialog box.

How to Work with AutoText

AutoText is a great tool that saves you time when entering text. If you find yourself repeatedly typing the same company name, phrase, or address, make the text an AutoText entry. Assign the entry a brief abbreviation, and the next time you enter the abbreviation, AutoText inserts the entire text entry for you. AutoText entries can be of any length—from a short sentence to an entire letter—and they are easy to save and use.

Begin

1 Select the Text

Type the text you want to include in your AutoText entry (for example, **Human Resources Department**) and apply any formatting you want.

> Memo
>
> Subject: New Benefit Policies
> To: All Full-time Employees
> From: Human Resources Department

2 Choose the AutoText Command

Open the **Insert** menu and select **AutoText, New.**

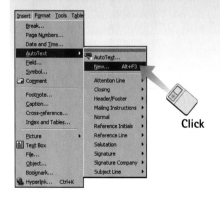

Click

3 Enter a Name

In the Create AutoText dialog box, type a name for the entry in the **Please Name Your AutoText Entry** box (such as **Human Resources** or use the default suggestion) and choose **OK**. Although AutoText names can be more than one word long, you're better off using a name or abbreviation that's short and memorable.

Click

4 Insert AutoText

The next time you're ready to use the entry, click your document where you want the entry inserted and type the first few letters of an AutoText entry's name. As you type, an AutoComplete tip containing the name may appear next to the characters you typed. If you press **Enter**, the AutoText entry is inserted at the location.

5 Open the AutoText Tab

You can also choose which AutoText entry you want to use by opening the **Insert** menu and selecting **AutoText**, **AutoText**. This opens the AutoCorrect dialog box with the AutoText tab displayed.

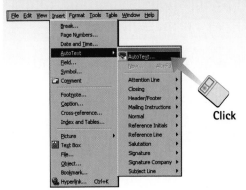

Click

6 Choose an Entry

On the list of AutoText categories, point to the category where your entry is stored and click the name of the entry. Click the **Insert** button, and the entry is pasted into your document.

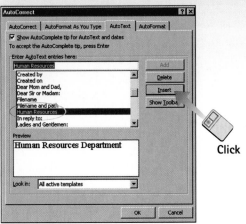

Click

End

How-To Hints

Delete Entries

To delete an AutoText entry, open the **Insert** menu and select **AutoText**, **AutoText** to display the AutoText tab of the AutoCorrect dialog box. Click the entry you want to delete from the list, click the **Delete** button, and click **OK**.

Use the AutoText Toolbar

Another way to create and insert AutoText entries is with the AutoText toolbar. Display the toolbar on your screen (select **View**, **Toolbars**, **AutoText**) and use the **New** button to add new entries as you encounter them. To insert an entry, click the **AutoText** button, choose the entry from the list, and click **Insert**.

Turn AutoComplete On or Off

To turn automatic AutoText entries on or off, choose **Tools**, **AutoCorrect**, **Next**, at the top of the AutoText tab, mark or clear the **Show AutoComplete Tip for AutoText and Dates** check box.

Task

How to Use Word's Formatting Tools

*T*he term *formatting* refers to all the techniques that enhance the appearance of your document: including character, paragraph, and page formatting. *Character formatting* refers to all the features that can affect individual text characters, such as fonts, sizes, bold, or italic. *Paragraph formatting* includes line spacing, indents, alignment, tabs, and paragraph spacing. *Page formatting* includes page orientation, margins, and page breaks.

Word's numerous formatting tools are what make the program such a valuable part of the Office suite. In this chapter, you'll learn about many of these formatting features and how they can help make your own documents more professional-looking and polished. ●

How to Apply Bold, Italic, and Other Formatting

By far the easiest formatting to apply is bold, italic, and underline. These three formatting commands are the most commonly used formatting commands. They are so frequently used, in fact, that they have their own buttons on the Formatting toolbar. You can easily turn these three formatting options on or off as needed using the toolbar buttons.

In addition, you can also find them in the *Font dialog box*, a comprehensive dialog box for applying formatting options in one fell swoop.

Begin

1 Use Bold, Italic, and Underline

Select the text you want to format, or choose the formatting commands before typing in the text. To boldface text, click the **Bold** button on the Formatting toolbar. To italicize text, click the **Italic** button. To underline text, click the **Underline** button.

Bold Underline

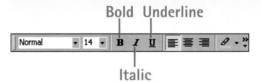

Italic

2 Formatting Applied

Depending on which buttons you select, the formatting is immediately applied to your selected text. You can also apply more than one format to your text. For example, you can choose to make a word bold, italicized, and underlined.

Bold

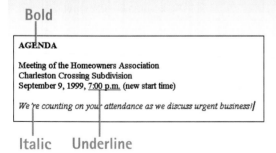

AGENDA

Meeting of the Homeowners Association
Charleston Crossing Subdivision
September 9, 1999, 7:00 p.m. (new start time)

We're counting on your attendance as we discuss urgent business!

Italic   Underline

3 Open the Font Dialog Box

If you want to see what the formatting will look like before you apply it, open the **Format** menu and choose **Font**. This opens the Font dialog box with the Font tab displayed.

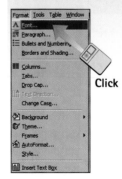

Click

_4_ Use the Font Dialog Box

In the **Font Style** list, choose **Bold**, **Italic**, or **Bold Italic** to boldface and/or italicize your text. To underline text, click the down arrow on the **Underline Style** list box to display the list of choices, and click the desired underline style.

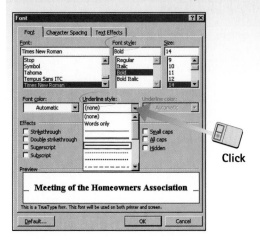

Click

_5_ Preview Your Selections

In the **Preview** area at the bottom of the dialog box, you can preview how your choices will affect the text.

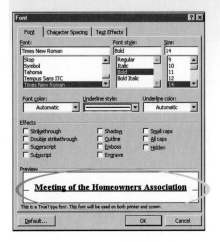

_6_ Exit the Dialog Box

When you've made your selections, choose **OK** to close the dialog box and apply the changes to the selected text.

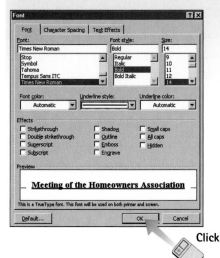

Click

End

How-To Hints

Toggle On or Off

The Bold, Italic, and Underline buttons on the Formatting toolbar toggle on or off. To remove the formatting, click the appropriate toolbar button again.

Keyboard Shortcuts

To format text from the keyboard, select the text, and use these keyboard shortcuts: **Ctrl+B** for boldface, **Ctrl+I** for italic, **Ctrl+U** for underline, or **Ctrl+Shift+D** for double underline.

Adding Color

To color text, click the **Font Color** drop-down arrow in the Font dialog box to display the list of choices, then click the color you want to use. To add color to an underline, click the **Underline Color** drop-down arrow and select a color. You can also use the **Font Color** button on the Formatting toolbar: Click the button's arrow and choose a color from the palette that appears.

How to Change the Font and Size

Changing fonts and sizes provides an easy way to alter the appearance of words and of the document. By default, Word assigns Times New Roman, 10 point, every time you open a new document, but you can easily apply another font or size any time you want. You can change the font or size for one word, a paragraph, or the entire document.

Don't go overboard and use so many fonts and sizes that the document becomes excessively busy and difficult to read. Two or three fonts per document is usually enough.

Begin

1 Select the Text

Select the text with the font you want to change.

> **AGENDA**
>
> Meeting of the Homeowners Association
> Charleston Crossing Subdivision
> September 9, 1999, 7:00 p.m. (new start time)

2 Choose a Font

On the Formatting toolbar, click the down arrow on the **Font** box to display a list of your installed fonts. Scroll through the list to find the font you want, and click it to apply it to the selected text. (Word places the fonts you've used recently above a double line at the top of the list; below the double line is an alphabetical list of all the fonts.)

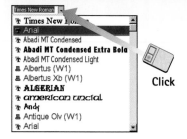

Click

3 Choose a Size

After you have chosen a font, you can make it larger or smaller by changing the font size. On the Formatting toolbar, click the down arrow on the **Font Size** box to display the list of font sizes. Scroll, if necessary, to find the size you want, and click it to apply it to the selected text. (You can also click in the **Font Size** box and type a point size that's not on the list.)

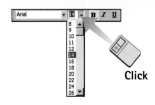

Click

4 Open the Font Dialog Box

The quickest way to experiment with fonts, sizes, and other characteristics all at the same time is to use the Font dialog box. Select the text you want to format, and choose **Format**, **Font**.

Click

5 Preview Font and Size

Use the Font tab to change the font and size, and check the results in the **Preview** area. Choose a font from the **Font** list, for example, to see what it looks like in the **Preview** area. Click **OK** to exit the Font dialog box and apply the new settings.

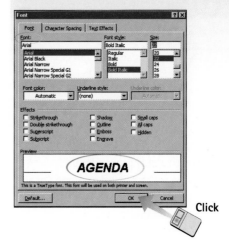

Click

End

How-To Hints

Don't Like It?

If, after applying a new font or size, you decide you don't like it, click the **Undo** button on the Standard toolbar; the text will revert back to the previous font or size.

Change the Default Font and Size

By default, Word uses the font Times New Roman and the font size 10, which can be pretty hard to read. To change the default font or size, change it in the Font dialog box, and click the **Default** button. Click **Yes** to confirm and the new default settings are applied.

Different Fonts

The number and type of available fonts depend on what has been installed on your computer, but most computers have a wide selection of fonts. The fonts shown in my font list will vary from those installed on your computer.

What's Assigned?

The buttons and list boxes on the Formatting toolbar—for font, font size, style, and so on—always reflect the formatting at the current location of the insertion point. This comes in handy when you aren't sure which font is applied to a particular block of text. Just click in the text, and look at the Formatting toolbar to see what characteristics are in effect.

How to Copy Text Formatting

If you have applied several character formats—such as a font, a font size, and a format (bold, italic, underline)—to a block of text in your document and later decide you would like to apply the same formatting to another block of text, you don't have to apply those formats one by one to the new location. Instead, you can use the Format Painter button to take all the formats from the original block of text and "paint" them across the new text.

Begin

1 Select the Text

Select the text that has the formatting you want to copy (characters, words, whole paragraphs, headings, and so on).

> **The Constitution of the United States of America**
>
> We the people of the United States, in order to form a more perfect union, establish justice, insure domestic tranquillity, provide for the common defense, promote the general welfare, and secure the blessings of liberty to ourselves and our posterity, do ordain and establish this Constitution for the United States of America.
>
> **Article I**
> **Section 1.**
>
> All legislative powers herein granted shall be vested in a Congress of the United States, which shall consist of a Senate and House of Representatives.
>
> **Section 2.**

2 Choose Format Painter

Click the **Format Painter** button in the Standard toolbar.

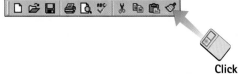

Click

3 Mouse Pointer Changes

Your mouse pointer changes to the paintbrush pointer.

> **The Constitution of the United States of America**
>
> We the people of the United States, in order to form a more perfect union, establish justice, insure domestic tranquillity, provide for the common defense, promote the general welfare, and secure the blessings of liberty to ourselves and our posterity, do ordain and establish this Constitution for the United States of America.
>
> **Article I**
> **Section 1.**
>
> All legislative powers herein granted shall be vested in a Congress of the United States, which shall consist of a Senate and House of Representatives.
>
> **Section 2.**

4 Drag to Copy Formatting

Drag the paintbrush pointer across the text where you want to paint the format.

> **The Constitution of the United States of America**
>
> We the people of the United States, in order to form a more perfect union, establish justice, insure domestic tranquillity, provide for the common defense, promote the general welfare, and secure the blessings of liberty to ourselves and our posterity, do ordain and establish this Constitution for the United States of America.
>
> **Article I**
> Section 1.
>
> All legislative powers herein granted shall be vested in a Congress of the United States, which shall consist of a Senate and House of Representatives.
>
> **Section 2.**

 Click & Drag

5 Formatting Is Applied

Release the mouse. The formatting is painted to the block of text (click anywhere to de-select the text).

> **The Constitution of the United States of America**
>
> We the people of the United States, in order to form a more perfect union, establish justice, insure domestic tranquillity, provide for the common defense, promote the general welfare, and secure the blessings of liberty to ourselves and our posterity, do ordain and establish this Constitution for the United States of America.
>
> **Article I**
> Section 1.
>
> All legislative powers herein granted shall be vested in a Congress of the United States, which shall consist of a Senate and House of Representatives.
>
> **Section 2.**

End

How-To Hints

Keep Painting

To paint the same formatting to several blocks of text more quickly, double-click the **Format Painter** button. Format Painter remains turned on so you can paint the formatting repeatedly. For example, you could paint across all the headings in the document shown here. When you're finished painting the formatting, click the **Format Painter** button again to turn it off.

Another Route

Another way to copy formatting is to use the Repeat command. Apply formatting to a selection of text with the Font dialog box (by using the Font dialog box, you can apply several formatting characteristics at once) and click **OK**. To apply that same formatting to another section of text, don't bother opening the Font dialog box again. Just select the block of text where you want to copy the formatting, choose **Edit, Repeat Font Formatting**, and the same formatting is applied to the new text. (This only works if your previous action was to assign formatting.)

Use AutoFormat

Don't like the pressures of coming up with formatting yourself? Use Word's AutoFormat feature to format your documents automatically. Open the **Format** menu and select **AutoFormat**. In the AutoFormat dialog box, select the type of document you're creating and click **OK**.

How to Use Styles

A *style* is a collection of formatting specifications that has been assigned a name and saved. You might have a report, for example, that uses specific formatting for every heading. Rather than reapply the formatting for every heading, assign the formatting to a style. You can then quickly apply the style whenever you need it. Word comes with a few predefined styles, but you can easily create your own and use them over and over.

Begin

1 Format the Text

Format the text as desired. You can apply any of Word's formatting commands, including character, paragraph, and page formatting. Then select the text or click anywhere in the formatted text.

How to Use Styles

A *style* is a collection of formatting specifications that has been assigned a name and saved. You might have a report, for example, that uses specific formatting for every heading. Rather than reapply the formatting for every heading, assign the formatting to a style. You can then quickly apply the style whenever you need it. Word comes with a few pre-made styles, but you can easily create your own and use them over and over.

Format the Text

Format the text as desired. You can apply any of Word's formatting commands, including character, paragraph, and page formatting. Then select the text or click anywhere in the formatted text.

Use the Style List Box
Click inside the Style list box on the Formatting toolbar.

Enter a Name
Type a name for the new style. Be careful not to use any of the existing style names. Press Enter when finished. The style is added to the list and ready to assign. For example, I assigned a new style called Paragraph Title.

Assign a Style
To assign a style to text, select the text first.

Open the Style List
Click the Style drop-down arrow and select the style you want to apply.

---

2 Use the Style List Box

Click inside the **Style** list box on the Formatting toolbar.

Click

3 Enter a Name

Type a name for the new style. Be careful not to use any of the existing style names. Press **Enter** when finished. The style is added to the list and ready to assign. For example, I assigned a new style called **Paragraph Title**.

Paragraph Title

4 Assign a Style

To assign a style to text, select the text first.

How to Use Styles

A *style* is a collection of formatting specifications that has been assigned a name and saved. You might have a report, for example, that uses specific formatting for every heading. Rather than reapply the formatting for every heading, assign the formatting to a style. You can then quickly apply the style whenever you need it. Word comes with a few pre-made styles, but you can easily create your own and use them over and over.

Format the Text
Format the text as desired. You can apply any of Word's formatting commands, including character, paragraph, and page formatting. Then select the text or click anywhere in the formatted text.

Use the Style List Box
Click inside the Style list box on the Formatting toolbar.

Enter a Name
Type a name for the new style. Be careful not to use any of the existing style names. Press Enter when finished. The style is added to the list and ready to assign. For example, I assigned a new style called Paragraph Title.

Assign a Style
To assign a style to text, select the text first.

Open the Style List
Click the Style drop-down arrow and select the style you want to apply.

---

5 Open the Style List

Click the **Style** drop-down arrow and select the style you want to apply.

Click

---

6 Formatting Is Applied

The style is immediately applied to the selected text. Continue applying the style to other text in your document as needed.

How to Use Styles

A *style* is a collection of formatting specifications that has been assigned a name and saved. You might have a report, for example, that uses specific formatting for every heading. Rather than reapply the formatting for every heading, assign the formatting to a style. You can then quickly apply the style whenever you need it. Word comes with a few pre-made styles, but you can easily create your own and use them over and over.

Format the Text
Format the text as desired. You can apply any of Word's formatting commands, including character, paragraph, and page formatting. Then select the text or click anywhere in the formatted text.

Use the Style List Box
Click inside the Style list box on the Formatting toolbar.

Enter a Name
Type a name for the new style. Be careful not to use any of the existing style names. Press Enter when finished. The style is added to the list and ready to assign. For example, I assigned a new style called Paragraph Title.

Assign a Style
To assign a style to text, select the text first.

Open the Style List
Click the Style drop-down arrow and select the style you want to apply.

End

How-To Hints

Use the Style Dialog Box

Another way to assign styles is with the **Format**, **Style** command. Open the **Format** menu and select **Style** to display the Style dialog box where you can select a style to apply, modify an existing style, or delete styles.

Adding Style Shortcuts

You can assign keystroke combinations to styles to help speed up style assignment. Open the **Format** menu and select **Style**. Select the style you want to add a keyboard shortcut to, and click the **Modify** button. Click the **Shortcut Key** button and assign a keystroke combination to the style in the **Press New Shortcut Key** text box. If the keystroke combination is already in use by another feature, the dialog box will tell you and you can try another. When you find one that's available, click **Assign** and exit the dialog boxes. Of course, now you have to remember what the shortcut key is to use the style.

How to Insert Symbols

Need to insert a special character or symbol not found on the keyboard? Tap into Word's collection of characters and symbols to find exactly what you seek. You can insert a copyright or trademark symbol, for example, into your text for products you mention. Depending on what fonts you have installed, you may have access to additional symbols, such as mathematical or Greek symbols, architectural symbols, and more.

Begin

1 Open the Symbol Dialog Box

Click the insertion point where you want the symbol inserted, open the **Insert** menu, and select **Symbol**.

Click

2 Choose a Symbol

From the **Symbols** tab, click a symbol to magnify it. Each symbol you click is magnified so you can see clearly what it looks like (for example, click the ® symbol).

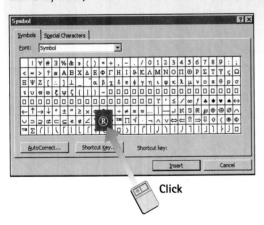

Click

3 Insert the Symbol

After selecting the symbol you want to use, click the **Insert** button and the symbol is placed in your text.

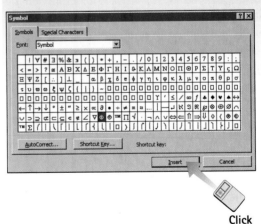

Click

4 Choose a Special Character

If you want a special character inserted, click the **Special Character** tab to view what's available.

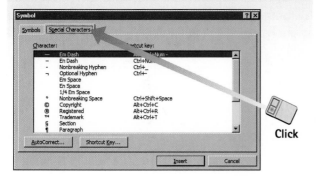

Click

5 Insert the Special Character

Select the special character you want to insert, and click the **Insert** button. The character is added to your text.

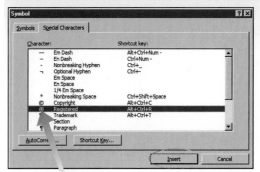

Click

6 Close the Dialog Box

The Symbol dialog box remains open in case you want to add another symbol. Click the **Close** button to exit the dialog box.

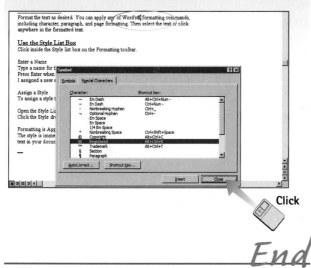

Click

End

How-To Hints

Customize the Symbols

Use the **Font** drop-down list in the Symbol dialog box to change the font used. Use WingDings, for example, to insert character icons such as clocks and telephones. Be sure to check out the symbols available for the fonts you have installed on your computer.

Symbols Ready to Go

Word's AutoCorrect feature watches out for common symbols you need to type, such as the copyright or trademark symbols, and automatically inserts them for you. For example, if you type (c), AutoCorrect automatically replaces the keystrokes with the © symbol. For more information about using AutoCorrect, turn to the task "How to Work with AutoCorrect" in Chapter 4, "How to Use Word's Proofing and Printing Tools."

How to Set Margins

The default margins in Word are 1 inch on the top and bottom of the page and 1.25 inches on the left and right. These margins are fine for most documents, but like all features in Word, they can be changed.

Wider margins can give the page a more spacious appearance, for example. Or you may find you have just a line or two more than will fit on a page, but if you adjust the margins slightly, everything fits.

Begin

1 Open the Page Setup Dialog Box

Open the **File** menu and select **Page Setup**.

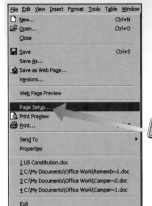

Click

2 View the Margins Tab

In the Page Setup dialog box, click the **Margins** tab if it's not already displayed.

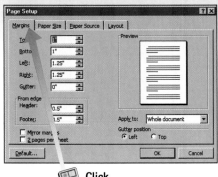

Click

3 Change the Margins

Type new margin settings in **Top**, **Bottom**, **Left**, and **Right** boxes; the settings are measured in inches. You can also use the spin arrows to set new measurements: Click the up arrow to increase the measurement, and click the down arrow to decrease the measurement.

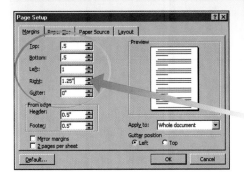

Click

4 Apply the New Settings

Click **OK** to apply the new margins to your document.

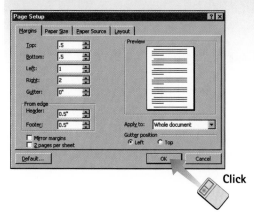

Click

5 View the New Margin Settings

On the Standard toolbar, click the **Print Preview** button to switch the document to print preview. In Print Preview you see a whole-page view of your document, and it's easier to check margin settings for a good visual appearance.

Print Preview

6 Change Margins Manually

Instead of setting inch measurements, you can change margins manually in either Print Preview or Print Layout view. The margins are displayed as gray bars at each end of the horizontal and vertical rulers. You can drag a margin to reset it.

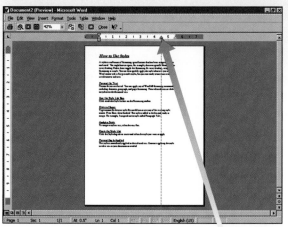

Click & Drag

End

How-To Hints

Use Caution

Be careful about setting margins too narrow or wide: Most printers have a minimum margin that's not printable. (Commonly, less than .25 inches is outside the printable area.)

Changing the Default Margins

If your company wants margin settings on all its documents that differ from Word's default margins, you can set the default margins to match those used in your company (then you won't have to change the margins each time you start a new document). To set new default margins, follow steps 1 through 3, but before you choose OK in step 4, click the **Default** button. When Word asks if you want to change the default settings for page setup, click **Yes**, and choose **OK**. You can change the default margins as often as you like.

How to Set the Line Spacing

Line spacing is the amount of space between lines within a paragraph. By default, Word starts each new document with single spacing, which provides just enough space between lines so that letters don't over-lap. You might want to switch to double-spacing for rough drafts of documents because it gives you extra room to write in edits by hand. Or try one-and-a-half spacing, which makes text easier to read by separating lines with an extra half-line of blank space.

You can also control the amount of space between paragraphs. For example, documents with an extra half-line of space between paragraphs are easier to read, and you don't need to type an extra blank line between paragraphs.

Begin

1 Select the Paragraph

To change the line spacing of only one paragraph, click in the paragraph. To change the line spacing of several paragraphs, select them first. To change the line spacing for the entire document, press **Ctrl+A** to select the entire document.

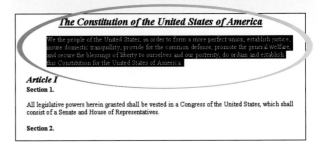

2 Open the Paragraph Dialog Box

Open the **Format** menu and select **Paragraph** to display the Paragraph dialog box.

Click

3 Choose a Line Spacing

At the top of the Paragraph dialog box, click the **Indents and Spacing** tab if it's not already in front. Then click the down arrow on the **Line Spacing** list box. Select a line spacing: **Single**, **1.5 Lines**, or **Double**.

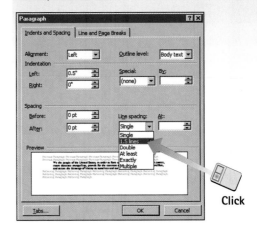

Click

4 Change Paragraph Spacing

To change paragraph spacing for the selected text, designate a new setting in the **Before** and **After** boxes under **Spacing**. Use the spin arrows to set paragraph spacing in points, or type in a setting. The **Before** box sets spacing at the top of the paragraph; the **After** box sets spacing at the bottom of the paragraph.

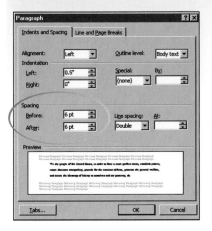

5 Exit the Dialog Box

Choose **OK** to close the dialog box.

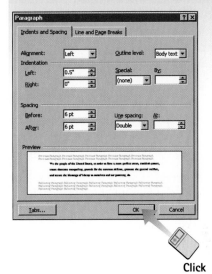

Click

6 Apply Line Spacing

Any changes you made in the Paragraph dialog box are applied to the selected text.

The Constitution of the United States of America

We the people of the United States, in order to form a more perfect union, establish justice, ensure domestic tranquility, provide for the common defense, promote the general welfare, and secure the blessings of liberty to ourselves and our posterity, do ordain and establish this Constitution for the United States of America.

Article I
Section 1.

All legislative powers herein granted shall be vested in a Congress of the United States, which shall consist of a Senate and House of Representatives.

End

How-To Hints

Preview First

When changing the settings in the Paragraph dialog box, check out the effects in the Preview area to see how similar effects will appear in your own text.

How to Align Text

Use Word's alignment commands to change the way your text is positioned horizontally on the document page. By default, Word automatically aligns your text with the left margin as you type. You can choose to align text to the right margin, center text between the left and right margins, or justify text so it aligns at both the left and right margins.

For example, if you're creating a title page for a report, you might want to center the title text. If you're creating a newsletter or columns of text, justify the text to create even alignments on both sides.

Begin

1 Select the Text

Select the text or paragraphs you want to align.

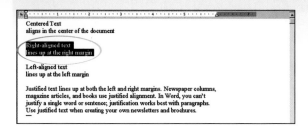

2 Use the Alignment Buttons

The alignment buttons on the Formatting toolbar will quickly align the text for you. Click **Align Left** to left-align text. Click **Center** to center text, click **Align Right** to right-align text. Click **Justify** to justify text between the left and right margins.

3 Word Aligns Your Text

Depending on which alignment button you chose, Word aligns your text accordingly. The figure below shows several alignment examples in effect.

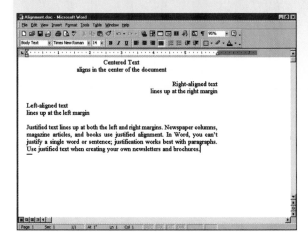

4 Use the Paragraph Dialog Box

Another way to apply alignment is with the Paragraph dialog box: one-stop shopping for Paragraph formatting commands. Open the **Format** menu and choose **Paragraph**.

Click

5 Choose an Alignment

In the **Indents and Spacing** tab, click the **Alignment** drop-down arrow to display a list of alignment options. Click the one you want to use.

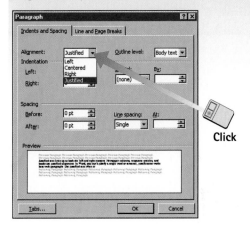

Click

6 Exit the Dialog Box

Notice the **Preview** area gives you a glimpse at what the alignment will do to your text. Click **OK** to exit the dialog box and apply the settings to your document.

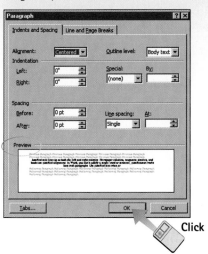

Click

End

How-To Hints

Undo Alignment

To undo any alignment you assign, select the text again and choose a new alignment. Unlike Bold or Italic, the alignment buttons don't toggle on or off.

Keyboard Shortcuts

To center text using only the keyboard, press **Ctrl+E**. Press **Ctrl+L** for left alignment, **Ctrl+R** for right alignment, and **Ctrl+J** for justified alignment.

Vertical Alignment

To change your document's vertical alignment, use the Page Setup dialog box. Open the **File** menu and select **Page Setup**. Click the **Layout** tab and use the **Vertical Alignment** drop-down list to choose a new alignment: **Top** (default), **Center**, or **Justified**. Click **OK** to exit and apply the alignment to the document.

How to Indent Text

Indentations are simply margins that affect individual paragraphs or lines. Indentations can help make paragraphs easier to distinguish. The quickest way to indent a line of text is with the Tab key; however, other ways will indent text more precisely. You can set exact measurements for left and right indentations, choose to indent only the first line of text, or create a hanging indentation that leaves the first line intact but indents the rest of the paragraph.

Begin

1 Use the Indent Buttons

For quick indentations, use the Indent buttons on the Formatting toolbar. To increase the indentation, click in the paragraph or sentence you want to indent, and click the **Increase Indent** button. To decrease the indentation, click **Decrease Indent**.

Increase Indent

Decrease Indent

2 Use the Paragraph Dialog Box

For specific kinds of indentations or to set an exact indentation, open the Paragraph dialog box. Click in front of the paragraph or text you want to indent, and display the **Format** menu and select **Paragraph**.

Click

3 Set an Indent Measurement

From the **Indents and Spacing** tab, use the **Left** or **Right** indentation boxes to set a specific measurement for the indentation. You can type directly into the boxes, or use the spin arrows to increase the settings.

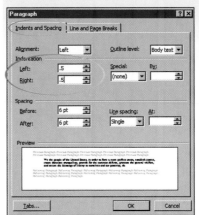

4 Set a Special Indent

To set a First line or a Hanging indentation, click the **Special** drop-down list and make a selection.

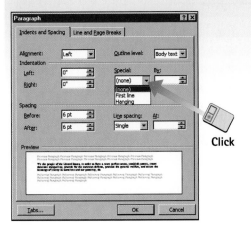

Click

5 Exit the Dialog Box

After setting the indent, check the **Preview** area to see how it will look. Click **OK** to exit the dialog box.

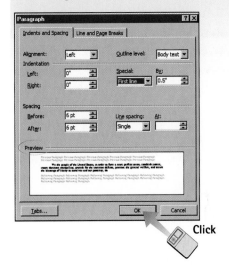

Click

6 Indents Applied

Word applies your indent specifications to the selected text. The figure below shows an example of a first-line indentation and a hanging indentation.

First line indentation

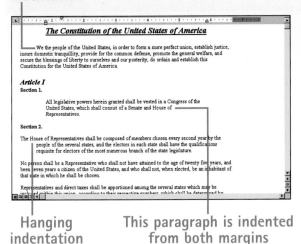

Hanging indentation

This paragraph is indented from both margins

End

How-To Hints

Another Quick Indentation

For a quick indentation while you're typing a new paragraph, press the Tab key. This indents your text line by 1/2", which is perfect for starting most paragraphs.

Indentations on the Ruler

You can also set indentations on the ruler, including First line and Hanging indentations. To set an indentation, drag the appropriate indentation marker on the ruler bar. The indentation markers are funny looking triangle shapes on the left side of the ruler. If you hover your mouse pointer over an indentation marker, a ScreenTip appears identifying the marker.

Other Indentation Ideas

Use both a left and right indentation to indent quotes or special text you want to set off in a document.

TASK *10*

How to Work with Bulleted and Numbered Lists

Use Word's Bulleted and Numbered List features to set off lists of information in your documents. For example, a bulleted list can make a list of related information easy to spot on a page, and a numbered list organizes items that must be listed in a certain order.

You can start a bulleted or numbered list before typing in text, or you can turn existing text into an organized list.

Begin

1 Select Text

To turn existing text into a list, first select the text.

2 Use the Formatting Buttons

To add bullets, click the **Bullets** button on the Formatting toolbar. To turn the text into a numbered list, click the **Numbering** button.

Numbering

Bullets

3 Word Applies Bullets or Numbers

If you selected Bullets, the text is immediately indented with bullet points in front of each line. If you selected Numbering, the list is numbered sequentially, as shown in the following figure.

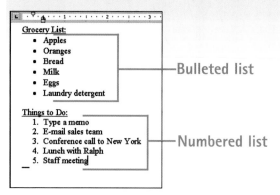

Bulleted list

Numbered list

4 Add to the List

To add more items to the list, click at the end of the line before the place where you want to add another item and press **Enter**. Word inserts a new bullet or numbered step for you; just type in the new text. After you type the last item in the list, press **Enter** twice to turn the numbered or bulleted list off, or click the **Numbering** or **Bullets** button on the toolbar to turn the feature off.

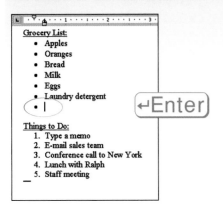

5 Change the Style

If you prefer to use a different bullet or numbering style in your list, open the Bullets and Numbering dialog box. Select the list text, and open the **Format** menu and choose **Bullets and Numbering**.

Click

6 Bullets and Numbering Dialog

To change the bullet style, click the **Bulleted** tab and choose another style. To change the number style, click the **Numbered** tab and select another style. Click **OK** to exit the dialog box and apply the new style.

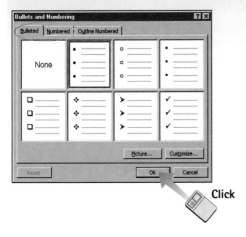

Click

End

How-To Hints

Create the List from Scratch

You can also create a bulleted or numbered list as you type. For a numbered list, type **1.** followed by a space, type the text for the first item, and press Enter. To create a bulleted list, type an asterisk (*) followed by a space, type the text for the first item, and press Enter. Continue entering list items as needed. Press Enter twice after the last item to turn off the list feature.

Customize Bullets or Numbers

Use the **Customize** button in the Bullets and Numbering dialog box to set another font for the bullets or numbers you use, or customize the way in which they are positioned in the document. Learn more about customizing in Task 11, "How to Customize Bulleted and Numbered Lists."

How to Customize Bulleted and Numbered Lists

Word automatically assigns a default bullet style or a default number style when creating bulleted and numbered lists. You can customize the appearance of the bullets or numbers used in such lists. For example, you may prefer larger bullets, or picture bullets instead. If you're using Word to create a Web page, for instance, you may want to use a colorful bullet image that really shows up on the page. Use the Bullets and Numbering customizing features to change the style and position of the bullets or numbers used in your lists.

Begin

1 Select Text

To customize an existing bulleted or numbered list, first select the list. You can also follow these steps to set custom bullets or numbers before typing in the list.

2 Open the Dialog Box

Open the **Format** menu and choose **Bullets and Numbering**. This opens the Bullets and Numbering dialog box.

Click

3 Open the Customize Dialog Box

To customize the placement of the bullets or numbers in the list text or change the bullet style, click the **Customize** button (be sure to select a bullet style first). This opens the Customize Bulleted List or Customize Numbered List dialog box.

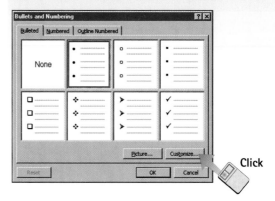

Click

4 Change the Position

Use the position controls to change how the bulleted or numbered list is indented. Enter a new measurement in the Indent at text box or use the spin arrows to set a new setting. Check the **Preview** area to see how the indents look. Click **OK** to exit and apply the new indents.

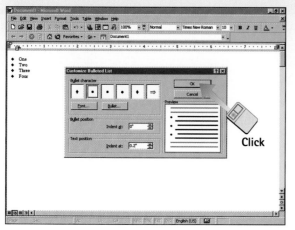

Click

5 Assign a Picture Bullet

You can assign Web page bullets to a bulleted list. Click the **Picture** button in the Bullets and Numbering dialog box to open the Picture Bullet dialog box.

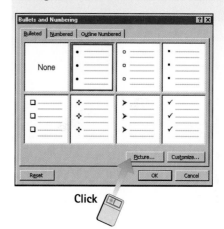

Click

6 Choose a Picture Bullet

Scroll through the list of picture bullets in the **Pictures** tab and select the one you want to use.

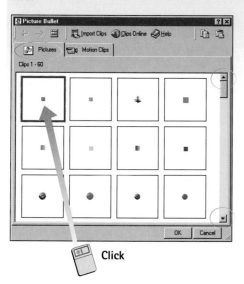

Click

7 Exit and Apply

A balloon list pops up; click the **Insert Clip** icon and click **OK**. The bullet pictures replace any default bullets in the list.

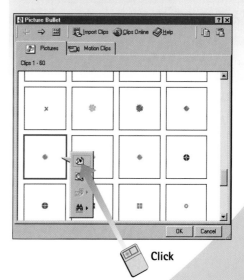

Click

End

How to Set Tabs

Tabs are used to indent and create vertically aligned columns of text. By default, Word has tab stops set at every .5-inch interval in your document; the tab text is always aligned at the left, which means it lines up at the left edge of the tab column. You can create your own tab stops and change how the tab text is aligned at a tab stop. You can, for example, align tab text to the right edge of the tab column, center the text in the column, or use the decimal point tab to line up decimal points in the tab column. You can even apply a bar tab which sets a vertical bar between tab columns.

You can use the ruler to set tabs, or open the Tabs dialog box. Both methods are explained in this task.

Begin

1 Set a Tab Stop on the Ruler

To set a tab stop on the ruler, first select the type of tab alignment. By default, the Left Tab alignment is selected. To select another, you must cycle through the selections. Each click on the alignment button displays a different tab alignment symbol (hover your mouse pointer over the button to display the tab alignment name).

Tab alignment button

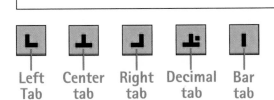

| Left Tab | Center tab | Right tab | Decimal tab | Bar tab |

2 Click in Place

On the ruler, click where you want the tab inserted; the tab symbol is added to the ruler.

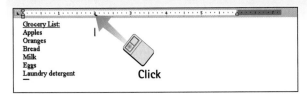

Click

3 Apply a Tab

To use the new tab stop, place the cursor at the beginning of the line and press **Tab**, or place your cursor in front of the text you want to reposition and then press **Tab**. The tab is in effect until you change it to another setting.

Tab

4 Open the Tabs Dialog Box

Another way to set tabs is to use the Tabs dialog box. Open the **Format** menu and choose **Tabs**.

Click

5 Enter a Tab Stop

In the **Tab Stop Position** text box, enter a new tab stop measurement. Use the **Alignment** options to change the tab stop alignment.

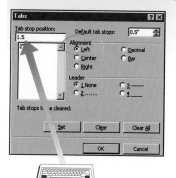

6 Exit the Dialog Box

Click **OK** to exit the dialog box. The new tab stop is ready to go.

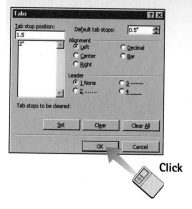

Click

End

How-To Hints

Deleting Tabs

To delete a tab, drag it off the ruler, release the mouse button, and it's gone. To delete tabs from the Tabs dialog box, select the tab from the list box and click **Clear**.

Leader Tabs

Use the Tabs dialog box to set leader tabs. Leader tabs are tabs separated by dots or dashes. They're used to help the reader follow tabbed information from column to column.

Changing the Default Tab

If you prefer a different default tab setting than ? inch intervals, set a new default tab measurement in the Tabs dialog box. Click inside the **Default Tab Stops** text box and enter a new setting or use the spin arrows to change the existing setting. Click **OK** and the new default tab stop is applied.

How to Create Columns

If you're creating a newsletter or brochure with Word, consider formatting the text into columns, much like a newspaper or magazine. Word's columns are *newspaper-style columns*, which means the text flows to the bottom of a column and then continues at the top of the next column.

Begin

1 Select Text

Select the text you want to format into columns, then open the **Format** menu and choose **Columns**.

Click

2 Select a Column Type

Under the Presets area, click the type of column style you want to use, such as **Two** or **Three**. Use the **Width and Spacing** options to set an exact measurement for the columns and the space between them (or go with the default settings). The **Preview** area lets you see what the columns will look like.

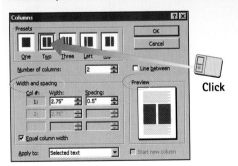

Click

3 Apply To

To apply the column format to a specific area, click the **Apply To** drop-down arrow and choose the extent to which the columns apply in the document. Alternatively, choose **Whole Document** if you want the entire document to use columns.

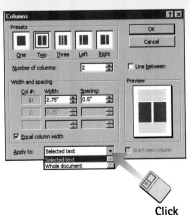

Click

4 Exit the Dialog Box

Click **OK** to exit the dialog box and apply the column format to your text.

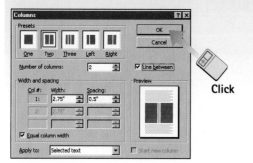

Click

5 Quick Columns

Another way to set columns is with the Columns button on the Standard toolbar. Select the text you want to apply columns to, then click the **Columns** button on the Standard toolbar and drag the number of columns you want to use.

Click & Drag

6 Column Format Applied

Release the mouse button and the columns are assigned. Word will display the columns in Print Layout view, the best view for seeing columns in Word.

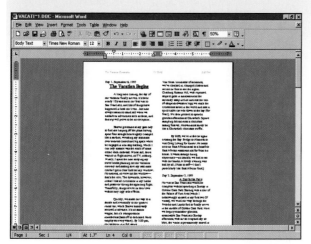

End

How-To Hints

Can't See Them?

The best view for columns is Print Layout view. You can only see columns in Print Layout view or in the Print Preview window. Click the **Print Layout View** button to switch views as needed.

Setting Column Breaks

To make a break within a column and cause the text to flow to the next column, click where you want the break to occur, then press **Ctrl+Shift+Enter**. To remove a column break, select it and press **Delete**.

Turning Columns Off

To turn your column text back into normal text (which is really just one column anyway), select the text, click the **Columns** button on the Standard toolbar, and drag to select a single column.

Inserting a Divider Line

One of the options in the Columns dialog box lets you add a divider line between columns, which defines the columns and gives a nice visual appeal. Click the **Line Between** check box to add such a line to your columns.

How to Insert a Table

If you want to create a complex list or chart, the best option is to use a Word table. A *table* is a grid of rows and columns; each box in a table is called a *cell*. You can use tables to create anything from simple charts to invoices and employee lists. Tables are useful for any kind of information that needs to be organized in a row-and-column format. Tables are flexible; you can specify exactly how many rows or columns, control the size and formatting of each cell, and include anything from text to graphics.

Begin

1 Create a Quick Table

To create a table the quick way, click in the document where you want to place the table, then click the **Insert Table** button on the Standard toolbar. A grid appears where you can tell Word how many columns and rows you want in the initial table; drag to select squares that represent cells in the table (for example, drag to select 3 columns by 4 rows).

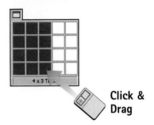

Click & Drag

2 Instant Table

Release the mouse button, and a table with the number of rows and columns you selected appears on the page. The table stretches across the width of the page; to make a column narrower, point to a vertical border and drag it to a new position (drag the right table border to narrow the entire table).

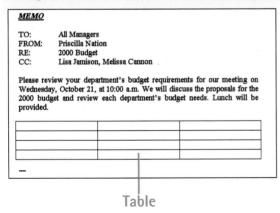

Table

3 Enter Table Text

Click in a cell and begin typing. The text in each cell behaves like a paragraph; if you press Enter, a new paragraph is started in the same cell. You can format the text in each cell the same way you format text in a normal paragraph.

MEMO

TO:	All Managers
FROM:	Priscilla Nation
RE:	2000 Budget
CC:	Lisa Jamison, Melissa Cannon

Please review your department's budget requirements for our meeting on Wednesday, October 21, at 10:00 a.m. We will discuss the proposals for the 2000 budget and review each department's budget needs. Lunch will be provided.

10:00	Department A	Tina Daniels
10:30	Department B	

4 Draw Your Own Table

To draw an asymmetrical table, cell by cell, click the **Tables and Borders** button on the Standard toolbar. The Tables and Borders toolbar appears, the view changes to Print Layout view, and the mouse pointer becomes a pencil.

Tables and Borders

5 Choose Table Options

Click the **Draw Table** button if it isn't already selected, then use the **Line Style**, **Line Weight**, and **Border Color** buttons on the Tables and Borders toolbar to choose the type and color of line you want for the outside border of your table. Drag the mouse to draw a rectangle for the outside border of the table.

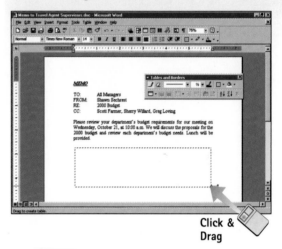

Click &
Drag

6 Draw the Table Lines

Select a different line type or color for the inside borders, if you want; then draw internal lines to delineate rows and columns. As you drag, a dashed line shows you where the line will be inserted. Release the mouse as the line extends across the entire width or height of the table. You can draw a table as complex as you want with this method.

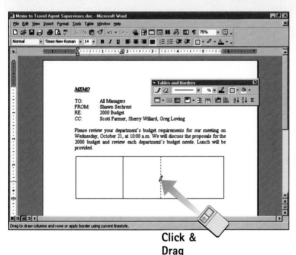

Click &
Drag

End

How-To Hints

Navigate a Table

Press **Tab** to move cell by cell to the right, and **Shift+Tab** to move cell by cell to the left. (To insert a tab character in a cell, press **Ctrl+Tab**.)

Add and Delete Rows

To insert a new row within a table, click in the row below where you want the new row inserted, then click the **Insert Table** drop-down arrow on the Tables and Borders toolbar and choose **Insert Rows Above**; or choose **Table, Insert, Rows Above**. To delete a row, click in the row, choose **Table, Select, Row**, then choose **Table, Delete, Rows**.

Formatting Gridlines

You can show your table's gridlines and format them with the Borders formats or hide them (which makes the table look like a neat list). To hide gridlines, click in the table, then choose **Table, Hide Gridlines**; to show them again, click in the table and choose **Table, Show Gridlines**.

How to Use Headers and Footers

A *header* is text that appears at the top of every page, and a *footer* is text that appears at the bottom of every page. You might want to use headers and footers to display the document title, your name, the name of your organization, and so on. You can also insert *fields* in headers and footers—a field is a holding place for information that Word updates automatically, such as the current date.

Begin

1 Open the Header and Footer

To add a header and/or a footer to a document, open the **View** menu and select **Header and Footer**.

Click

2 Enter Header Text

Word switches to Print Layout view, places the insertion point in the header area, and displays the Header and Footer toolbar. You type and format text in a header or footer just like normal text. By default, Word places the cursor in the header section. Type in any header text. (You may have to zoom your view with the Zoom percentage button on the Standard toolbar.)

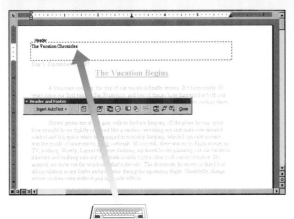

3 Enter Footer Text

To create a footer, click the **Switch Between Header and Footer** button on the Header and Footer toolbar to place the insertion point in the footer area. You can switch between the header and footer by clicking this button.

Switch Between Header and Footer

4 Insert Fields

You can select built-in header and footer entries from the **AutoText** button on the Header and Footer toolbar or insert fields. For example, click the **Date** button to insert a field for the current date. You can also click the **Page Number** button to insert the current page number. To add both to a single header line, click the **Tab** key to space out the entries, as shown in this figure.

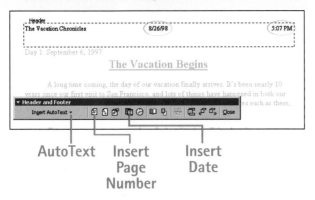

AutoText Insert Page Number Insert Date

5 Close Header and Footer

Click the **Close** button in the Header and Footer toolbar to return to the body of the document.

Click

6 View Headers and Footers

Headers and footers aren't visible in Normal view, but you can see them in both Print Layout view and in Print Preview.

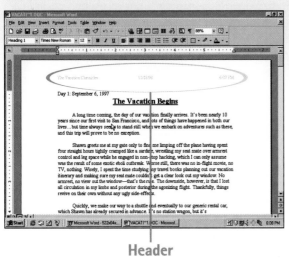

Header

End

How to Insert a Comment

Comments can help you identify various users who work on a document. For example, your office situation may require you to pass along reports for feedback from various department heads. Rather than guess which person contributed which text to the document, use comments to add text to the document.

Begin

1 Start a Comment

Click in the document where you want to insert a comment, then open the **Insert** menu and select **Comment**.

Click

2 Enter a Comment

A separate pane opens at the bottom of the document with space for entering your own comment. Enter the comment text just like you do any other text in Word.

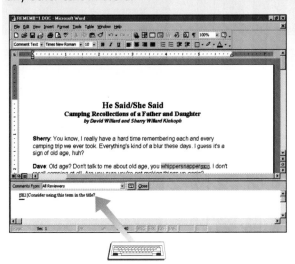

3 Click Close

When finished composing your comment, click the **Close** button on the comment pane.

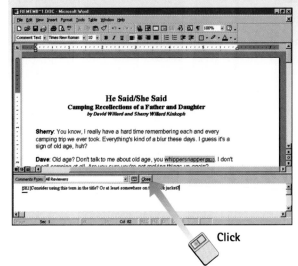

Click

4 View the Comment

The word to the left of where you clicked to insert the comment is highlighted in yellow. To view the comment, hover your mouse pointer over the highlighted word. The comment box appears revealing the comment as well as the name of the person who wrote it.

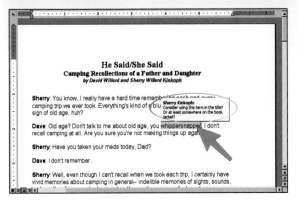

5 Edit a Comment

To edit a comment, right-click over the highlighted word and select **Edit Comment** from the shortcut menu. This reopens the comment pane and you can make changes to the comment text.

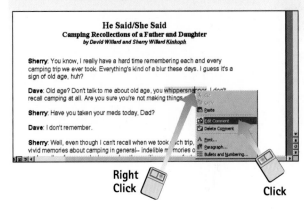

Right Click

Click

6 Remove a Comment

To delete a comment, right-click over the highlighted area and select **Delete Comment** from the shortcut menu.

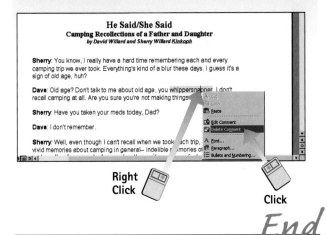

Right Click

Click

End

How-To Hints

Printing Comments

To print comments in a document, open the **File** menu and select **Print**. This opens the Print dialog box. Click the **Print What** drop-down arrow and select **Comments**. Click **OK**.

Reviewer Options

If your workplace requires frequent document sharing, you'll be pleased to note the numerous reviewing tools offered in Word for tracking changes, saving versions, and more. You'll find all the options available from a single toolbar, the Reviewing toolbar. To access this toolbar, open the **View** menu and select **Toolbars, Reviewing**.

How to Insert Page Numbers and Page Breaks

By default, Word keeps track of how much text can fit onto a document page and makes page breaks automatically for you. However, you will encounter times where you need to insert a page break yourself.

If you're creating a document with two or more pages, you should consider adding page numbers. Word inserts them and adjusts them according to changes you make to the document. When you're ready to print, the page numbers print too.

Begin

1 Insert a Manual Page Break

To insert a manual page break yourself, just click in the document where you want the break to occur, then press **Ctrl+Enter** on the keyboard.

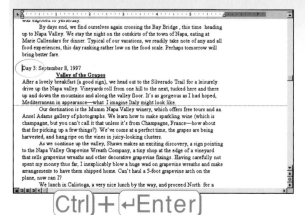

2 View the Break

This inserts a dotted line in the document that represents a page break (seen in Normal view in the figure below).

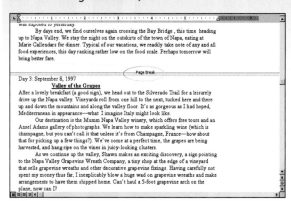

3 Open the Page Break Dialog Box

For a greater variety of page breaks, column breaks, and section breaks, open the Page Break dialog box; choose **Insert, Break**.

4 Select an Option

To set a page break, click the **Page Break** option. If you're setting a column or section break, select the appropriate options. Click **OK** to exit the dialog box and apply the break.

 Click

5 Open the Page Numbers Dialog

To add page numbers to your document, open the **Insert** menu and select **Page Numbers**. This opens the Page Numbers dialog box.

Click

6 Choose Position and Alignment

Click the **Position** drop-down arrow to change whether your page numbers appear at the top of the page or the bottom. Click the **Alignment** drop-down arrow to change how the numbers are aligned on the page. Click **OK** to exit.

Click

End

How-To Hints

Viewing Page Numbers

You won't be able to view page numbers in Normal view. Switch to Print Layout view to see page numbers, headers and footers, columns, and other special formatting options.

First Page Numbers

If you prefer the first page in your document not print with a page number, be sure to deselect the **Show Number on First Page** check box in the Page Numbers dialog box.

Formatting Page Numbers

To change the number format of your page numbers, click the **Format** button in the Page Numbers dialog box to open the Page Number Format dialog box. Use this box to specify a number style, control page numbering and chapter numbering.

How to Insert Footnotes and Endnotes

Some documents you create in Word may require footnotes or endnotes for identifying the source of your text or referencing other materials. You can easily add such notes to your document pages using the Footnote and Endnote dialog box. Footnotes appear at the bottom of each page and endnotes appear at the end of the document.

Begin

1 Place the Insertion Point

To add a footnote or endnote, click the insertion point in the document where you want to add a reference number.

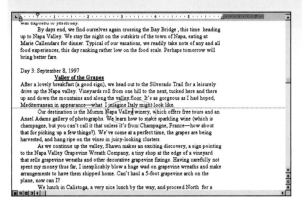

2 Open Footnote and Endnote

Open the **Insert** menu and select **Footnote**. This opens the Footnote and Endnote dialog box.

Click

3 Choose an Option

Under the **Insert** area of the dialog box, select either **Footnote** or **Endnote**.

Click

4 Click OK

Click **OK** to exit the dialog box and return to the document page.

Click

5 Add a Reference

Word adds a superscript reference number to the text and a pane opens at the bottom of the window to enter the reference text. Click inside the pane and type in the reference.

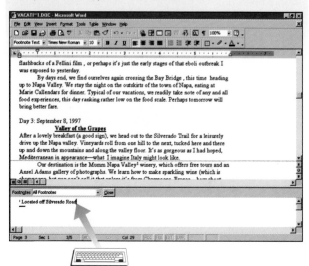

6 Click Close

Click the **Close** button to exit the pane. To view the footnote or endnote, switch to Print Layout view and scroll to the bottom of the page where the reference was entered (or end of the document).

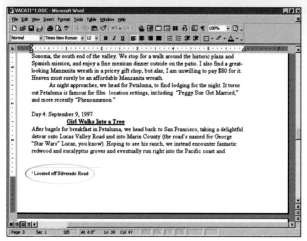

End

How-To Hints

AutoNumbering

By default, Word automatically numbers the references for you. Each new note you add is assigned the next consecutive number. If you prefer another mark, such as a letter or symbol, click the **Custom mark** option in the Footnote and Endnote dialog box and enter the mark. To use a symbol, click the **Symbol** button and select a symbol from the Symbol dialog box.

Changing the Placement

To change the location of footnotes and endnotes, and the format used for the numbers, click the **Options** button in the Footnote and Endnote dialog box to open another dialog box for setting such controls.

Task

4

How to Use Word's Proofing and Printing Tools

After you have created and formatted a Word document, you're ready to print it out or distribute it to others. Before you do, you need to proof it and make sure everything is in order. Word has several proofing tools you can use to make sure your documents are accurate and readable.

You can use the Spelling and Grammar check to go over your document and locate any spelling and grammar problems. Word's AutoCorrect feature helps you proof your document as you type. Use the Find and Replace tools to quickly locate text in your document and correct it as needed. When you finally have the document the way you want it, use the Print command to create a hard copy of the file. Printing is a common feature for all Office programs, so you will find specific instructions for printing in Chapter 1, "How to Use Common Office Features." Because some of your documents present different printing needs, this chapter shows you how to change the paper size and how to print envelopes and labels for Word. ●

How to Find and Replace Text

When you need to search your document for a particular word or phrase, don't bother scrolling and reading; use Word's Find command. This feature searches your entire document for the word or phrase you want. If you need to locate and change every occurrence of a word, use the Replace command. If you misspelled a client's name throughout a report, for example, you can quickly fix the mistake by using Find and Replace.

Begin

1 Find a Word or Phrase

To perform a quick search of your document for a particular word or phrase, open the **Edit** menu and select **Find**. This opens the Find and Replace dialog box, with the Find tab displayed.

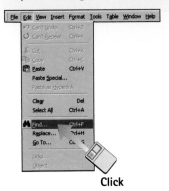

Click

2 Enter the Text

In the **Find What** text box, type the text you want to search for (for example, type **palace**). If you want to specify search criteria, such as matching case or finding whole words only, click the **More** button to reveal search options you can choose.

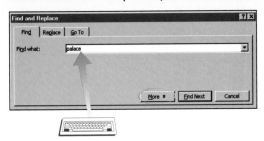

3 Conduct the Search

Click the **Find Next** button to locate the first occurrence of the word or phrase. Word highlights the text in your document, and the Find and Replace dialog box remains open on your screen. Click **Find Next** again to search for the next occurrence, or click **Cancel** to close the dialog box.

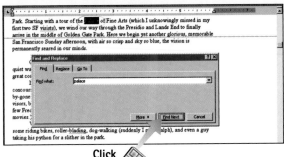

Click

4 Find and Replace Text

To find the text and replace it with new text, use the Replace command. Open the **Edit** menu and select **Replace**. This opens the Find and Replace dialog box with the Replace tab up front.

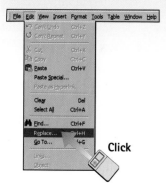

Click

5 Enter the Text

Type the word or words you're looking for in the **Find What** text box (such as **trip**), and type the replacement text in the **Replace With** text box (such as **journey**). If you want to specify any search criteria, click the **More** button and select from the available options.

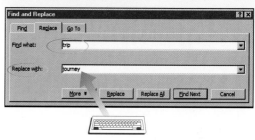

6 Search and Replace

Click the **Find Next** button to locate the first occurrence. Word highlights the text in the document. Click the **Replace** button to replace the highlighted text with the new text. Click **Replace All** to replace every occurrence in the document, or click **Find Next** to ignore the first occurrence and move on to the next.

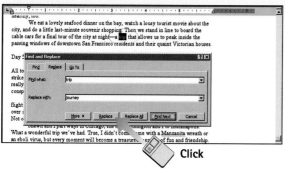

Click

End

How-To Hints

Search Complete

When Word completes a search, it displays a prompt box telling you the search is complete. Click **OK**. If the search didn't reveal any occurrences of the text, a prompt box alerts you; click **OK** and try another search.

Search and Delete

Use the Find and Replace tools to delete text from your document. Open the **Find and Replace** dialog box and enter the word you're looking for in the **Find What** text box, but leave the **Replace With** box empty. Word searches for the text and deletes it from your document without replacing it with new text.

How to Check Your Spelling and Grammar

The Spelling and Grammar Checker enables you to check the spelling and grammar of a document as you type, or to check the entire document all at once. Because most of us tend to forget about running the Spelling Checker when we finish typing, the Automatic Spelling Checker can save errors by pointing them out as we type and making them difficult to ignore.

If Automatic Spelling Checker is not on, choose **Tools**, **Options**, and click the **Spelling and Grammar** tab. Click the **Check Spelling as You Type** check box to turn it on (click the **Check Grammar as You Type** check box if you want to turn on Automatic Grammar Checking).

Begin

1 A Red Wavy Line

As you type, any word Word can't find in its dictionary gets a red wavy line under it to tell you it might be misspelled (in this figure, for example, Word points out `eboli` as a possible misspelling).

A long time coming, the day of our vacation finally arrives. It's been nearly 10 years since our first visit to San Francisco, and lots of things have happened in both our lives...but time always seems to stand still when we embark on adventures such as these, and this trip will prove to be no exception.

Shawn greets me at my gate only to find me limping off the plane having spent four straight hours tightly cramped like a sardine, wrestling my seat mate over armrest control and leg space while he engaged in non-stop hacking, which I can only assume was the result of some exotic eboli outbreak. Worse still, there was no in-flight movie, no TV, nothing. Wisely, I spent the time studying my travel books planning out our vacation itinerary and making sure my seat mate couldn't get a clear look out my window. No armrest, no view out the window—that's the rule. The downside, however, is that I lost all circulation in my limbs and posterior during the agonizing flight. Thankfully, things revive on their own without any ugly side-effects.

Quickly, we make our way to a shuttle and eventually to our generic rental car, which Shawn has already secured in advance. It's no station wagon, but it's transportation nonetheless (hats off to dedicated Hertz employees everywhere). By 2:00 pm, our vacation is in full swing.

2 Display the Shortcut Menu

Right-click the word to open a shortcut menu displaying possible alternative spellings (at the top) and a few additional commands. Click an alternative spelling to choose it from the shortcut menu. If your spelling is correct (for example, someone's last name), click **Add**; the word is added to Word's dictionary and won't be picked up by the Spelling Checker ever again.

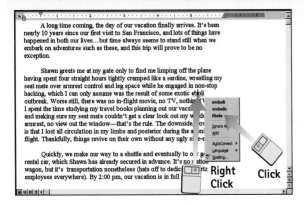

3 Ignore the Spelling

If you don't want to add the word to the dictionary but want to leave the word the way you spelled it in the current document, click **Ignore All**. To add the correct spelling to your AutoCorrect list so future misspellings will be corrected automatically as you type, click **AutoCorrect** (see Task 4, "How to Work with AutoCorrect"). To open the Spelling dialog box, click **Spelling**.

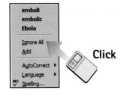

4 A Green Wavy Line

If the wavy underline is green, Word detects a possible grammatical error. Follow steps 2 and 3 to fix the error.

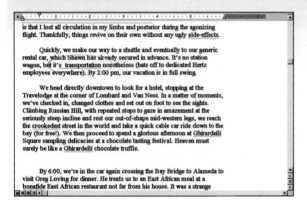

5 Spell Check Your Document

To run the Spelling and Grammar Checker for the whole document at one time, click the **Spelling and Grammar** button on the Standard toolbar, or open the **Tools** menu and select **Spelling and Grammar**.

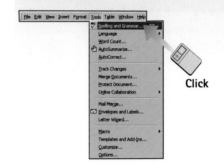

Click

6 Spelling and Grammar Dialog Box

Word checks every word in your document against its dictionary and list of grammatical rules and presents the Spelling and Grammar dialog box when it encounters a word that is not in its dictionary or a sentence that does not conform to a grammatical rule. You can choose to ignore the problem, change it, or select from other options in the dialog box.

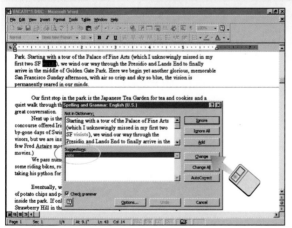

End

How-To Hints

Turn It Off

To turn the Automatic Spelling checker off, choose **Tools, Options**. On the **Spelling and Grammar** tab, clear the **Check Spelling as You Type** check box. To turn the Automatic Grammar Checker off, clear the **Check Grammar as You Type** check box. Click **OK** to exit.

Check a Section

To check the spelling and grammar of only a portion of the document, select that portion before starting the check. When Word finishes checking the selection, it asks if you want to check the rest of the document. Click **No** to end the check.

Check the Writing Style

To modify what Word looks for in a grammar check, choose **Tools, Options**, and click the **Spelling & Grammar** tab. In the **Writing Style** drop-down list, select a style that best describes your document. You can choose which items Word checks by clicking the **Settings** button. Mark or clear check boxes for items such as wordiness or passive sentences. Click **OK**.

How to Use the Thesaurus

In addition to spelling and grammar checking, Word provides the Thesaurus tool to help you with your writing endeavors. With the Thesaurus, you can look up synonyms (words that mean the same or nearly the same) and other meanings for words you type into your document. Use this tool to help you make a better impact on readers when you find yourself overusing a word.

Begin

1 Select a Word

Select the word in your document you want to look up by using the Thesaurus tool.

Shawn greets me at my gate only to find me limping off the plane having spent four straight hours tightly cramped like a sardine, wrestling my seat mate over armrest control and leg space while he engaged in non-stop hacking, which I can only assume was the result of some exotic eboli outbreak. Worse still, there was no in-flight movie, no TV, nothing. Wisely, I spent the time studying my travel books planning out our vacation itinerary and making sure my seat mate couldn't get a clear look out my window. No armrest, no view out the window—that's the rule. The downside, however, is that I lost all circulation in my limbs and posterior during the agonizing flight. Thankfully, things revive on their own without any ugly side-effects.

Quickly, we make our way to a shuttle and eventually to our generic rental car, which Shawn has already secured in advance. It's no station wagon, but it's transportation nonetheless (hats off to dedicated Hertz employees everywhere). By 2:00 pm, our vacation is in full swing. Let the adventure begin.

We head directly downtown to look for a hotel, stopping at the Traveledge at the corner of Lombard and Van Ness. In a matter of moments, we've checked in, changed clothes and set out on foot to see the sights. Climbing Russian Hill, with repeated stops to gaze in amazement at the seriously steep incline and rest our out-of-shape mid-western legs, we reach

2 Open the Thesaurus

Open the **Tools** menu and select **Language**, **Thesaurus**. This opens the Thesaurus dialog box.

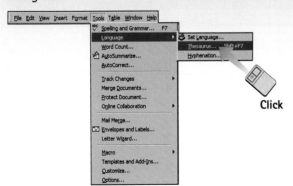

Click

3 View Synonyms

The Thesaurus dialog box displays your selected word in the **Looked Up** text box. A list of synonyms appears in the list box on the right.

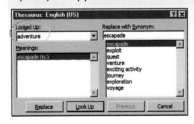

4 Look Up a Word

To look up a word's meaning, select it from the **Replace with Synonym** list box. For example, in the figure below, I've selected **journey**. Click the **Look Up** button.

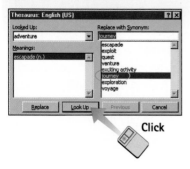

Click

5 View a Meaning

The Thesaurus displays the word you selected, along with its meanings and another synonym list. Continue looking up words and meanings until you find the word you want to use. To return to the previous word viewed, click the **Previous** button.

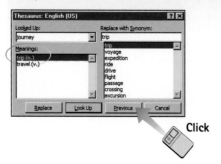

Click

6 Replace the Word

Highlight the word you want to use and then click the **Replace** button. This replaces the word you selected in the document with the new word you found.

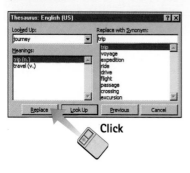

Click

End

How-To Hints

Forget It

To exit the Thesaurus without choosing a word, simply click the **Cancel** button.

How to Work with AutoCorrect

Word's AutoCorrect feature can save you time by automatically correcting misspelled words as you type—no need to run a spelling checker. AutoCorrect comes with a list of common misspellings, but the list isn't comprehensive; you can add your own common misspellings to the list to personalize it to your work habits.

What makes AutoCorrect even more useful is that you can use it to do your typing for you. If you often type a particular word or long phrase, you can create an AutoCorrect entry that types the word for you when you type a short acronym. For example, I got tired of typing the word "AutoCorrect," so I made it an AutoCorrect entry; now when I type "ac" and a space, Word types out the whole word for me, capitals and all. You also turn a long phrase, such as "Lake City High School Alumni Association," into an AutoCorrect entry that responds to a short acronym such as "lca."

Begin

1 Try It Out

To test AutoCorrect to see how it performs, type **teh** and then press the spacebar or type a punctuation mark such as a comma or a period. Because "teh" is a common misspelling, AutoCorrect corrects it to "the" before you realize you mistyped it.

2 Undo AutoCorrect

If you type something you don't want corrected (for example, **Mr. Edmund Teh**), press **Ctrl+Z** to undo the correction before you type any other characters. The AutoCorrection is undone, and you can continue typing.

3 Remove a Word from AutoCorrect

To remove a word from the AutoCorrect list, open the **Tools** menu and select **AutoCorrect**.

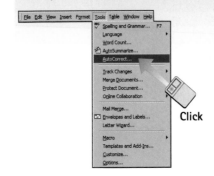

Click

4 Delete the Word

Click the **AutoCorrect** tab. In the **Replace** box, type the first few letters of the word you want to delete from AutoCorrect; the list of words and replacements scrolls to the point where you can find your word. Click your word in the list and then click **Delete**. Click **OK** to exit the dialog box.

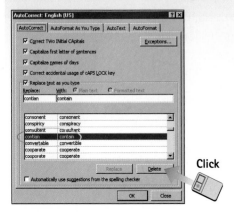

Click

5 Add a Misspelling

To add a word you frequently misspell to the AutoCorrect list, open a document and type the correct spelling. (You can also add a long phrase for which you want to create a shortcut; type in the phrase, including any special capitalization.) Select the word or phrase and then choose **Tools, AutoCorrect**.

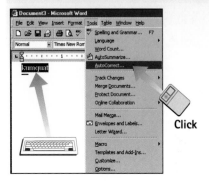

Click

6 Click Add

Click the **AutoCorrect** tab. Your word or phrase appears in the **With** box. In the **Replace** box, type the incorrect word (for example, **kumqat**) or acronym you want to replace (this text is what you expect to mistype in your document). If you want to add only a single item, choose **OK** to close the dialog box; if you want to add more words to the AutoCorrect list, click **Add** to add each word and choose **OK** when you finish.

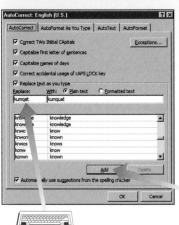

Click

How-To Hints

Turn It Off

Turn AutoCorrect on or off by clearing or marking the **Replace Text as You Type** check box on the AutoCorrect tab in the AutoCorrect dialog box.

Other Options

As you can see on the AutoCorrect tab, Word will automatically correct other items. Set or turn off other convenient automated options, such as capitalization of weekday names and the first word in sentences, by marking or clearing those check boxes.

AutoCorrect Long Phrases

To add a long word or phrase to the AutoCorrect list, enter the complete phrase in the **With** box. Enter an abbreviation or acronym you want to substitute for the phrase in the **Replace** box. Next time you need to insert the phrase, type the abbreviation or acronym you assigned, and let AutoCorrect handle the rest.

End

How to Change Paper Size

By default, Word assumes your document is a standard 8 1/2" by 11" page. If you need to create a document that uses a different paper size, open the Page Setup dialog box and change the settings. From the Paper Size tab, you can change the paper size or orientation or enter the measurements for a custom paper size.

Begin

1 Open Page Setup

Open the **File** menu and select **Page Setup**. This opens the Page Setup dialog box.

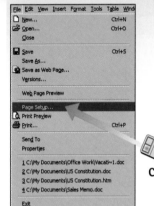

Click

2 Select the Paper Size Tab

Click the **Paper Size** tab to view the options associated with paper sizes and orientation.

Click

3 Change the Paper Size

Use the **Paper Size** drop-down list to select another paper size. As you scroll through the list, you might notice Word is ready to handle legal-size paper and a variety of envelope sizes. To create a custom size, select **Custom** from the list and enter the parameters of the paper.

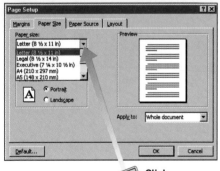

Click

4 Change the Page Orientation

With some documents, you might need to change the way the text is printed on the page—the Orientation settings. By default, Word prints the document "shortways" across the 8 1/2" page. This is called **Portrait**. You can switch to **Landscape** to print across the length of the page (longways across the 11" page).

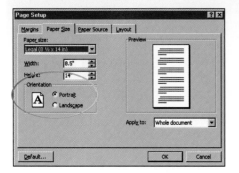

5 Change the Paper Source

Depending on your printer, you might have to change the paper source option before printing. To do so, click the **Paper Source** tab and select the appropriate tray.

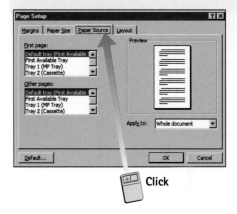

Click

6 Exit the Dialog Box

After you have set your paper size and source options, click **OK** to exit the Page Setup dialog box and start creating the document. When you're ready to print, click the **Print** button on the Standard toolbar.

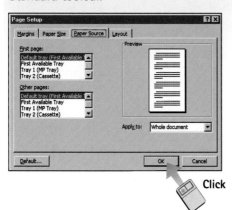

Click

End

How-To Hints

Need Help Printing?

To find out more about printing files, see Task 8, "How to Print a File," in Chapter 1.

Caution!

If you choose to set a new paper size after you have already designed and created the document, you might need to make a few adjustments. Be sure to check the document in Print Preview (click the **Print Preview** button on the Standard toolbar) to see if everything still fits properly or needs adjusting.

Changing the Default

If you find yourself using a different paper size over and over, you can select it from the **Paper Size** tab and click the **Default** button to make it the new default paper size.

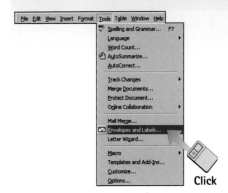

How to Print an Envelope

Task 8 in Chapter 1 covers the basics of printing your Office files; however, some Word projects you tackle involve some special printing needs, such as envelopes. When you create letters in Word, you can create envelopes to go with them. Use Word's Envelopes and Labels dialog box to enter addresses and select from a variety of envelope sizes.

Begin

1 The Envelope and Labels Dialog Box

If you have created a letter with an address you want to print on an envelope, open the letter document. If not, you can open the Envelope feature from any document and create a quick envelope. Open the **Tools** menu and select **Envelopes and Labels**.

2 Use the Envelopes Tab

Click the **Envelopes** tab. If needed, type the delivery address and the return address in the appropriate text boxes. If you're using this feature with a letter file, Word borrows the addresses you entered in the letter document.

3 Open the Envelope Options

To choose an envelope size other than the default size, click the **Options** button to open the Envelope Options dialog box.

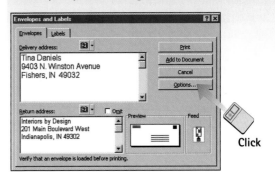

4 Choose an Envelope Size

Select another size from the **Envelope Size** drop-down list.

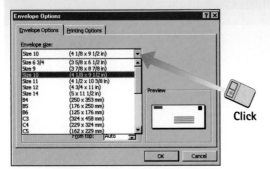

Click

5 Exit Envelope Options

You can also change the font used for the addresses and control the spacing between the addresses and the edges of the envelope. Click **OK** to return to the Envelopes and Labels dialog box after you finish setting envelope options.

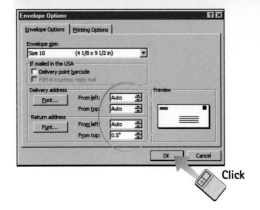

Click

6 Print

To print the envelope, click the **Print** button. Be sure to feed the envelope into your printer correctly. Depending on your printer setup, the Feed area in the dialog box gives you a clue about how to feed the envelope.

Click

End

How-To Hints

Omit

Select the **Omit** check box in the Envelopes and Labels dialog box if you have preprinted envelopes that already have a return address or company logo.

Add to Document

Select the **Add to Document** button in the Envelopes and Labels dialog box to add the envelope style and contents to the document to save them for later use.

Task

5

How to Use Excel

*T*he second most popular program included in Office is Excel. Excel is an excellent tool for keeping track of data and crunching numbers. With Excel, you can create worksheets to add up sales for your department or to track your personal expenses. You can use Excel to set up a budget or to create an invoice. You can even use Excel as a simple database program. With Excel, you can perform any kind of mathematical calculation, from the simplest to the most complex, and organize data so that it becomes meaningful and useful.

Although at first it resembles an accounting spreadsheet, Excel is much easier to use because you're not always erasing data and rewriting it somewhere else. To reorganize data on a worksheet, you can either drag it around or tell Excel to sort it or filter it for you. In this chapter, you will learn how to use Excel's basic features, such as entering data, adding and deleting rows and columns, and working with worksheets. ●

How to Use the Excel Window

When you first open Excel, a blank *workbook* opens. A workbook is an Excel file, just as a document is a Word file. By default, each workbook file contains three *worksheets*, which look like an accountant's spreadsheet divided into a grid of columns and rows that intersect to form *cells*. Surrounding the workbook are tools that you can use to help you enter and work with data that you place in the worksheet cells. Take a few moments and familiarize yourself with the Excel environment.

Begin

1 The Program Window Controls

The Excel program window opens along with a blank workbook window. Usually, both windows are maximized: The program window fills the entire screen, and the workbook window fills the program window. (When both are maximized, two Restore buttons—one for each window—are displayed in the set of buttons in the top right corner of the window's screen.) If your program window isn't maximized, click its **Maximize** button. To minimize the program window to a button on the Windows taskbar, click the **Minimize** button.

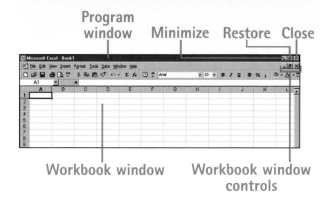

Program window   Minimize   Restore   Close

Workbook window   Workbook window controls

2 View the Title Bar

Excel's title bar tells you what is in the window. When the workbook window is maximized, it has to share the title bar with the program window, so the title bar contains the names of both the program (Microsoft Excel) and the file. ("Book1" is a temporary name for your file. When you save it for the first time, you can assign a better name.

Title bar

3 Select from the Menu Bar

The Excel menu bar contains menus, which in turn contain all the available Excel commands. All the tasks you need to perform are available through menu commands. To use the menu commands, click the menu name to display the menu and then click the command you want.

Menu bar

4 Use the Worksheet Grid

Each cell is identified by its address on the worksheet, also called a *cell reference*. A cell address consists of the column label and the row number, such as A1. The Name box, located at the far left end of the Formula bar identifies the active cell, as sort of a "you-are-here" marker.

The cell reference appears in the Name box

Active cell

Row number

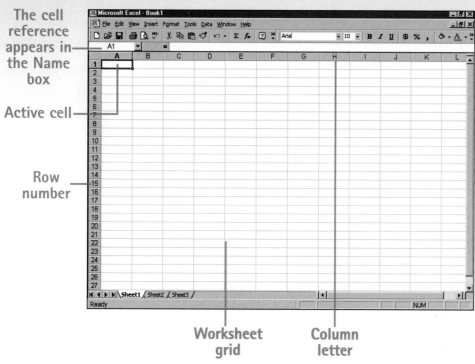

Worksheet grid

Column letter

Continues

How-To Hints

The Worksheet Is Bigger Than You Think

The worksheet grid you see is only a small part of the whole worksheet: a worksheet is actually 256 columns wide and 65,536 rows long. When you scroll past column Z, the columns are labeled AA, AB, and so on. The last column in any worksheet is labeled IV.

What Toolbars?

If you don't see the Standard or Formatting toolbar or if you see other toolbars you would like to hide, choose **View, Toolbars**. Select the **Standard** or **Formatting** toolbar. A check mark next to the toolbar name means the toolbar is displayed.

5 A Look at the Toolbars

The Standard and Formatting toolbars may share a row onscreen (Standard on the left, Formatting on the right). Both toolbars contain shortcuts for frequently used commands. To activate a toolbar button, click it. To see a button name, hover the mouse pointer over the button for a moment. A ScreenTip appears with the button name. (Learn all about using and customizing toolbars in Chapter 1, "How to Use Common Office Features.")

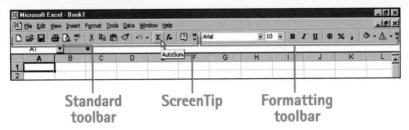

Standard   ScreenTip   Formatting
toolbar   toolbar

6 View the Formula Bar

Below the toolbars you'll find the Formula bar where you can build formulas to calculate your worksheet data. You can learn all about creating formulas using the Formula bar commands in Chapter 6, "How to Use Formulas and Functions."

Formula bar

7 Use the Scrollbars

The vertical and horizontal scrollbars allow you to view different portions of your worksheet. Use the arrows on the scrollbars to scroll in the appropriate direction. Drag the scroll box to move your view of the worksheet in larger portions.

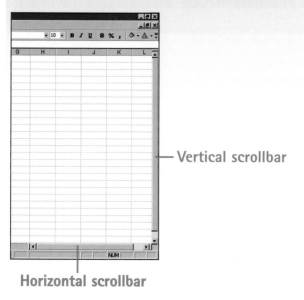

— Vertical scrollbar

Horizontal scrollbar

8 View Worksheets

A tab at the bottom of the workbook window represents each worksheet in a workbook. By default, Excel starts you out with three worksheets in each workbook, but you can add and subtract worksheets as needed. To display a sheet, click its tab. Learn more about working with worksheets in Task 16, "How to Work with Worksheets."

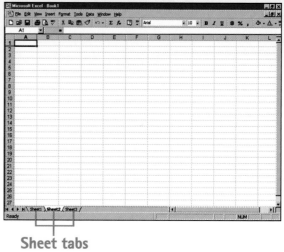

Sheet tabs

End

How-To Hints

No Scrollbars?

If either of your scrollbars isn't showing, choose **Tools, Options**. Click the **View** tab and click any check box that isn't already marked (**Formula Bar, Status Bar, Horizontal Scrollbar**, and/or **Vertical Scrollbar**) and then choose **OK**.

Use the Shortcut Menu

To open a shortcut menu that contains often-used commands, click an object with the right mouse button (called a *right-click*). Then use the left mouse button to click the command you want. Almost everything in the Excel window contains its own shortcut menu, including the status bar (located at the very bottom of the program window).

Keyboard Shortcuts

To choose menu commands with the keyboard, press the **Alt** key, then press the underlined letter in the desired menu, and press the underlined letter in the desired command. To display the **Format** menu, for example, press **Alt+O**. When the Format menu is displayed, press **E** to choose the **Cells** command.

How to Enter and Edit Cell Data

Data in a worksheet is always entered in cells. To enter data, just click a cell, type the data, and press **Enter** (or press **Tab**, or click another cell in the worksheet). The data you enter into Excel can be broken down into three categories: labels (text), values (numbers, dates, and times), and formulas (calculations). Text data always lines up to the left of the cell, and number data aligns to the right, unless you change the alignment. Based on the type of data you enter, Excel can perform various calculations.

Begin

1 Select a Cell

Click the cell in which you want to enter data. The cell you click becomes the active cell, and a highlighted border surrounds the cell. Its reference appears in the Name box to the left of the Formula bar.

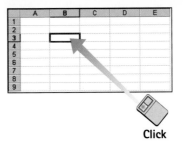

Click

2 Enter Data in the Selected Cell

Type your entry (numbers and/or letters). As you type data, the data appears in both the active cell and in the Formula bar. When finished, press **Enter**. The active cell border moves down one cell, and your characters are entered in the cell in which you typed them.

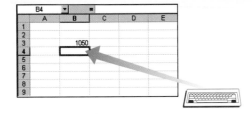

3 Enter a Multicolumn List

To enter a multicolumn list, begin at the top left corner of the list. As you type the entries, press **Tab** to move to the right to enter the data for each cell in the row. After you type the last entry in the row, press **Enter** instead of **Tab**; the active cell moves to the beginning of the next row. This maneuver is called *AutoReturn*.

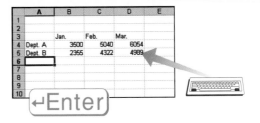

↵Enter

4 Copy the Cell Above

To copy the entry from the cell above the active cell, press **Ctrl+'** (press **Ctrl** and the apostrophe key simultaneously) and then press **Enter**.

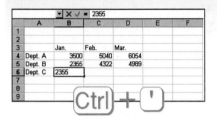

5 AutoComplete an Entry

If you want to repeat an entry from anywhere in the same column (which not only saves time, but also prevents typing mistakes), type the first few letters of the entry. A possible match appears in the cell. This function is called *AutoComplete*. If the entry is correct, press **Enter**. If you don't want that entry, just continue typing.

6 Pick a Repeated Entry

If you want to repeat an entry that already exists in the column somewhere, you can select it from a list instead of retyping it. Right-click the active cell, and choose **Pick From List**. A list of all the entries in the column appears. Click the entry you want.

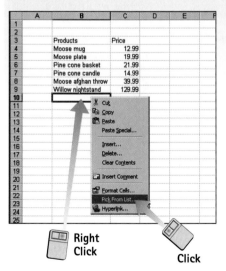

Right Click

Click

End

How-To Hints

Edit Data

To edit data in a cell, simply select the cell again and make changes to the existing data. You can edit the data in the cell or in the Formula bar. Double-click the cell to edit directly in the cell. To edit data in the Formula bar, click in the Formula bar and make your changes. You can use the Backspace and Delete keys to remove data, type over existing data, or enter new data.

Ways to Move

You can move the active cell using the arrow keys, the PgUp, PgDn, Home, and End keys. You can jump to the end of a row or column of filled cells or blank cells by pointing to the border of the active cell and double-clicking. For example, if you double-click the top border of the active cell and it contains data, you jump to the top of the column of cells containing data.

How to Navigate Worksheets

Each worksheet comprises 256 columns and 65,536 rows. With so much space in a single worksheet, you can easily lose yourself in the vast forest of worksheet cells. You need to know how to read cell addresses. Each cell in the worksheet grid has an address or *reference* based on which row and column it's in. Excel labels columns with letters and rows with numbers. Cell addresses always list the column letter first and then the row number. For example, the cell in the top left corner of the worksheet is A1.

Begin

1 Use the Mouse

One way to navigate the worksheet is to use the mouse. To move to a particular cell, simply click on the cell. This makes the cell active. If the cell is not in view, use the scroll bars to locate the cell.

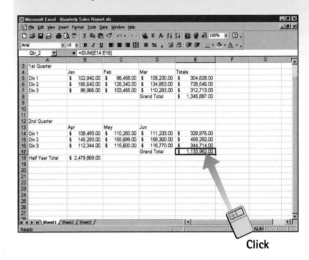

Click

2 Use the Keyboard

If you prefer to use the keyboard to navigate, press the keyboard arrow keys to move around the worksheet. The active cell changes with each press of the arrow keys.

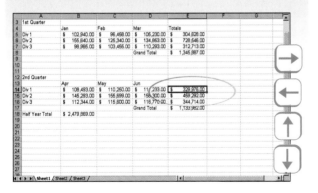

3 Double-click a Cell Border

To jump to the bottom of a list of data, click a cell in the list and point to the bottom edge of the cell. When your mouse pointer becomes an arrow, double-click. Excel takes you to the bottom cell in the range.

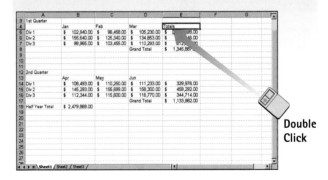

Double Click

4 Jump Home or Jump to the End

To jump back to the first cell in the worksheet, A1, press **Ctrl+Home**. To jump to the lower-right corner of the working area of the worksheet, press **Ctrl+End**.

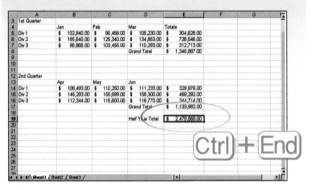

5 Jump Around Rows and Columns

To jump to the beginning of the row (column A), press **Home**. To jump to the right-most cell in the row (within the working area of the worksheet), press **End** and then press **Enter**.

6 Use the Go To Command

Yet another way to move to a particular cell in a worksheet is to use the Go To command. Open the **Edit** menu and select **Go To**. Enter the cell address you want to reach in the **Reference** text box and click **OK**.

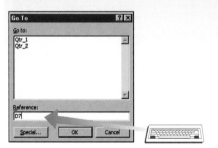

End

How-To Hints

Jump to the End of the Data

When you double-click the left, right, top, or bottom of a cell border, the active cell jumps to the end of a contiguous block of data. If you have a list of data, for example, double-clicking the edge of a cell in the list sends you to the end of the list and stops short of the first empty cell.

Other Ways to Use Go To

You can open the Go To dialog box by pressing **F5** or **Ctrl+G**. The Go To dialog box remembers the name of the reference you just came from, so to go back again quickly, press **F5** and press **Enter**.

Enter a Reference Directly

Another way to make a particular cell active is to type the name of the cell into the **Name** box and press **Enter**.

Scrollbar Tip

As you drag the vertical scroll box, a ScreenTip appears telling you which row appears at the top of the window. If you drag the horizontal scroll box, the ScreenTip tells you what column is at the left side of the window. To return the view to the active cell, press **Ctrl+Backspace**.

TASK 4

How to Select a Range of Cells

If cells are the building blocks of worksheets, ranges are the mortar for holding them together. A *range* is a rectangular group of related cells that you can connect in a column, a row, or a combination of columns and rows. After you select a range of cells, you can perform a variety of tasks upon them in one simple step.

You can format a group of cells all at once, for example, rather than one cell at a time. You can use a range to print a specific group of cells from your worksheet. You can also use ranges in formulas, which can really save you time. (Learn how to name ranges in Task 12, "How to Define a Range Name.")

Begin

1 Click the First Cell

To select a range, start by clicking the first cell in the range.

Click

2 Drag to Select

Hold down the mouse button and drag across the cells you want to include in the range.

Click & Drag

3 Release the Mouse Button

When you release the mouse button, the range is selected. Ranges are referred to by their anchor points, the top left corner and the bottom right corner. After selecting a range, you can format the cells using Excel's formatting features (see Chapter 7, "How to Use Excel's Formatting Tools"), or you can use the range in a formula (see Chapter 6, "How to Use Formulas and Functions").

Release

108 CHAPTER 5: HOW TO USE EXCEL

4 Select a Range with the Keyboard

To select a range using the keyboard, use the arrow keys to move to the first cell in the range.

	A	B	C	D	E	F
1	1998 Sales Report	4/12/98				
2						
3	1st Quarter					
4		Jan	Feb	Mar	Totals	
5	Div 1	$ 102,940.00	$ 96,458.00	$ 105,230.00	$ 304,628.00	
6	Div 2	$ 155,640.00	$125,340.00	$ 134,853.00	$ 728,546.00	
7	Div 3	$ 98,965.00	$103,455.00	$ 110,293.00	$ 312,713.00	
8				Grand Total	$ 1,345,887.00	
9						
10						
11						
12	2nd Quarter					
13		Apr	May	Jun		
14	Div 1	$ 108,493.00	$110,250.00	$ 111,233.00	$ 329,976.00	
15	Div 2	$ 145,293.00	$155,699.00	$ 158,300.00	$ 459,292.00	
16	Div 3	$ 112,344.00	$115,600.00	$ 116,770.00	$ 344,714.00	
17				Grand Total	$ 1,133,982.00	
18						
19				Half Year Total	$ 2,479,869.00	
20						
21						
22						
23						

5 Use the Shift Key

Press and hold the **Shift** key and use the arrow keys to select the range.

	A	B	C	D	E	F
1	1998 Sales Report	4/12/98				
2						
3	1st Quarter					
4		Jan	Feb	Mar	Totals	
5	Div 1	$ 102,940.00	$ 96,458.00	$ 105,230.00	$ 304,628.00	
6	Div 2	$ 155,640.00	$125,340.00	$ 134,853.00	$ 728,546.00	
7	Div 3	$ 98,965.00	$103,455.00	$ 110,293.00	$ 312,713.00	
8				Grand Total	$ 1,345,887.00	
9						
10						
11						
12	2nd Quarter					
13		Apr	May	Jun		
14	Div 1	$ 108,493.00	$110,250.00	$ 111,233.00	$ 329,976.00	
15	Div 2	$ 145,293.00	$155,699.00	$ 158,300.00	$ 459,292.00	
16	Div 3	$ 112,344.00	$115,600.00	$ 116,770.00	$ 344,714.00	
17				Grand Total	$ 1,133,982.00	
18						
19				Half Year Total	$ 2,479,869.00	
20						
21						
22						
23						
24						
25						

⬆Shift → ↓

6 Select the Entire Worksheet

To select the entire worksheet as a range, click the **Select All** button located at the top of the worksheet to the left of the column labels.

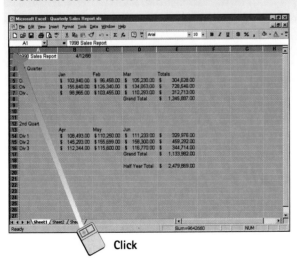

Click

End

How-To Hints

Select Cells

Remember, to select a cell, click the cell. A selector, a black outline around the cell, surrounds it. When you select a cell, its reference or *address* appears in the Name box in the Formula bar.

To deselect a range, click outside the range or press any arrow key.

Select a Row or Column

To quickly select an entire row, click the row's header label. For example to select row 23, click on the number 23 on the far left edge of the worksheet. To select a column, click the column's header label.

How to Use AutoFill

A feature called *AutoFill* can speed up data entry dramatically by filling in a data series or duplicate entries for you. By dragging the mouse across the worksheet, you can use AutoFill to fill in lists of day or month names, a series of numbers, or a list of identical text entries.

Day and month names, and their standard three-letter abbreviations, are built-in lists in Excel. That's how AutoFill knows what to enter. You can create custom lists (of people or product names, for example), and AutoFill will fill them, as well.

Begin

1 Start a Month List

To AutoFill a list of month names, enter a single month name in a cell, and then select that cell. You can enter an abbreviation or type in the entire month name.

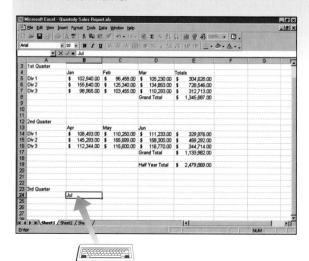

2 Drag the Fill Handle

Move the mouse pointer over the *fill handle* (the small black square in the bottom right corner of the cell) until it takes the shape of a crosshair. Next, click and hold down the left mouse button while you drag across a row or column of cells (you can fill cells in any direction). A ScreenTip shows what's being filled into each cell you drag (so you can tell when you've dragged far enough).

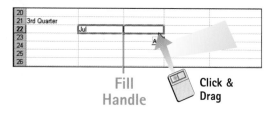

Fill Handle

Click & Drag

3 Release the Fill Handle

Release the mouse button at the end of the row or column of cells you want to fill. The series is entered in the cells, in the proper order.

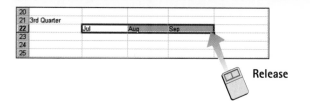

Release

4 Start a Text Series

To enter a text series, such as Div 1, Div 2, and so on, click inside the cell and enter the first entry in the series. Select the cell and drag the fill handle in the direction you want to go.

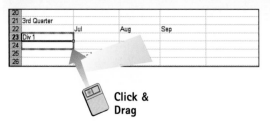

Click & Drag

5 Release the Fill Handle

Release the fill handle and the text series appears in the selected cells.

Release

6 Start a Number Series

To fill a number series that increases by 5, start the series by entering **5** and **10**, select the two cells, and drag the fill handle to fill the series. AutoFill automatically fills in the rest of the series based on the first two cell entries.

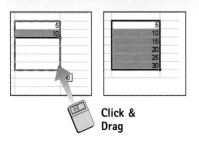

Click & Drag

End

How-To Hints

Copy Data

To fill a list with a repeated text entry, type the entry, select it, and drag the fill handle to copy the entry repeatedly.

Copy a Formula with AutoFill

You can use AutoFill to copy a formula down the side or across the bottom of a table. The cell references in the formula adjust so that the formula calculates the correct cells (see Chapter 6, Task 3, "How to Use Absolute and Relative Cell Addresses," to learn how to use cell references).

Create a Custom List

To create a custom list, enter the whole list in any worksheet. Select the list, and then choose **Tools, Options**. On the **Custom Lists** tab, click **Import** and click **OK**. The list is saved in the Custom lists window. You can fill the list in any workbook by typing any entry in the list and then dragging with the fill handle.

How to Move and Copy Data with Drag-and-Drop

If you need to move or copy data to another location on a worksheet and the new location is only a short distance from the original location, the easiest way is to drag it and drop it with the mouse. Whether you're moving or copying a single cell or a range of cells, the drag-and-drop method makes it easy and fast.

Begin

1 Select Cells to Move

To move cells, select the range of cells you want to move and point to any border of the selected range so that the mouse pointer becomes an arrow. Drag the range to a new location.

Click & Drag

2 Drop the Cells

While you drag, an outline of the range moves across the worksheet, and a ScreenTip tells you the reference of the range location. When the range border is where you want it, drop the data by releasing the mouse button.

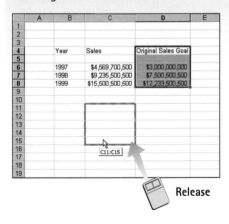

Release

3 The Range Moves

The range moves to its new location.

4 Select Cells to Copy

To copy cells, select the range of cells you want to copy and point to any border of the selected range so that the mouse pointer becomes an arrow. Drag the range to a new location.

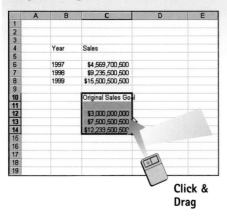

Click & Drag

5 Drag the Cells

While you drag, an outline of the range moves across the worksheet, and a ScreenTip tells you the reference of the range location.

6 Press Ctrl and Drop the Cells

When the range border is where you want it, press and hold **Ctrl** and then drop the data by releasing the mouse button. When you press **Ctrl**, the mouse pointer acquires a small plus symbol that tells you it's copying. A copy of the data is dropped in the new location.

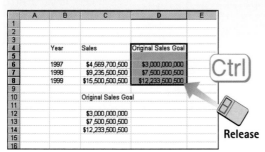

Release

End

How-To Hints

Press Ctrl Only When You Drop

Many books will tell you that you must hold down **Ctrl** while you drag a range you want to copy. This is not so. You must press and hold down **Ctrl** while you release the mouse button. It doesn't matter whether you press **Ctrl** while you drag. This is true of any drag-and-drop copy operation in any Microsoft software.

Drag with the Right Mouse Button

You can drag data with the right mouse button and then choose a command—choose from several Move and Copy commands—on the shortcut menu that appears when you drop the data in its new location.

How to Move and Copy Data with the Clipboard

If you need to move or copy data over a long distance or to another worksheet or workbook (or even to another Office program, such as Word), it's easier to cut or copy the text to the Windows Clipboard and then paste it where you want it.

The *Windows Clipboard* is a temporary holding area in Windows for data you have cut or copied in any of the Office programs. Data on the Clipboard can be pasted repeatedly. If you're using Windows 95, the data is kept on the Clipboard until you cut or copy another chunk of data, or until you close Windows. If you're using Windows 98, you can cut or copy multiple items to the Clipboard and paste them when you need them.

Begin

1 Select the Data to Move

To move data, you will use the cut and paste commands. Select the data you want to move.

	A	B	C	D	E
3	1st Quarter				
4		Jan	Feb	Mar	Totals
5	Div 1	$ 102,940.00	$ 96,458.00	$ 105,230.00	$ 304,628.00
6	Div 2	$ 155,640.00	$125,340.00	$ 134,853.00	$ 728,546.00
7	Div 3	$ 98,965.00	$103,455.00	$ 110,293.00	$ 312,713.00
8				Grand Total	$ 1,345,887.00
9					
10					
11					
12	2nd Quarter				
13		Apr	May	Jun	
14	Div 1	$ 108,493.00	$110,250.00	$ 111,233.00	$ 329,976.00
15	Div 2	$ 145,293.00	$155,699.00	$ 158,300.00	$ 459,292.00
16	Div 3	$ 112,344.00	$115,600.00	$ 116,770.00	$ 344,714.00
17				Grand Total	$ 1,133,982.00
18					
19	Half Year Total	$2,479,869.00			
20					

2 Cut the Selected Data

Right-click the selected cells and choose the **Cut** command on the shortcut menu. The selected data will have a moving border around it that disappears when you paste it somewhere else.

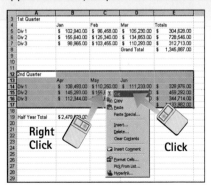

Right Click   Click

3 Paste the Cut Data

Right-click the top left cell of the range where you want to paste the data, and choose **Paste** on the shortcut menu. The data is pasted into its new location and disappears from its original location.

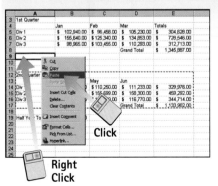

Click   Right Click

4 Select the Data to Copy

To copy data, you will use the Copy and Paste commands. Select the data you want to copy.

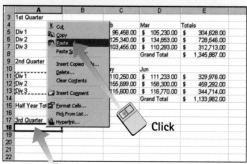

5 Copy the Selected Data

Right-click the selected cells and choose the **Copy** command on the shortcut menu. The selected data will have a moving border around it.

6 Paste the Copied Data

Right-click the top left cell of the range where you want to paste the copied data and choose **Paste** on the shortcut menu. The data is pasted into its new location. (the moving border remains around the copied data until you begin typing in another cell, or until you press **Enter** or **Esc**.)

End

How-To Hints

Paste with Windows 98

If you copy or cut multiple items, use the **Paste** command. A Clipboard box appears for you to choose which item to paste. The Windows 98 Clipboard feature holds up to 12 cut or copied items.

Use the Toolbar Buttons

Another way to move and copy data quickly is to use the **Cut**, **Copy**, and **Paste** buttons on the Standard toolbar.

Keystrokes

You can also cut data with the keystroke **Ctrl+X**, copy with the keystroke **Ctrl+C**, and paste with the keystroke **Ctrl+V**.

Paste with Enter

You can also paste cut or copied data by pressing **Enter**. If you press Enter to paste data, the data is removed from the Clipboard and is not available for more pasting.

Undo a Mistake

If you make a mistake, click the **Undo** button on the Standard toolbar, choose **Edit**, **Undo**, or press **Ctrl+Z** to undo the mistake.

How to Insert Columns and Rows

You may find that you need to add a row or column after you've already inserted data into your worksheet. You can easily insert a new row or column wherever you like using Excel's Insert commands. For example, if you need to add a row or column of data in the middle of a table, you could move the existing data by dragging and dropping it to make room for the new row or column. It's faster to insert a new row or column instead.

Begin

1 Select the Row

To insert a row, select the row you want to appear below the inserted row (click the row number to select it).

Click

2 Choose Insert

Right-click the selected row and choose **Insert** on the shortcut menu.

Right Click

3 A New Row Is Inserted

A new row is inserted above the row you selected.

4 Select the Column

To insert a column, select the column you want to appear on the right of the new column (click the column letter to select it).

Click

5 Insert a New Column

Right-click the selected column and select **Insert** on the shortcut menu. A new column is inserted to the left of the column you selected.

Click

Right Click

6 Insert Adjacent Rows or Columns

To insert several adjacent rows or columns at one time, select that many rows or columns in the table, right-click the selection, and choose **Insert**. An equal number of rows or columns is inserted.

Right Click   Click

End

How-To Hints

Formulas Usually Self-Adjust

If you have written formulas that calculate across the range of cells, the formulas adjust themselves automatically after you insert new rows or columns. (If you insert a row immediately above a subtotal, though, you will need to adjust the formula.)

Insert a Whole Row or Column

If you select the entire row or column before you click the **Insert** command, a new row or column is added. If you select only a cell, an Insert dialog box appears for you to choose what to insert—new cells, an entire row, or an entire column. Make your selection and click **OK**.

9

How to Delete Columns and Rows

You can delete rows and columns just as easily as you can add them. For example, you may find you no longer need a particular row or column of data in a range. You could delete the data and then move the remaining data to close the empty space. It's faster, however, to delete the entire row or column because the Excel closes up the empty space for you.

If you have written formulas that calculate across the table, the formulas adjust themselves automatically after you delete rows or columns.

Begin

1 Select the Row

To delete a row, select the row you want to delete (click its row number to select it).

Click

2 Delete the Selected Row

Right-click the selection and select **Delete** on the shortcut menu.

Right Click   Click

3 The Row Is Removed

Excel immediately deletes the entire row, and the existing rows move up to fill its place.

4 Select the Column

To delete a column, select the column you want to delete (click its column letter to select it).

Click

5 Delete the Selected Column

Right-click the selected column and select **Delete** on the shortcut menu. As soon as you select the command, the column is immediately deleted.

Right Click

Click

6 Delete Multiple Rows

To delete several adjacent rows all at the same time, select the adjacent rows in the worksheet, right-click the selection, and choose **Delete** from the shortcut menu.

Click

Right Click

7 Delete Multiple Columns

To delete several adjacent columns at the same time, select the adjacent columns in the table, right-click the selection, and choose **Delete** from the shortcut menu.

Click

Right Click

End

How to Delete Cells

It's easy to delete data from cells; you select the cells and press **Delete**. Sometimes you will want to remove the cells themselves or just the data or formatting. Excel has several delete options that you can apply.

You might want to remove a row of data from a table, for example, but another table is next to it. If you delete the data by deleting the row from the worksheet, you will affect the second table because the row will be deleted all the way across the worksheet. If you delete the cells in the one table, however, the table closes up the space where the cells were, but the table next to it is unaffected.

Begin

1 Select the Cells

Select the cells you want to delete.

2 Choose Delete

Right-click the selected cells and choose **Delete** from the shortcut menu.

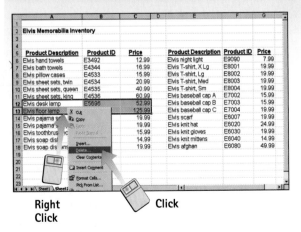

Right Click   **Click**

3 Shift Replacement Cells Up

In the Delete dialog box, click the **Shift Cells Up** option and click **OK**.

Click

4 Replacement Cells Move

The cells are removed from the worksheet, and the cells below move up to fill in the empty space. The cells on either side of the deleted cells are unaffected.

	A	B	C	D	E	F	G
1							
2	Elvis Memorabilia Inventory						
3							
4							
5	**Product Description**	**Product ID**	**Price**		**Product Description**	**Product ID**	**Price**
6	Elvis hand towels	E3492	12.99		Elvis night light	E9090	7.99
7	Elvis bath towels	E4344	16.99		Elvis T-shirt, X Lg	E8001	19.99
8	Elvis pillow cases	E4533	15.99		Elvis T-shirt, Lg	E8002	19.99
9	Elvis sheet sets, twin	E4534	20.99		Elvis T-shirt, Med	E8003	19.99
10	Elvis sheet sets, queen	E4535	40.99		Elvis T-shirt, Sm	E8004	19.99
11	Elvis sheet sets, king	E4536	60.99		Elvis baseball cap A	E7002	15.99
12	Elvis pajama sets	E3221	19.99		Elvis baseball cap B	E7003	15.99
13	Elvis pajama sets, knit	E3222	19.99		Elvis baseball cap C	E7004	15.99
14	Elvis toothbrush holder	E3299	15.99		Elvis scarf	E6007	19.99
15	Elvis soap dish	E3230	14.99		Elvis knit hat	E6020	24.99
16	Elvis soap dispenser	E3240	19.99		Elvis knit gloves	E6030	19.99
17					Elvis knit mittens	E6040	14.99
18					Elvis afghan	E6080	49.99

5 If You Shift Cells Left...

If you select the **Shift Cells Left** option in the Delete dialog box (in step 3), cells on the right side of the deleted cells move over, and cells above and below the deleted cells are unaffected.

	A	B	C	D	E	F	G
1							
2	Elvis Memorabilia Inventory						
3							
4							
5	**Product Description**	**Product ID**	**Price**		**Product Description**	**Product ID**	**Price**
6	Elvis hand towels	E3492	12.99		Elvis night light	E9090	7.99
7	Elvis bath towels	E4344	16.99		Elvis T-shirt, X Lg	E8001	19.99
8	Elvis pillow cases	E4533	15.99		Elvis T-shirt, Lg	E8002	19.99
9	Elvis sheet sets, twin	E4534	20.99		Elvis T-shirt, Med	E8003	19.99
10	Elvis sheet sets, queen	E4535	40.99		Elvis T-shirt, Sm	E8004	19.99
11	Elvis sheet sets, king	E4536	60.99		Elvis baseball cap A	E7002	15.99
12		Elvis baseball (	E7003	16			
13		Elvis baseball (	E7004	20			
14	Elvis pajama sets	E3221	19.99		Elvis scarf	E6007	19.99
15	Elvis pajama sets, knit	E3222	19.99		Elvis knit hat	E6020	24.99
16	Elvis toothbrush holder	E3299	15.99		Elvis knit gloves	E6030	19.99
17	Elvis soap dish	E3230	14.99		Elvis knit mittens	E6040	14.99
18	Elvis soap dispenser	E3240	19.99		Elvis afghan	E6080	49.99

6 Clear the Formatting Only

If you don't want to delete the cells or the contents but you want to remove their formatting (cell borders and colors) without affecting the data, select the cells and choose **Edit**, **Clear**, **Formats**.

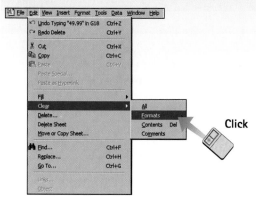

Click

End

How-To Hints

What Happens to the Worksheet?

When you delete cells (or rows/columns) from a worksheet, you don't reduce the total size of the worksheet. New cells, rows, or columns are added to the bottom and right edges of the worksheet so that every worksheet still contains 256 columns and 65,536 rows.

Delete Contents Only

To delete only the cell's contents and not the cell or formatting, open the **Edit** menu and choose **Clear**, **Contents**.

Oops!

If you make a mistake about deleting something, click the **Undo** button on the Standard toolbar.

How to Set the Column Width and Row Height

In a new worksheet, all the columns and rows are the same size. As you enter data, you will find that the default sizes aren't going to work for all your entries. It's quite common to exceed your column width when entering data. If it's a text entry, the text flows over into the cell to the right, until you enter data in the cell on the right. Then, the wide entry is cut off at the cell border. (It's all there, but it's hidden.) If it's a number entry, it won't flow over. Instead it appears as ######## in the cell.

You can quickly adjust the column width or row height in your worksheets. You can drag a row or column to a new size, or you can specify an exact size.

Begin

1 Drag a New Column Width

To adjust the column width, point at the right border of the column letter for the column you want to widen. The mouse pointer becomes a two-headed arrow. Hold down the left mouse button and drag the border in either direction to adjust the width. A ScreenTip lets you know the width measurement. Release the mouse button when the column is the width you want.

Click & Drag

2 Resize Multiple Columns

To make several columns the same width, select all the columns by dragging over their column letters, and then adjust the width for any one of them while they're all selected. They will all adjust to the same width.

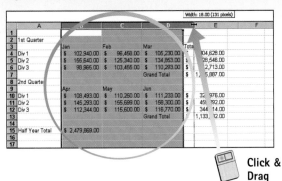

Click & Drag

3 Open the Column Width Dialog Box

To enter an exact value for the column width, select the column, open the **Format** menu, and choose **Column, Width**.

Click

4 Specify an Exact Size

Enter a measurement (in points) for the column width, click **OK** to exit, and apply the new setting.

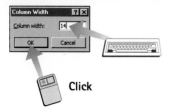

Click

5 Drag a New Row Height

You can adjust row height the same way you adjust column width. Point to the bottom border of the row number for the row you want to deepen. The mouse pointer becomes a two-headed arrow. Hold down the left mouse button and drag the border in either direction to adjust the row height. A ScreenTip lets you know the measurement. Release the mouse button when the row is the height you want.

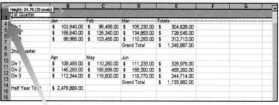

Click & Drag

6 Open the Row Height Dialog Box

You can also specify an exact value for the row height. Select the row or rows to which you want to apply a new measurement, open the **Format** menu, and select **Row**, **Height**. Enter a new value (in points) and click **OK** to exit.

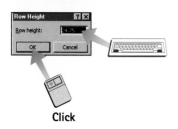

Click

End

How to Define a Range Name

Excel's default range names don't readily identify a range's contents. To clarify your data, you can assign range names. It's much easier to refer to your data by a name than with a meaningless cell address. For example, a range named *Sales_Totals* is a lot easier to decipher than *B2:F1*. The formula *=INCOME-EXPENSE* is easier to understand than *=B8:B24-C8:C24*. Giving ranges recognizable names will make your formulas easier to follow.

Range names appear in the Name box at the top of your worksheet. When you have at least one defined range name in a worksheet, you can click the Name box drop-down list to see a list of ranges.

Begin

1 Select a Range

To name a range, first select the range in the worksheet.

2 Click the Name Box

Click inside the **Name** box located at the far left end of the Formula bar.

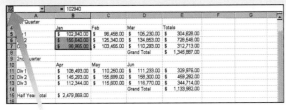

Click

3 Type a Name

Type a name for the range. Names must begin with a letter or an underscore (_), and after that you can use any other character. Don't use spaces. Use the underscore (_) instead, or a period (.).

4 Press Enter

Press **Enter** when finished typing in a range name. The name appears in place of the cell reference in the Name box when the range is selected in the worksheet.

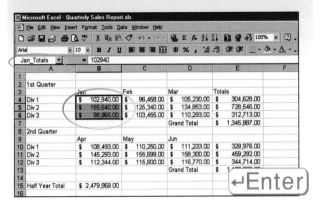

5 Go to the Range

To jump to the named range from anywhere in the workbook, click the drop-down arrow next to the **Name** box and click the range name in the list.

Click

6 Use the Define Name Box

Another way to name a range or edit an existing range name is to use the Define Name dialog box. Open the **Insert** menu and select **Name**, **Define**. In the Define Name box, you can enter a new range name, enter its cell references and click the **Add** button, or you can edit an existing name. Click **OK** to exit the dialog box.

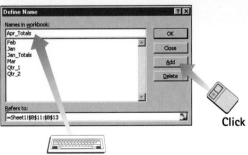

Click

End

How-To Hints

Delete a Range Name

To delete a range name, open the worksheet that contains the named cell or range. Choose **Insert**, **Name**, **Define**. In the Define Name dialog box, select the name and click **Delete** and then click **OK**.

Use Range Names in Formulas

To use the name in a formula, write the formula and click the range to include it; the range name appears in the formula in place of cell references.

Not Case Sensitive

Names are not case sensitive: If you create the name *Total_Sales*, Excel reads the names *TOTAL_SALES* and *total_sales* as the same name.

How to Find and Replace Data

As in Microsoft Word, you can search for and replace any character in a worksheet. You can find and/or replace text strings, such as a company or employee name, and you can find and/or replace numbers, either single digits or strings of numbers. You can also choose to search for characters in cell values, formulas, and worksheet comments.

If you have used Microsoft Word, you will discover that Find and Replace procedures are almost identical in the two programs. If you're new to the procedure, I will teach you how to use them in Excel, and you will know how to use them in Word.

Begin

1 Use the Find Command

To search for a word or number in a worksheet, open the **Edit** menu and select **Find**.

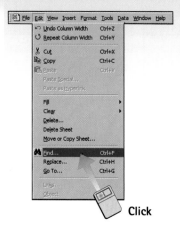

Click

2 Enter the Search Data

In the Find dialog box, click inside the **Find What** text box and type the characters (numbers, text, symbols) for which you want to search.

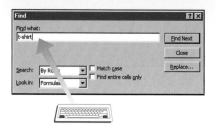

3 Select What to Search

Click the **Look In** drop-down arrow and select what you want to search. For example, if you're searching for text, select **Values**; if you're searching formulas, select **Formulas**; and if you're searching cell comments, select **Comments**.

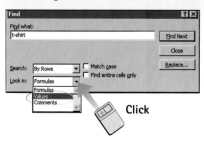

Click

4 Start the Search

Click the **Find Next** button to start the search. Excel locates the first cell containing your search characters and highlights it in the worksheet. Click **Find Next** repeatedly to find each occurrence of the character string.

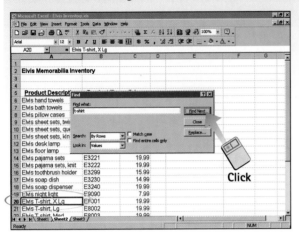

Click

5 Use the Replace Command

To conduct a search and replace, you must first open the Replace dialog box. Open the **Edit** menu and select **Replace**.

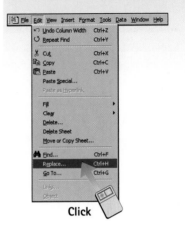

Click

6 Replace the Data

In the Replace dialog box, type the data you want to replace in the **Find What** box. Type the replacement data in the **Replace With** box. Click **Find Next,** and Excel highlights the first occurrence in the worksheet. Click the **Replace** button to replace the data; click **Replace All** to replace all occurrences at once.

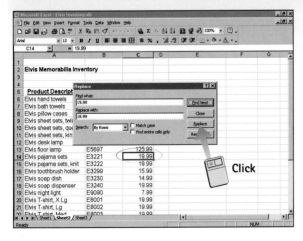

Click

How-To Hints

Keyboard Shortcuts

The keyboard shortcut for Edit, Find is Ctrl+F, and the shortcut for Edit, Replace is Ctrl+H. You can open the Replace dialog box without first opening the Find dialog box.

Narrow Your Search

To limit your search to text with specific capitalization, mark the **Match Case** check box. To limit your search to complete entries instead of including partial entries (if you want to search for 100, for example, and not find 1,000 or 20,100), mark the **Find Entire Cells Only** check box.

Speed Up the Search

In a large table, sometimes the search is faster if you select **By Rows** or **By Columns** in the **Search** drop-down list, especially if you start by selecting a cell in the specific row or column you want to search. In a small table, it makes no difference what's selected in the **Search** list.

End

How to Sort Data

Excel can be used as database, a tool for organizing data. Its grid of columns and rows makes it perfect for entering *fields* and *records*. For example, an inventory database might contain fields (columns) for product name, product number, and price. A record (row) is a complete entry in the database with data recorded for each field.

A priority of any database is the capability to sort data. You can sort a data list to see product names in alphabetical order, for example, and then sort the list to see product prices from highest to lowest. When you sort a list, the whole list is sorted and each record (row) in the list retains its integrity. Other tables on the same worksheet are not affected by the sort.

Begin

1 Select a Field

To sort by a single *key*, or field (column), click any cell in that column. For example, in this figure, I want to sort the Product ID column.

Click

2 Sort in Ascending Order

To sort the data alphabetically or in lowest-to-highest order, click the **Sort Ascending** button. To sort in reverse order or highest-to-lowest order, click the **Sort Descending** button.

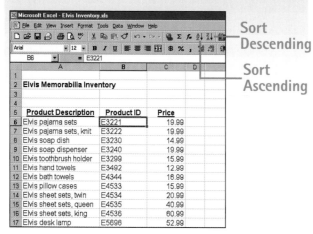

Sort Descending

Sort Ascending

3 Sort by Multiple Fields

To sort the data by multiple fields, called a multikey sort, click anywhere in the data list and then open the **Data** menu and select **Sort**.

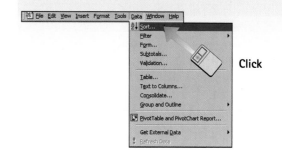

Click

4 Set the First Field

In the Sort dialog box, click the **Sort By** drop-down arrow and select the field you want for your major sort. Next to the column heading, click the sort order option you want (**Ascending** or **Descending**). In this figure, I'm sorting an address table by the Last Name column.

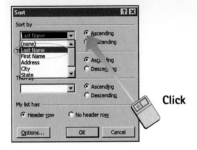

Click

5 Set the Second Field

For the second key in the sort, click the **Then By** drop-down arrow and select the column (in this example, my second key sort is the State column) and click a sort order option. To sort by a third key within the second key, use the second **Then By** box. Click **OK** to run the sort.

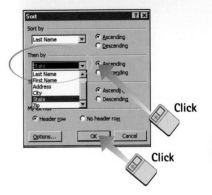

Click

Click

6 Results of a Multikey Sort

Shown here is the result of the two-key sort by Last Name and then by State.

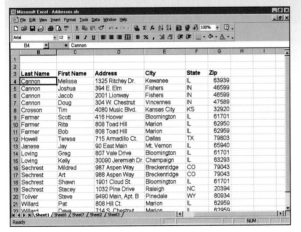

End

How-To Hints

Undo a Sort

To return your data list to its former state, click the **Undo** button on the Standard toolbar to undo the sort immediately.

Sort One Column, Not the Whole List

If you want to sort a single column within a list but not sort the rest of the list with that column, select all the cells in the table column that you want to sort. Only the cells in that column are sorted.

Lose Your Headings?

If your column headings are similar enough to the data in your list that Excel doesn't guess that they're headings, they may get sorted into the data. To fix that, click the **Undo** button to undo the sort. Choose **Data, Sort**. In the Sort dialog box, click the **Header Row** option before you run the sort.

How to Filter Data

Another activity you can do when using Excel as a database is to *filter* data. Filtering shows only the records you want to see and hides the rest. Records aren't removed, they're just hidden temporarily.

Filtering is based on *criteria*, data that's shared by all the records you want to see. For example, in an inventory database, you might sort the data to only show records of a certain price range. You don't have to sort a list before you filter, and you can have blank cells in the list. The top row, however, should contain column headings or labels, and the list should contain no completely blank rows.

Begin

1 Click a Cell

To begin a filter, click any cell in the list or table.

	A	B	C	D
4				
5	**Product Description**	**Product ID**	**Price**	
6	Elvis hand towels	E3492	12.99	
7	Elvis bath towels	E4344	16.99	
8	Elvis pillow cases	E4533	15.99	
9	Elvis sheet sets, twin	E4534	20.99	
10	Elvis sheet sets, queen	E4535	40.99	
11	Elvis sheet sets, king	E4536	60.99	
12	Elvis desk lamp	E5696	5.99	
13	Elvis floor lamp	E5697	125.9	
14	Elvis pajama sets	E3221	19.99	
15	Elvis pajama sets, knit	E3222	19.99	
16	Elvis toothbrush holder	E3299	15.99	
17	Elvis soap dish	E3230	14.99	
18	Elvis soap dispenser	E3240	19.99	
19	Elvis night light	E9090	7.99	
20	Elvis T-shirt, X Lg	E8001	19.99	
21	Elvis T-shirt, Lg	E8002	19.99	
22	Elvis T-shirt, Med	E8003	19.99	
23	Elvis T-shirt, Sm	E8004	19.99	
24	Elvis baseball cap A	E7002	15.99	
25	Elvis baseball cap B	E7003	15.99	
26	Elvis baseball cap C	E7004	19.99	

Sheet1 \ **Sheet2** \ Sheet3 /

Click

2 Click the Filter Command

Open the **Data** menu and select **Filter**, **AutoFilter**.

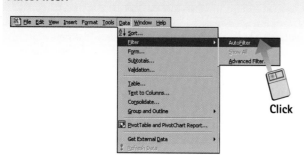

File Edit View Insert Format Tools Data Window Help

Sort...
Filter ▶ AutoFilter
Form... Show All
Subtotals... Advanced Filter...
Validation...
Table...
Text to Columns...
Consolidate...
Group and Outline ▶
PivotTable and PivotChart Report...
Get External Data ▶
Refresh Data

Click

3 Click a Filter Arrow

Filter arrows appear in each column label cell. In the column that contains the criteria you want to filter, click the filter arrow to drop a list of all the values in the column.

	A	B	C	D
4				
5	**Product Description** ▾	**Product ID** ▾	**Price** ▾	
6	Elvis hand towels	E3492	(All)	
7	Elvis bath towels	E4344	(Top 10...)	
8	Elvis pillow cases	E4533	(Custom...)	
9	Elvis sheet sets, twin	E4534	7.99	
10	Elvis sheet sets, queen	E4535	12.99	
11	Elvis sheet sets, king	E4536	14.99	
12	Elvis desk lamp	E5696	15.99	
13	Elvis floor lamp	E5697	16.99	
14	Elvis pajama sets	E3221	19.99	
15	Elvis pajama sets, knit	E3222	20.99	
16	Elvis toothbrush holder	E3299	24.99	
17	Elvis soap dish	E3230	40.99	
18	Elvis soap dispenser	E3240	49.99	
19	Elvis night light	E9090	52.99	
			60.99	
			125.99	
16	Elvis toothbrush holder	E3299	15.99	
17	Elvis soap dish	E3230	14.99	
18	Elvis soap dispenser	E3240	19.99	
19	Elvis night light	E9090	7.99	
20	Elvis T-shirt, X Lg	E8001	19.99	
21	Elvis T-shirt, Lg	E8002	19.99	
22	Elvis T-shirt, Med	E8003	19.99	
23	Elvis T-shirt, Sm	E8004	19.99	
24	Elvis baseball cap A	E7002	15.99	
25	Elvis baseball cap B	E7003	15.99	
26	Elvis baseball cap C	E7004	19.99	

Sheet1 \ **Sheet2** \ Sheet3 /

Click

4 Click Filter Criteria

Click the criteria you want. All records that don't meet that criteria are hidden. The filter arrow where you set the criteria turns blue, and the row numbers where records are hidden turn blue.

	A	B	C	D
4				
5	Product Description▾	Product ID▾	Price ▾	
14	Elvis pajama sets	E3221	19.99	
15	Elvis pajama sets, knit	E3222	19.99	
18	Elvis soap dispenser	E3240	19.99	
20	Elvis T-shirt, X Lg	E8001	19.99	
21	Elvis T-shirt, Lg	E8002	19.99	
22	Elvis T-shirt, Med	E8003	19.99	
23	Elvis T-shirt, Sm	E8004	19.99	
26	Elvis baseball cap C	E7004	19.99	
27	Elvis scarf	E6007	19.99	
29	Elvis knit gloves	E6030	19.99	
32				
33				

5 Set Multiple Criteria

To set multiple criteria to further filter the results of the first filter, set criteria in multiple columns (repeat steps 1-4). Shown is a list filtered to show all sheet sets that are priced at $40.99.

	Product Description▾	Product ID▾	Price ▾
4			
5	Product Description▾	Product ID▾	Price ▾
9	sheet sets	E4534	40.99
10	sheet sets	E4535	40.99
12	sheet sets	E4544	40.99
13	sheet sets	E4545	40.99
34			
35			
36			

6 Remove the Filter

To remove the filter and show all the records in the list again, either click the filter arrow where you set the criteria and click **(All)** or choose **Data**, **Filter**, **AutoFilter** to turn AutoFilter off.

5	Product Description▾	Product ID▾	Price ▾
9	(All)	E4534	40.99
10	(Top 10...)	E4535	40.99
	(Custom...)		
12	afghan	E4544	40.99
	sheet sets		
13	sheet sets	4545	40.99
34			
35			

 Click

End

How-To Hints

Field or Column?

Excel (and Access, Word, and Outlook) uses the terms *column* and *field* interchangeably. A *field* is a database term that refers to a column in a table.

Top 10

To filter the top (or bottom) 10 (or another number) of number items in a list, select the **Top 10** filter criteria. Select **Top** or **Bottom**, select a number, select **Items** or **Percent**, and choose **OK**.

Comparison Criteria

To set complex criteria such as "prices greater than $4," click the filter arrow in the column in which you want to set the criteria, and click **(Custom)**. In the Custom AutoFilter dialog box, select comparison operators in the list box on the left, type or select criteria in the list box on the right, and click **OK**.

16

How to Work with Worksheets

By default, Excel opens every new workbook file with three worksheets. You can add or subtract worksheets as needed. You can also rename worksheets to better describe their contents. For example, you may have a quarterly sales report with sales totals for each quarter on separate worksheets. You can name each sheet with distinctive names such as *Quarter 1*, *Quarter 2*, and so on. You can even move and copy sheets from workbook to workbook. In this task, you'll learn the various ways you can work with worksheets.

Begin

1 Move from One Sheet to Another

To move from one sheet to another, click the sheet tab for the sheet to which you want to view. The selected sheet, or *active* sheet, is the one with the bright white-and-black sheet tab. Sheets that aren't selected have sheet tabs that are gray and black.

21	T-shirt, Lg	E8002	19.99
22	T-shirt, Med	E8003	19.99
23	T-shirt, Sm	E8004	19.99

Sheet1 \ Sheet2 / Sheet3 /
Ready

Click

2 Rename a Worksheet

Double-click the sheet tab, and the sheet name is highlighted. Type a new name and press **Enter**.

21	T-shirt, Lg	E8002	19.99
22	T-shirt, Med	E8003	19.99
23	T-shirt, Sm	E8004	19.99

Sheet1 \ Inventory / Sheet3 /

Double Click

3 Delete a Worksheet

Right-click the sheet tab for the worksheet you want to delete and choose **Delete**.

17	soap dish	E3230	14.99
18	soap dispenser	Insert...	19.99
19	night light	Delete	7.99
20	T-shirt, X Lg	Rename	19.99
21	T-shirt, Lg	Move or Copy..	19.99
22	T-shirt, Med	Select All Sheets	19.99
23	T-shirt, Sm	View Code	19.99

Sheet1 \ Inventory / Sheet3 /
Ready

Right Click

Click

4 Add Another Worksheet

Right-click a sheet tab and choose **Insert**. In the Insert dialog box on the **General** tab, double-click the **Worksheet** icon. The new worksheet is inserted on the left side of the sheet tab you initially right-clicked.

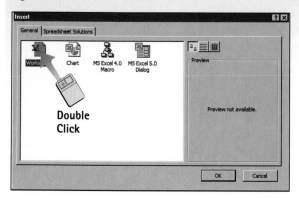

Double Click

5 Move a Worksheet

To move a worksheet within a workbook, drag its sheet tab. While you drag, the mouse pointer acquires a sheet-of-paper symbol, and a small black triangle points to the position where the sheet will be moved.

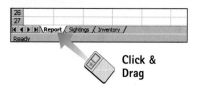

Click & Drag

6 Copy a Worksheet

To make a copy of a worksheet within a workbook, drag its sheet tab. While you drag, the mouse pointer acquires a sheet-of-paper symbol, and a small black triangle points to the position where the sheet will be copied. Before you release the mouse button, press **Ctrl** (the pointer will show a small plus symbol on its sheet-of-paper symbol, which indicates a copy).

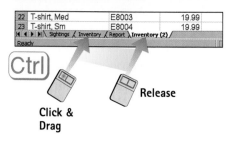

Ctrl

Release

Click & Drag

End

How-To Hints

Use the Shortcut Menu

Right-click over the worksheet tab to display a shortcut menu of commands that you can apply to the worksheet. Be sure to position the mouse pointer directly over the sheet tab name or the wrong shortcut menu will appear.

Another Way to Move or Copy

Another way to move or copy a worksheet is to use the Move or Copy dialog box. Right-click over the sheet tab you want to move or copy and select **Move or Copy** from the shortcut menu. Select the workbook you want to move or copy the worksheet to, and then choose where to place the sheet. Click **OK** to exit the dialog box and either execute the move or copy.

Add Several Sheets at Once

To add several worksheets all at once, select several sheets and then use the **Insert, Worksheet** command. Press and hold the **Ctrl** key while selecting two or more sheets and open the **Insert** menu and choose **Worksheet**.

Task

6

How to Use Formulas and Functions

*T*he real thrill of using a spreadsheet program such as Excel is in performing calculations. From the simplest addition and subtraction to complex scientific exponential equations, Excel worksheets use formulas to perform all kinds of calculations on your data. Based on the values you have entered, for example, you can create formulas that calculate the average sales for your department, total the commissions each sales representative receives, and compare the figures to last year's numbers.

You don't have to worry that a calculation might be incorrect: Excel won't make a mistake. Whenever you change a value included in a formula, Excel updates the formula results automatically. In this chapter, you will learn the basic steps for creating and using Excel formulas.

In addition to formulas you create yourself, Excel comes with hundreds of built-in functions: calculation tools you can use to perform more complex financial, analytical, or statistical calculations. You will also learn how to apply these functions to your own worksheet situations. ●

How to Use AutoSum

The most common mathematical calculation you'll perform in Excel is summing up data. For example, you might sum the sales results for several months or the total items in an invoice. Summing is so common that a toolbar button enters a **SUM** formula for you. You can add the contents of cells by writing a formula such as **=A1+B1+C1+D1+E1**, but using the **SUM** function in a formula is faster because Excel does the work for you. The **SUM** function is the perfect tool for quickly adding up multiple cells.

You will learn how to write a formula in Task 2, "How to Create Formulas," and you will learn more about functions (built-in equations) in Task 4, "How to Enter Functions." In this task, you'll learn to enter a fast sum with the AutoSum button.

Begin

1 Enter the Numbers

Enter the numbers you want to sum in a column, row, or rectangular block of cells. The formula ignores any text entries in the *range* of cells (the collection of cells you will sum).

	A	B	C	D	E
1					
2					
3		Sales - 3rd Quarter			
4				Totals	
5		Department A		1,389,588	
6		Department B		1,575,594	
7		Department C		1,675,900	
8		Department D		1,490,800	
9					

2 Select a Location for the Sum

Select the cell where you want the sum result to appear (usually at the end of the row or column of numbers).

	A	B	C	D	E	F
1						
2						
3		Sales - 3rd Quarter				
4				Totals		
5		Department A		1,389,588		
6		Department B		1,575,594		
7		Department C		1,675,900		
8		Department D		1,490,800		
9						
10						
11						

Click

3 Click AutoSum

On the Standard toolbar, click the **AutoSum** button.

Σ *f*ₓ A↓ Z↓ »
      Z↑ A↑

Click

4 The SUM Formula Is Entered

The AutoSum button inserts a formula that uses the SUM function and surrounds the cells being summed with a flashing border.

SUM	▼ X ✓ = =SUM(D5:D8)			
	A	B	C	D	E
1					
2					
3		Sales - 3rd Quarter			
4				Totals	
5		Department A		1,675,900	
6		Department B		1,575,594	
7		Department C		1,490,800	
8		Department D		1,389,588	
9				=SUM(D5:D8)	
10					
11					

5 Complete the Entry

If the flashing border is surrounding all the cells you want to sum, press **Enter** to complete the formula. If the surrounded cells are wrong, drag to select the cells you want summed (the flashing border surrounds the cells you drag), and press **Enter**. The result of the formula is displayed in the cell.

D10	▼ =			
	A	B	C	D	E
1					
2					
3		Sales - 3rd Quarter			
4				Totals	
5		Department A		1,675,900	
6		Department B		1,575,594	
7		Department C		1,490,800	
8		Department D		1,389,588	
9				6,131,882	
10					
11					
12					

↵Enter

6 The Formula and the Result

To see the formula and the result, click the cell where you entered the formula. The results appear in the cell, and the formula appears in the Formula bar.

D9	▼ = =SUM(D5:D8)			
	A	B	C	D	E
1					
2					
3		Sales - 3rd Quarter			
4				Totals	
5		Department A		1,675,900	
6		Department B		1,575,594	
7		Department C		1,490,800	
8		Department D		1,389,588	
9				6,131,882	
10					

Click

End

How-To Hints

Sum a Whole Table at Once

To AutoSum all the columns in a table at once, select all the cells in the row below the table and click the **AutoSum** button. Each column is summed in the cell below the column. To sum all the rows in a table at once, select all the cells in the column next to the table and click the **AutoSum** button. Each row is summed in the cell at the end of the row.

Put the AutoSum Anywhere

You can place an AutoSum formula anywhere on the worksheet, not just next to the range you're summing. To place the AutoSum formula away from the range of cells, click the cell where you want to display the result and click the **AutoSum** button. Drag to select the cells you want to sum, and press **Enter**.

How to Create Formulas

On paper, formulas are written like this:

2+2=4

In Excel, a formula takes a slightly different form:

=2+2

The answer, 4, is displayed in the cell. All formulas in a worksheet begin with an equal sign (=).

In Excel, you're not limited to writing =2+2; you can type **=(a cell)+(another cell)**, and the values entered in those cells are added together. If you change the values in those cells, the formula continues to add together their current values. You can also use *mathematical operators* to perform other calculations, such as subtraction (-), multiplication (*), or division (/).

Begin

1 Select a Cell

Click the cell where you want to enter the formula and type an equal sign (=).

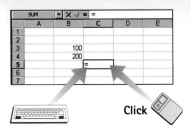

Click

2 Build the Formula

Click the first of the cells you want to add to the formula. The cell's reference is immediately added to the equation. Type an operator for the formula, such as a plus symbol (+), or use another operator: subtract (-), multiply (*), or divide (/).

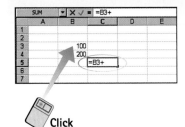

Click

3 Finish the Formula

Click the next cell you want to add to the formula. As you click each cell, its cell address, or *cell reference*, appears in the formula.

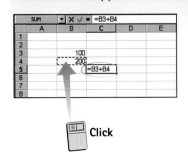

Click

4 Press Enter

Press **Enter** to complete the formula. The formula is entered, and the result appears in the formula cell. The formula itself is displayed in the Formula bar. To view the formula, click the cell containing the formula results.

┌─ ┘Enter ─┐

5 Test the Formula

Now change the values in the cells you referenced in the formula; the formula result changes automatically because the formula adds whichever values are in the cells.

End

How-To Hints

Calculate a Large Range

To calculate a large range of cells on a worksheet without entering each cell into the formula separately, you can sum a *range* of cells by including the first and last cell; Excel includes all the cells in between. If you want to sum cells A1, A2, A3, A4, and A5 (the first five cells in column A), for example, a more convenient formula is **=SUM(A1:A5)**. This formula tells Excel to sum all the cells between A1 and A5. (**SUM** is a specific Excel function; you will learn more about functions in Task 4.)

What's Really in the Cell?

You can't tell by looking at a cell whether the value you see is a simple number or the result of a formula. To find out, select the cell and look at the Formula bar (what's actually entered in the cell is always displayed in the Formula bar).

Group Operators Within Parentheses

To use different operators in the same formula, use parentheses to divide the formula appropriately. If you want to add 4+6 and divide the result by 2, for example, the formula **=4+6/2** gives the wrong answer (7), but the formula **=(4+6)/2** gives the right answer (5). Operations within parentheses are performed first.

How to Use Absolute and Relative Cell Addresses

Cell references are the addresses of cells in a worksheet. Three types exist: *relative*, *absolute*, and *mixed*. *Relative references* give a cell's location relative to the active cell, as in "two cells left and one cell up." *Absolute references* give an address that's unchanging, such as "the intersection of row 3 and column B." *Mixed references* return a mixture of the two: for example, "two cells below the active cell, in column D."

A relative reference looks like **A1,** absolute references are always preceded by a dollar sign (such as **A1**), and a mixed reference looks like **A$1** or **$A1**. Use absolute references when you always want the address to refer to a specific location on the worksheet.

Begin

1 Enter a Formula

To demonstrate the difference between relative and absolute references, enter a formula that sums the two cells left of the formula. In this figure, the cells in columns C and D are summed.

2 AutoFill the Formula

Copy the formula down the column using AutoFill. The formula for each cell adjusts to sum the two cells to its left, as shown in the figure. A click on any of the cells in column E reveals a formula relative to the cell addresses.

3 Rewrite the Formula

Now rewrite the original formula so it multiplies the cell to its left (cell D2) by the value in cell F2. The formula will read **=D2*F2**. Notice the results displayed in cell E2.

4 AutoFill the Formula

Use AutoFill to copy the formula down the column again. This time you'll notice the results are all wrong for the remaining cells in column E. This is because relative references tell each formula to multiply the cell to its left by the cell on its right (instead of the value in F2). You need to change the F2 reference to an absolute reference so that each formula multiplies the cell on its left by the value in cell F2.

E5	▼	=	=D5*F5		
	A	B	C	D	E	F
1						
2			10	20	40	2
3			20	30	0	
4			30	40	0	
5			40	50	0	
6						
7						

5 Change the Reference Type

To change the reference type, click the cell that contains the original formula. In the Formula bar, click the reference **F2**, and press **F4**. (Pressing F4 cycles the cell reference repeatedly through all the reference types.) When the reference in the Formula bar reads **F2**, press **Enter** to complete the formula.

SUM	▼	X ✓ =	=D2*F2		
	A	B	C	D	E	F
1						
2			10	20	=D2*F2	2
3			20	30	0	
4			30	40	0	
5			40	50	0	
6						
7						

[F4]

6 AutoFill the Formula

Use AutoFill to copy the formula down the column again. Now each formula multiplies the cell on its left by the value in cell F2.

E5	▼	=	=D5*F2		
	A	B	C	D	E	F
1						
2			10	20	40	2
3			20	30	60	
4			30	40	80	
5			40	50	100	
6						
7						
8						

End

How-To Hints

Manual References

You can also enter absolute references by typing in the appropriate symbol in the Formula bar. To make cell reference B4 absolute, for example, type **B4**.

Edit References

To edit a reference in a formula, click in the Formula bar where you want to edit and make your changes. Use the **F4** command to change relative, absolute, or mixed references. Press **Enter** when finished editing.

Reference Other Sheets

You can also reference cells from other worksheets in your workbook. To do this, type the sheet name, an exclamation point, and the cell reference. For example, **Sheet2!B4** would refer to cell B4 in worksheet 2.

How to Enter Functions

Task 2 shows you how to write formulas, and it briefly mentions functions. A *function* is a built-in formula with a name that Excel recognizes. A function saves you time you would have spent setting up the math yourself. Excel has more than 300 functions available, so you're sure to find one for the type of mathematical calculation you want to perform.

To use a function, write a formula that includes the function name, the cells you want calculated, and any other information (called *arguments*) that the particular function needs. In Task 1, you learned how to use AutoSum to create a **SUM** formula automatically: the formula consisted of an equal sign (=), the function name (**SUM**), and the cells you want summed (in parentheses).

Begin

1 Type =

Click the cell in which you want to write the formula and type an equal sign (=). On the Formula bar, click the down arrow next to the **Name** box. The Name box becomes a list of common function names.

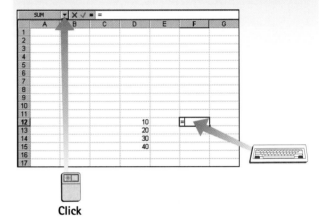

Click

2 Select a Function

Click a function name from the list box. The steps in this task will demonstrate the **AVERAGE** function. The **AVERAGE** function is better than a manual adding-and-dividing-cells formula because it ignores empty cells, which give an incorrect result.

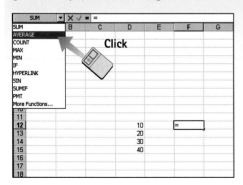

Click

3 Use the Formula Palette

The Formula palette appears (if the Office Assistant appears, click the **No, I Don't Need Help Now** option to make it go away). The palette may guess which cells you want to average, but you can select exactly which cells to use with the function if Excel guesses incorrectly. If the Formula palette is in the way, you can drag it out of the way to uncover cells (click anywhere on the gray palette and drag).

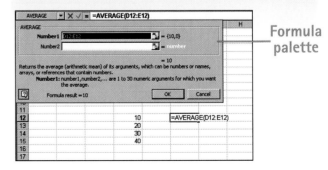

Formula palette

4 Drag the Cells to Be Calculated

If the correct cells you want to calculate aren't listed in the **Number1** argument box, drag over the cell references in the worksheet to highlight them. A moving border appears around the cells, and the correct cell references now appear in the Formula palette's **Number1** argument box. (Ignore the other argument boxes: They're for including other ranges in the calculation.)

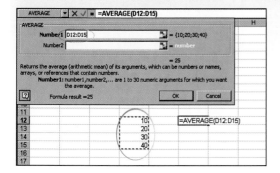

5 Complete the Formula

Click **OK** to complete the formula. The palette disappears, and the formula result appears in the worksheet. The formula itself, including the function, appears in the Formula bar.

6 Try the Other Functions

The **MIN**, **MAX**, and **COUNT** functions work the same way as the **AVERAGE** and **SUM** functions. Shown here are the results of each of these formulas for the same range of cells. If you don't see the function you want on the Functions list, click **More Functions** and find the function in the Paste Function dialog box.

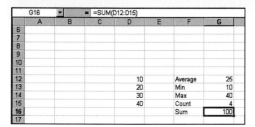

End

How-To Hints

Write Your Own Formulas

You can write formulas yourself by typing them. When you type a function name in a formula, it must be spelled correctly and written correctly.

Minimize and Maximize the Palette

If the Formula palette is so large that you can't drag it out of the way, minimize it temporarily by clicking the button on the right end of the argument box you want to fill (the small button looks like a busy grid with a little red arrow). After you drag the cells, click the button on the end of the minimized palette to return it to full size.

How to Use AutoCalculate

Sometimes you need an immediate calculation, but you don't need the formula permanently entered in a worksheet cell. *AutoCalculate* is a feature that's always turned on, always out of your way, and available any time you need a quick answer to a simple calculation while you work.

If you're entering a column of numbers and you want to know the total of what you have entered so far, select the cells you want to sum and look at the AutoCalculate box. You can also get a quick average, a count of cells, or other calculations by changing the AutoCalculate function.

Begin

1 Select Cells

Select the cells you want to calculate.

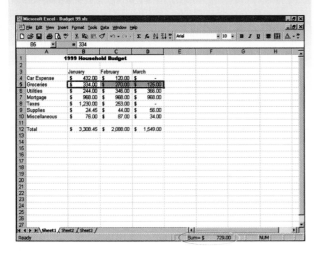

2 Look at AutoCalculate

Look at the AutoCalculate box on the status bar. The calculation result is displayed for the selected cells.

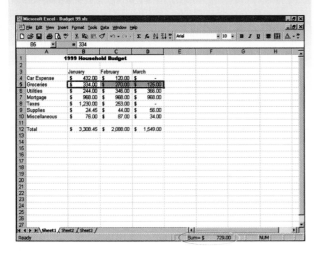

3 See the AutoCalculate Functions

To change the calculation function, right-click the **AutoCalculate** box on the status bar.

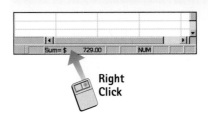

Right Click

4 Select a Function

Click a different function, or click **None** to turn it off.

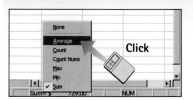

Click

5 Look at the Results

AutoCalculate changes to show the results of your selected function.

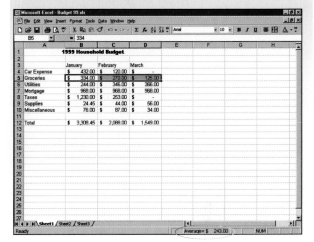

End

How-To Hints

If AutoCalculate Isn't There

If AutoCalculate doesn't appear, make sure its calculation is set to a function (not to None) by right-clicking the AutoCalculate box, and make sure a range of cells that contain numbers is selected.

If Your Status Bar Isn't There

If your status bar is missing, choose **Tools**, **Options**. On the **View** tab, mark the **Status bar** check box, and choose **OK**. If your status bar isn't turned on, you won't be able to use the AutoCalculate feature.

How to Fix Formula Errors

Not all formulas are perfect, and when they aren't, Excel lets you know by displaying an error value in the cell. Error values are preceded by a pound sign (#). For example, you may have entered an incorrect value or operator, the wrong cell reference, or function. The first thing to do when you see an error value is to recheck the formula and references used.

For complex worksheets, it's not always easy to see whether your formulas and data references are correct. Use Excel's auditing tools to help you find your mistakes. You can display tracer lines that locate precedents (cell references referred to in a formula) and dependents (cell references that are referenced in another cell, such as those used in a formula).

Begin

1 Select Cells

Select the cell or cells you want to examine for accuracy. For example, in the worksheet shown, the average sales per month figure seems a bit high, so I'm going to trace its precedents.

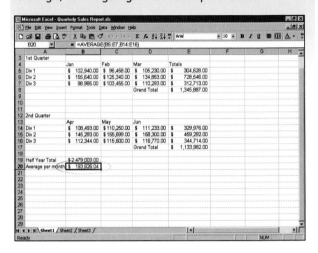

2 Open the Auditing Submenu

Open the **Tools** menu and select **Auditing**, then choose **Trace Precedents**.

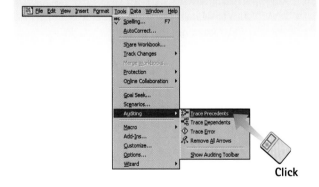

Click

3 Trace the Precedents

Excel immediately marks the cell references used in the formula in blue and traces them back to the cell you selected in step 1 with a blue arrow. In the figure, I can now see I selected the Totals column to be included in the formula, and it shouldn't be.

4 Remove the Trace

To turn off the trace marks, open the **Tools** menu and select **Auditing**, then **Remove All Arrows**.

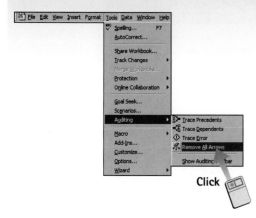

Click

5 Trace Errors

If your worksheet cell displays an error result, use the Trace Error auditing tool to help you track down the source of the error. Select the cell and then open the **Tools** menu and choose **Auditing**, then **Trace Error**. In this figure, cell A10 contains an error.

Click

6 View the Trace

Excel displays trace arrows pointing out the sources of the formula to help you track down the error. In this figure, I've tried to divide by a zero value in cell B10. Oops! After locating your error, make the necessary corrections and turn off the trace arrows (select **Tools**, **Auditing**, **Remove All Arrows**).

	A	B	C	D	E	F
	A10		=SUM(A9+Qtr_1)/B10			
3	1st Quarter					
4		Jan	Feb	Mar	Totals	
5	Div 1	$ 102,940.00	$ 96,458.00	$ 105,230.00	$ 304,628.00	
6	Div 2	$ 155,640.00	$ 125,340.00	$ 134,853.00	$ 728,546.00	
7	Div 3	$ 98,965.00	$ 103,455.00	$ 110,293.00	$ 312,713.00	
8				Grand Total	$ 1,345,887.00	
9	1345887					
10	#DIV/0!					
11						
12	2nd Quarter					
13		Apr	May	Jun		
14	Div 1	$ 108,493.00	$ 110,250.00	$ 111,233.00	$ 329,976.00	
15	Div 2	$ 145,293.00	$ 155,699.00	$ 158,300.00	$ 459,292.00	
16	Div 3	$ 112,344.00	$ 115,600.00	$ 116,770.00	$ 344,714.00	
17				Grand Total	$ 1,133,982.00	

End

How-To Hints

Tracing Dependents

In this task, you saw how to trace precedents, which showed you which cells were used to obtain the results in the selected cell. You can also choose to trace dependents, which is the reverse of tracing precedents. Instead of selecting the cell containing the results, you can select a cell and trace its use to a formula. To trace dependents, select **Tools**, **Auditing**, **Trace Dependents**.

Use the Auditing Toolbar

When working with complex worksheets, display the Auditing toolbar onscreen for easy access to auditing commands. To open the toolbar, open the **Tools** menu and select **Auditing**, **Show Auditing Toolbar**. To close the toolbar again, follow the same step, this time deselecting the **Show Auditing Toolbar** command.

Multiple Traces

You can use the Trace Precedent or Trace Dependent commands as many times as you want for any given cell.

Task

7

How to Use Excel's Formatting Tools

*B*y their very nature, *Excel worksheets* aren't the most appealing, eye-catching way to present data. Granted, your data may be well organized, but with the plain presentation of columns and rows, your data can quickly become lost in a sea of never-ending cells. To help make your data more presentable, use Excel's many formatting features to create worksheets that are visually appealing.

You can easily change fonts, sizes, and formatting of your text and number entries to make the data easier to read. You can also apply borders and shading to your worksheet cells. If you're not too confident about choosing your own formatting options, let Excel do the work for you with AutoFormat.

In this chapter, you will learn five important formatting features that can help you format your worksheets quickly and painlessly. Just remember that it doesn't matter how powerful your *formulas* and *functions* are if you can't clearly see the results. ●

How to Change Number Formats

Numeric values you enter into your worksheets are usually more than just numbers. They represent dollar values, dates, percentages, and other real values. By default, when you enter a number, it's displayed in General format, which is usually just the way you type it. You can also use Excel's other number formats to change its meaning.

For example, the entry 5.05 can mean different things. If you apply the currency format, the entry becomes $5.05; if you apply the percentage format, the entry becomes 500%. In this task, you learn how to change the number format using toolbar buttons and the Format Cells dialog box.

1 Select the Cell or Range

Select the cell or range where you want to change the number format.

2 Click Currency

To change a format to accounting format (which adds a $, rounds the number to two decimal places, and spaces the $ so that all the dollar signs in the column are aligned), click the **Currency Style** button on the Formatting toolbar.

Click

3 Click Percent

To change a format to percent format (which adds a % and changes the number from a fraction or integer to a percentage value), click the **Percent Style** button on the Formatting toolbar. (Remember, percent means hundredths, so 0.12 is displayed as 12%, but 12 is displayed as 1200%.)

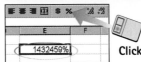

Click

4 Click Comma

To apply comma format (which rounds the number to two decimal places and adds a comma at each thousands mark), click the **Comma Style** button on the Formatting toolbar. To control the decimal point, you can also click the **Increase Decimal** or **Decrease Decimal** buttons on the Formatting toolbar.

Click

5 Use the Format Cells Dialog Box

To apply different formats that aren't on the Formatting toolbar, open the **Format** menu and select **Cells**. This opens the Format Cells dialog box. Click the **Number** tab and then choose a number format in the **Category** list. Your selected number is displayed with that format in the **Sample** area.

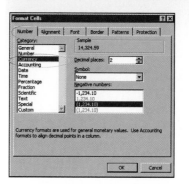

6 Set Format Options

Different formats in the Format Cells dialog box offer different options; select a **Category** and set the options for that format. A description of the selected category appears at the bottom of the dialog box. To exit the dialog box and apply the new format, click **OK**.

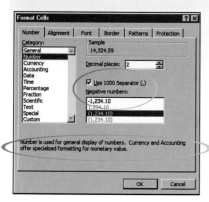

End

How to Adjust the Cell Alignment

By default, Excel automatically aligns your entries based on their data type. Text entries always line up to the left of the cells. Number entries always align to the right. Both text and numbers align vertically at the bottom of the cells, but you can change the alignment of any entry, both horizontally and vertically.

With Excel's alignment commands, you can also flip your text to read as if each letter is stacked on top of the next, or you can rotate the text to read sideways (top to bottom instead of left to right).

Begin

1 Quick Cell Alignment

For quick horizontal alignment changes, use the alignment buttons on the Formatting toolbar. Select the cell or range you want to align and click the appropriate button.

Align Center

Align Left Align Right

2 Center a Title over a Range

If you want to center text in a single row over a range of cells, select the entire range of blank cells you want to center, including the cell containing the text you want centered.

	A	B	C	D
1	1999 Household Budget			
2				
3		January	February	March
4	Car Expense	432	120	15
5	Groceries	334	270	125
6	Utilities	244	346	366
7	Mortgage	968	968	968
8	Taxes	1230	253	125
9	Supplies	15	44	23
10	Miscellaneous	76	87	34
11	Total	3299	2088	1656
12				

3 Click the Merge and Center Button

Next, click the **Merge and Center** button on the Formatting toolbar.

Click

4 The Text Is Centered

Excel centers the title over the range.

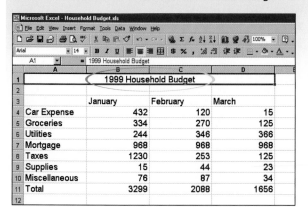

5 Change Orientation

If you want to change the horizontal alignment or flip or rotate your entry, use Excel's Format Cells dialog box. Open the **Format** menu and select **Cells**.

Click

6 Select an Alignment or Orientation

Click the **Alignment** tab. Use the **Vertical** alignment drop-down list to align your entry between the top and bottom cell borders. To change orientation, click the type of option you want to use from the **Orientation** settings. Click **OK** to exit the dialog box and apply the new settings.

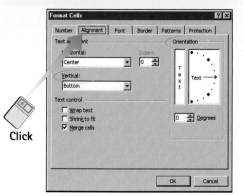

Click

End

How-To Hints

What About Fonts and Sizes?

You can format Excel data the same way you would format text in Word. You can use the Font and Font Size drop-down lists on the Formatting toolbar to change the font and size of your text. You can also apply bold, italic, or underline by clicking the appropriate toolbar buttons. To apply all these formatting options at once, open the **Format** menu, select **Cells**, and click the **Font** tab.

Format with Indents

You can indent text within a cell using Excel's Increase Indent button on the Formatting toolbar. Of course, this only works if the cell entry is left aligned.

Use Text Wrap

If you have a lot of text you're trying to fit into a single cell, consider using Excel's Wrap Text option found on the Alignment tab in the Format Cells dialog box. This option, when selected, wraps text to the next line in the cell without expanding the cell width.

How to Work with Borders and Patterns

The gridlines you see in your Excel worksheets are a little misleading. Normally, these lines do not print, and if you do print them, they may appear faint. To give your cells well-defined lines, use Excel's Border options. You can choose to add a border to a single cell or an entire range. You can specify a border on only one side or border the entire cell.

If borders don't set your cells off, try adding a background pattern, such as color shading or a pattern effect. Keep in mind, however, that a background that's too busy will make it difficult for the reader to see your data.

Begin

1 Open the Format Cells Dialog Box

Select the cell or range to which you want to add a border or pattern, open the **Format** menu, and select **Cells**.

Click

2 Use the Border Tab

Click the **Border** tab to see the various border options. To set a border around the outer edges of the cell or range, click the **Outline** preset. (To set gridlines within the range's inner cells, select **Inside**.)

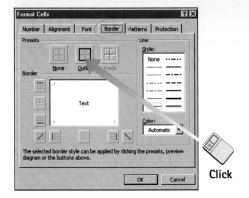

Click

3 Set a Custom Border

If you're customizing your border, use the **Border** buttons to select which sides to border. Click a side to place it on the border position box. Continue adding sides as needed.

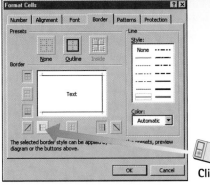

Click

4 Set a Line Style

From the **Style** list, choose a border style. Use the **Color** drop-down list to select a border color. Click **OK** to exit and apply the new settings.

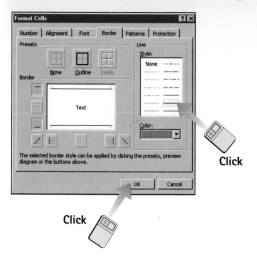

Click

Click

5 Use the Patterns Tab

To apply a pattern, click the **Patterns** tab. To select a color, click the color effect you want to apply from the palette. Click the **Pattern** drop-down list to select a pattern to apply. Click **OK** to exit the dialog box and apply the pattern or shading.

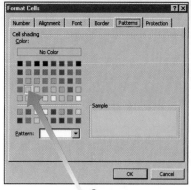

Click

6 The New Formatting Is Applied

As soon as you exit the Format Cells dialog box, the new settings are applied to your worksheet, as shown here.

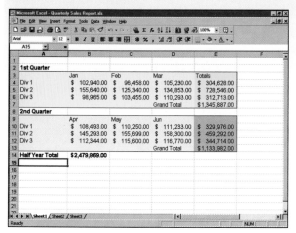

End

How-To Hints

Printing Gridlines

By default, Excel's gridlines don't print, but to turn them on, open the **File** menu and select **Page Setup**. Click the **Sheet** tab, select **Gridlines**, and click **OK**. Now print the worksheet to see how the gridlines look.

Using the Formatting Buttons

To add a quick border to any cell or cells, click the **Borders** drop-down arrow on the Formatting toolbar and select a border style. To add color to your cell background, click the **Fill Color** drop-down arrow and choose a color from the palette. If you want to change the font color, click the **Font Color** drop-down arrow and choose another color.

How to Copy Cell Formatting

If you have applied several formatting attributes (such as font, size, color, and borders) to a cell or range of cells and then later decide you would like to apply the same formatting to another range, you don't have to apply those formats one by one to the new location. Instead, you can use Excel's Format Painter button to take all the formats from the original range and "paint" them across the new range.

Begin

1 Select the Range

Select the range that has the formatting you want to copy.

2 Choose Format Painter

Click the **Format Painter** button in the Standard toolbar.

Click

3 Mouse Pointer Changes

Your mouse pointer changes to a paintbrush pointer.

4 Drag to Copy Formatting

Drag the paintbrush pointer across the range where you want to paint the format.

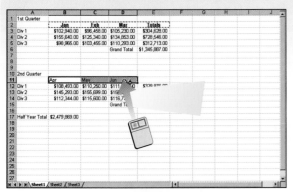

**Click &
Drag**

5 Formatting Is Applied

Release the mouse. The formatting is painted to the range of cells (click anywhere to deselect the range).

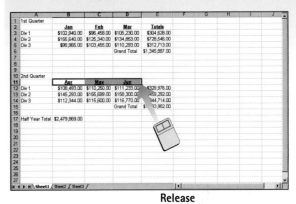

Release

End

How-To Hints

Keep Painting

To paint the same formatting to several ranges more quickly, double-click the **Format Painter** button. Format Painter remains turned on so that you can paint the formatting repeatedly. For example, you could paint across all the headings in the worksheet. When you're finished painting the formatting, click the **Format Painter** button again to turn it off.

Use AutoFormat

Don't like the pressure of coming up with formatting yourself? Use Excel's AutoFormat feature to format your worksheets automatically, as explained in Task 5, "How to AutoFormat a Range."

How to AutoFormat a Range

If formatting worksheets isn't your cup of tea, you will be happy to learn that Excel comes with pre-designed formats you can apply to your worksheet data. The AutoFormat features provide you with 16 table formats you can use to make your worksheet data look more presentable. Experiment with each one and see how it affects your data's presentation.

Begin

1 Select the Range

Select the range containing the data you want to format or click anywhere inside the range.

	A	B	C	D	E
1		1999 Household Budget			
2					
3		January	February	March	
4	Car Expense	$ 432.00	$ 120.00	$ 15.00	
5	Groceries	$ 334.00	$ 270.00	$ 125.00	
6	Utilities	$ 244.00	$ 346.00	$ 366.00	
7	Mortgage	$ 968.00	$ 968.00	$ 968.00	
8	Taxes	$ 1,230.00	$ 253.00	$ 125.00	
9	Supplies	$ 15.00	$ 44.00	$ 23.00	
10	Miscellaneous	$ 76.00	$ 87.00	$ 34.00	
11	Total	$ 3,299.00	$ 2,088.00	$ 1,656.00	
12					
13					

2 Open the AutoFormat Dialog Box

Open the **Format** menu and select **AutoFormat**. This opens the AutoFormat dialog box.

Click

3 Choose a Table Format

From the list box, choose a format style you want to use. Click the scroll arrow buttons to move up and down the list. When you find a format you like, click on it in the list box.

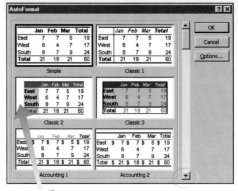

Click

4 View Your Options

To exclude certain elements from the format set, click the **Options** button.

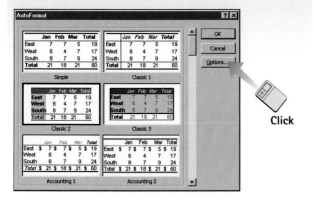

Click

5 Turn Off Elements

Select or deselect the format options you want to turn on or off. Click **OK** to exit the dialog box.

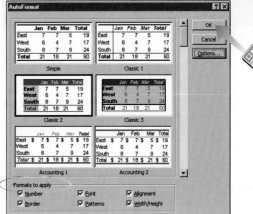

Click

6 Formatting Is Applied

The formatting is automatically applied to the selected cell or range.

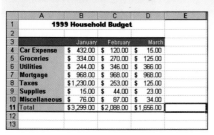

End

How-To Hints

Don't Like It?

If you decide you don't like the format you applied to your range with AutoFormat, click the **Undo** button. If you want to choose another instead, select the range again and reopen the AutoFormat dialog box. Choose another format and click **OK** to exit.

Warning

The AutoFormat you apply will overwrite any existing formatting the cells may already have.

Task

8

How to Use Excel's Chart Tools

*W*hen you look at a worksheet, it's not always easy to see the relationship between the numbers. Even the most seasoned bean counter may have trouble spotting trends or patterns easily. To show trends, patterns, and relationships visually, turn your Excel data into a chart. Charts make it easy to see how your numbers relate.

A chart takes your data and represents it visually, much like a snapshot. You can create a pie chart of your household spending, for example, to easily see which area takes the biggest slice of the pie. You can also create a bar chart that quickly tells you, or your audience, which division leads in sales. Not only can you visually see the relationship of numbers, but you can see any trends and patterns, and quickly summarize the data.

With Excel, you can create charts as part of the worksheet or as a separate worksheet. To make creating charts easy, use Excel's Chart Wizard feature. This feature leads you step-by-step through the process of turning your data into a chart. You can apply 14 chart types, as well as variations of each. Each type has a specific purpose. In this chapter, you will learn how to turn your Excel data into a chart using Chart Wizard and how to use Excel's chart tools to format and change the chart. ●

How to Create a Chart with Chart Wizard

A chart turns boring numbers into an instantly accessible, persuasive visual presentation. This task tells you how to create charts from your worksheet data.

The *Chart Wizard* builds the chart for you and asks for your input along the way. After the chart is built, you can resize it, rearrange it, recolor it, and personalize it so that it doesn't look like every other Excel chart in the computer world.

Begin

1 Select Data

Start by selecting the table or list of data you want to chart. Include headings and labels, but don't include subtotals or totals. On the Standard toolbar, click the **Chart Wizard** button.

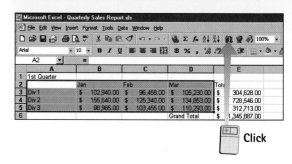

Click

2 Start the Chart Wizard

The Chart Wizard starts (if the Office Assistant shows up, click **No, I Don't Need Help Now** to send it away). Click the **Chart Type** you want on the left and the **Chart Sub-type** you want on the right, and then click **Next**.

Click

3 Check the Data Range

Check the **Data Range** to be sure it's correct. Click the two **Series In** options (**Rows** and **Columns**) to see which layout is best, and then click **Next**.

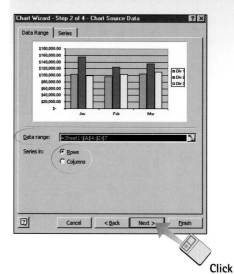

Click

4 Set Chart Features

Use the **Titles** tab to type a **Chart Title** and **Axis** titles, if you want them. Use the **Legend** tab to reposition or turn off the legend, and append a data table to the bottom of the chart by clicking the **Show Data Table** check box on the **Data Table** tab. Click **Next**.

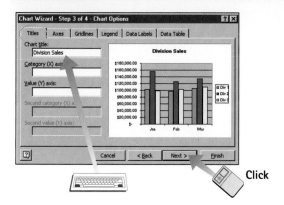

Click

5 Choose a Location

Choose a location for the chart: The **As New Sheet** option creates a separate *chart sheet* (this is similar to a worksheet, but it holds only a big chart), called CHART1, in the workbook. The **As Object In** option creates an embedded chart object on the worksheet you select from the **As Object In** drop-down list. Click **Finish**.

Click

6 View the Chart

Depending on the option you chose in step 5, the chart appears in your worksheet or as a separate sheet in the workbook, as shown in the figure below. The Chart toolbar may appear so you can make changes to the chart as needed.

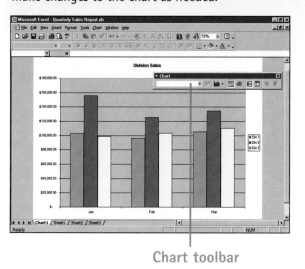

Chart toolbar

End

How-To Hints

Finish Fast

To create a chart quickly using all the default chart settings, click **Finish** in the very first Chart Wizard dialog box.

Another Route

Another way to open the Chart Wizard is to display the **Insert** menu and select **Chart**.

Preview Your Chart

To preview how your chart will appear, click the **Click and Hold to View Sample** button in the very first Chart Wizard dialog box. If you don't like the chart, you can select another type right then and there.

How to Move and Resize Charts

Once you've created a chart, whether in a separate worksheet or in the current worksheet, you can move and resize the chart as needed. For example, if you placed the chart on the active worksheet, it might cover some of the existing data. You can move the chart out of the way, or resize it to fit wherever you like.

When you select a chart or any other graphic object, it's surrounded by *selection handles*. You can use these handles to resize the object. When moving and resizing charts, you must click and hold the left mouse button and drag to move or resize. You'll learn how to accomplish both actions in this task.

Begin

1 Select the Chart

Start by selecting the chart you want to move or resize. Be sure to click on a blank area of the chart or you might end up selecting an individual chart element. As soon as you click on the chart to select it, it's surrounded by tiny black boxes, called *selection handles*.

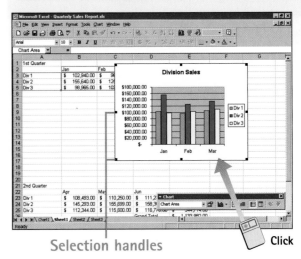

Selection handles

Click

2 Move the Chart

To move the chart, hold down the left mouse button and drag the chart to a new location on the worksheet. As you drag, the pointer becomes a four-sided arrow pointer.

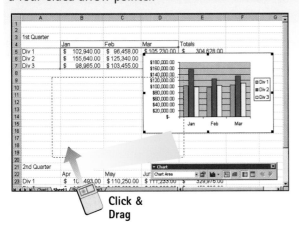

Click & Drag

3 Anchor the Chart

When the chart is at the location you want, release the mouse button.

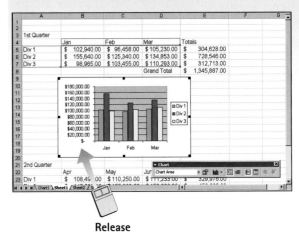

Release

4 Resize the Chart

To resize a chart, you must drag one of its selection handles. To resize a side of the chart, click and hold the left mouse button over a selection handle on the side of the chart object. The mouse pointer becomes a two-sided arrow. Start dragging to resize the chart.

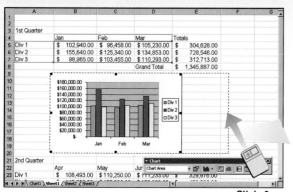

Click & Drag

5 Release

When the chart is at the size you want, release the mouse button.

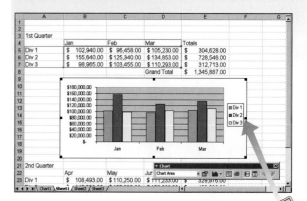

Release

6 Resize Two Sides at Once

To resize two sides at once, click and drag on a corner selection handle. As you drag, both sides of the chart are resized. Release the mouse button and the chart is resized.

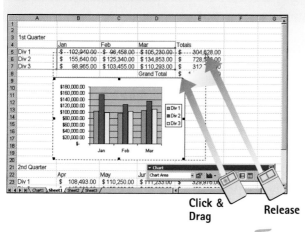

Click & Drag   **Release**

End

How-To Hints

Perfect Resizing

Press and hold the **Shift** key while dragging a corner of the chart object to resize all four sides proportionally.

Don't Like It?

If you're not happy with the new size, click the **Undo** button on the Standard toolbar to return the chart to its former size.

Delete Charts

To delete a chart from your worksheet, select it and press the **Delete** key.

How to Change the Chart Type

When you create a chart, you have many options for the *chart type*. Standard chart types use columns or bars, lines and points, or a sliced-up pie. Probably your best bet is to stick to standard chart types. If you use a chart type that your audience isn't used to seeing, they may have difficulty deciphering it, and the data may lose its impact.

After you have created a chart, you can easily change the chart type without having to re-create the chart, so you can try out different chart types to see which you like best.

Begin

1 Select the Chart

Click the chart to select it. If the chart is on a chart sheet, it is automatically selected when you click its sheet tab.

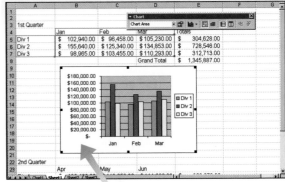

Click

2 Click the Chart Type Button

On the Chart toolbar, click the down arrow on the **Chart Type** button. Click a chart type icon on the button's list.

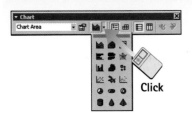

Click

3 The New Chart Type Is Applied

The chart type changes to the type you select (shown is the same column chart changed to a pie chart).

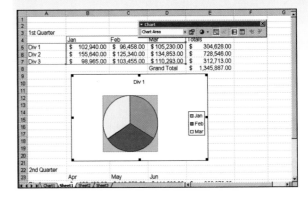

4 Use the Chart Type Command

With the chart selected, open the **Chart** menu and select **Chart Type**. In the Chart Type dialog box, select a **Chart Type** and **Chart Sub-type**. To preview the chart, click and hold the **Click and Hold to View Sample** button (shown is the same chart changed to a 3D bar chart). When you find the chart type you want, click **OK**.

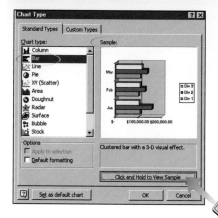

Click & Hold

5 Change the Markers

To change the chart type for a single series in a multiseries chart, right-click one of the data markers in the series and then choose **Chart Type**.

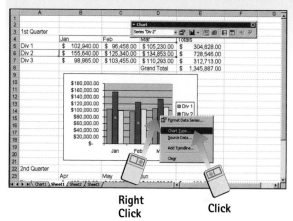

Right Click   Click

6 Select a Different Marker Type

In the Chart Type dialog box, select a new chart type for the selected series, and then choose **OK**. Shown here, one series in a column chart (Div 2) is changed to a line chart type.

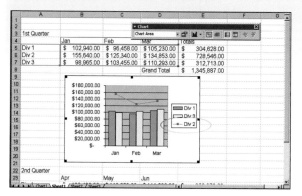

End

How-To Hints

Change Colors

To change the color of any element in the chart (data series, gridlines, axes, plot area, and so on), click the element to select it. Click the down arrow on the **Fill Color** button on the Formatting toolbar and click a different color.

Change Font Size for the Whole Chart

When you resize a chart, the axis and title characters may be too big or too small. To change the font size, click near the edge of the chart to select the **Chart Area** and select a new size in the **Font Size** box on the Formatting toolbar.

How to Work with Chart and Axis Titles

You don't need to spend a lot of time deciding on titles for your chart when you first create it because you can add, change, move, and delete titles at any time. For example, you may decide your chart needs a nice title centered above the chart data, or perhaps you want to rename the axes. You can easily make changes to the various chart elements until it looks just the way you want.

Begin

1 Move a Title

To move a title, click it to select it, and then drag it to a new location.

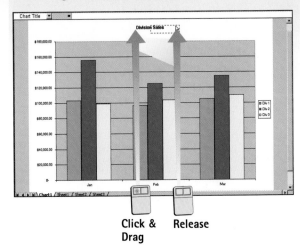

Click & Drag   Release

2 Change a Title's Text

Click the title to select it and click on the text and the mouse pointer becomes a cursor. Drag to select the characters you want to change or delete, or click to place the insertion point within the title and type new characters (when you click or drag within the title text, the title's border disappears). Click anywhere outside the title when finished with your edits.

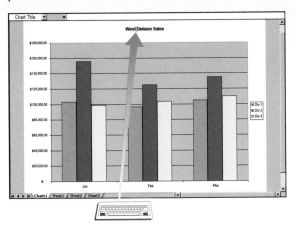

3 Delete a Title

To delete a title, click the title to select it, and then press **Delete**. You can also right-click the title and choose **Clear**.

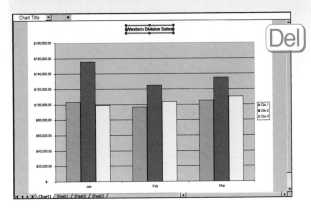

4 Add a Title

To add a new chart or axis title, open the **Chart** menu and select **Chart Options**. On the **Titles** tab of the Chart Options dialog box, type your title(s) and click **OK** to add them to your chart.

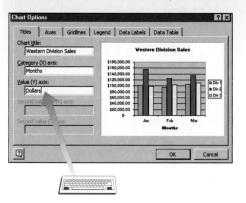

5 Use a Text Box

To add a text box as a title or as additional text to the chart, select the chart and start typing in your text. As you type, the text appears in the Formula bar. Press **Enter** and the text box appears on the chart. Move the text box by dragging it to a new location. Text boxes are similar to titles, except you can resize a text box.

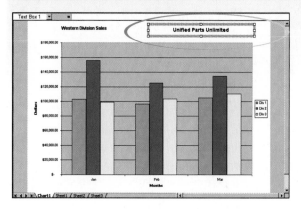

6 Change Colors

To format the colors in either a title or a text box, select the object and choose colors from the **Fill Color** and **Font Color** buttons on the Formatting toolbar. You can also right-click the object, choose **Format Chart Title** or **Format Text Box**, and set formatting details in the dialog boxes.

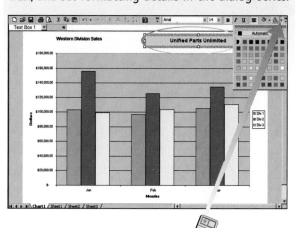

Click

7 Change the Font or Font Size

To change the font or font size in either a title or a text box, select the object and then select the characters you want to change. Make changes in the **Font** and **Font Size** boxes on the Formatting toolbar. You can also right-click the object, click **Format Chart Title** or **Format Text Box**, and set formatting details in the dialog boxes.

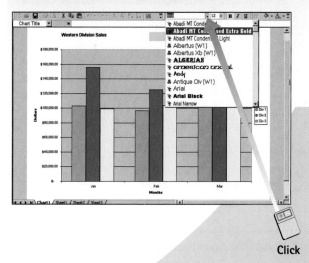

Click

End

How to Change the Chart Data

If you delete a column or row of data from a chart's source data table, the chart adjusts automatically. Nevertheless, if you add data to the source table (for example, if you add another month's sales figures), you need to add the new data to the chart. You can add expanded data to a chart in several quick ways.

If you have already created a highly formatted chart and you want to use it to display a different source data table (instead of creating a new chart), you can change the chart's source data range in the Chart Wizard.

Begin

1 Select the Source Range

Click the chart to select it. A colored border surrounds the source data.

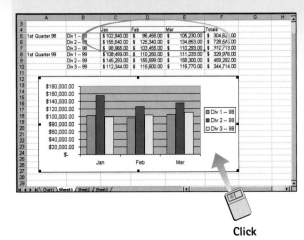

Click

2 Drag the Border

Click and drag the corner handle of the colored border to expand (or reduce) the source data range. For example, in this figure, I'm including the 1st Quarter's sales from '99.

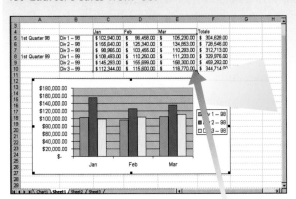

Click & Drag

3 Release

As soon as you release the mouse button, the source data range is redrawn, and the chart now reflects the new data. Notice the colored border now surrounds a larger data range than in step 1.

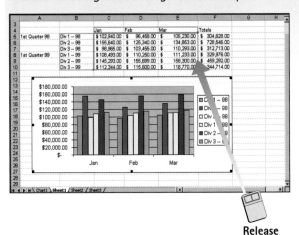

Release

4 Or Use the Add Data Command

Another method of adding new data to the chart is to use the **Add Data** command. Open the **Chart** menu and select **Add Data**. This opens the Add Data dialog box.

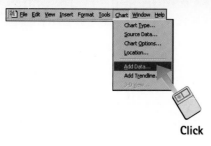

Click

5 Select the New Data

With the Add Data dialog box open, highlight the data in the worksheet that you want to add to the chart. (You can drag the Add Data dialog box out of the way if you need to: Click and drag its title bar.) After selecting the data, its range is inserted into the **Range** text box in the Add Data dialog box. Click **OK**.

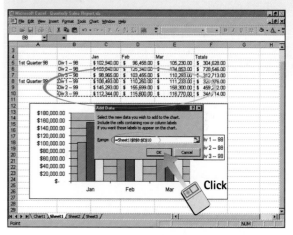

Click

6 The Data Is Added

Excel adds the new data to your chart.

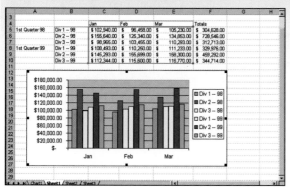

End

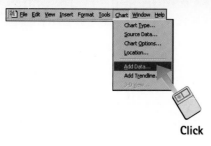

How-To Hints

Chart Help

For help with any chart, consult Excel's Help system. Open the **Help** menu and choose **Microsoft Excel Help**, or click the **Help** button on the toolbar to summon Office Assistant. To learn more about using the help features, see Tasks 10, "How to Use the Office Assistant," and 11, "How to Use the Office Help System," in Chapter 1, "How to Use Common Office Features."

Change the Source Data

You can make changes to the source data in your worksheet, and the changes are immediately reflected in the chart.

Print Charts

To print only your chart, first select the chart, open the **File** menu, and select **Print**. This opens the Print dialog box. Make sure the **Selected Chart** option is selected and click **OK**.

Task

How to Use PowerPoint

PowerPoint is a presentation program designed to help you create visual presentations and slide shows for an audience, whether it's one person or a roomful of people. With PowerPoint, you can create and combine slides into a visual presentation that easily communicates your message with style and pizzazz.

You can create, for example, professional, self-running, or interactive slide shows to give a training presentation. You can present the quarterly sales review as a slide show to the sales staff or present a new budget to your local civic organization. With PowerPoint, you can not only create visual presentations for any purpose, but you can also create speaker notes and audience handouts to go along with it.

In this chapter, you will learn about PowerPoint's basic features, including how to begin creating your first slide show presentation and using PowerPoint's specialized tools for adding text and graphics.

How to Get Around the PowerPoint Window

When you first start PowerPoint, the opening dialog box presents you with several options for starting a presentation. You can use PowerPoint's AutoContent Wizard to create a slide show, base the presentation on one of PowerPoint's many templates, build a show from scratch, or open an existing presentation file.

After you move beyond the opening dialog box, PowerPoint looks and feels the same as any other Office program. You will find the typical title bar, menu bar, toolbars, scrollbars, and status bar.

Begin

1 The Opening Dialog Box

From PowerPoint's opening dialog box, you can start a new presentation or open an existing one. Click the option you want to start. To close the dialog box without making a selection, click the **Cancel** button.

2 Use the Program Window Controls

The program window controls, located in the top right corner of the PowerPoint window, let you resize or close the program window. Use the Minimize button to reduce the window to an icon on the taskbar, use the Maximize button to enlarge the window to full screen size, use the Restore button to restore the window to its default size, and use the Close button to close and exit the program window.

Minimize   Close

Restore

3 View the Window Elements

The figure below points out the main on-screen elements found in the PowerPoint program window. The steps to follow will explain how to use each one.

Outline   Title bar   Menu bar Toolbars

Status bar Drawing toolbar Slide   Scrollbar

4 View the Title Bar

The title bar tells you what is in the window. When the presentation window is maximized, it has to share the title bar with the program window so that the title bar contains the names of both the program (Microsoft PowerPoint) and the file (such as Marketing Plan).

Title bar

5 Use the Menu Bar

The PowerPoint menu bar contains menus that, in turn, contain all the available PowerPoint commands. All the tasks you need to perform are available through menu commands. To use the menu commands, click the menu name to display the commands and click a command.

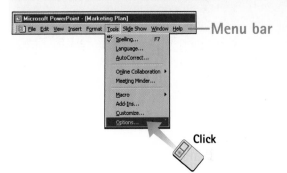

Menu bar

Click

6 Use the Toolbars

The Standard and Formatting toolbars share space on the PowerPoint window (although you can change this, as you learned in Chapter 1, "How to Use Common Office Features"). Both toolbars contain shortcuts for frequently used commands. To activate a toolbar button, click it. To see a button name, hover the mouse pointer over the button for a moment. A ScreenTip appears identifying the button.

Standard   Formatting
toolbar   toolbar

7 The Drawing Toolbar

In addition to the Standard and Formatting toolbars, a Drawing toolbar at the bottom of the PowerPoint window contains commands for drawing and working with graphics objects.

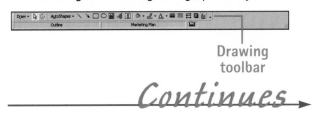

Drawing
toolbar

Continues

8 Use the Presentation Window

Use the presentation window to create your slides and arrange them into the presentation. By default, PowerPoint opens in Normal view, which shows the presentation outline, the slide, and the slide notes. (Learn more about views in Task 5, "How to Use PowerPoint's View Modes.")

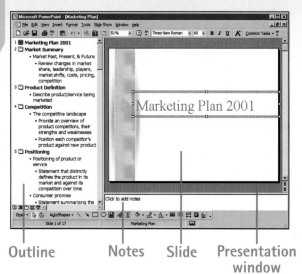

Outline   Notes   Slide   Presentation window

9 Use the Scrollbars

Use the vertical and horizontal scrollbars bordering the presentation window (depending on your view) to navigate the presentation and view the current slide.

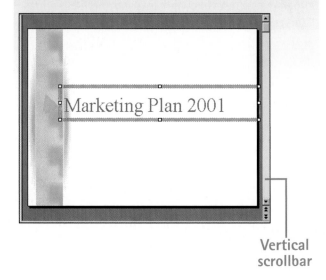

Vertical scrollbar

10 View the Status Bar

At the very bottom of the screen, the status bar tells you which slide you're currently viewing and displays the name of the current presentation.

Status bar

End

How-To Hints

Close the Opening Dialog Box

If you close the Opening dialog box using the Cancel button, you won't see the box again until you reopen PowerPoint. Don't worry: All the options in the dialog box are available through PowerPoint's File menu.

Other Toolbars

PowerPoint has different toolbars for different occasions. To add a toolbar to your window, right-click an existing toolbar, and you can see a list of available toolbars. Toolbars that are already displayed have a check mark next to their names. You can click the toolbar name to select or deselect it for display.

Use the View Buttons

The PowerPoint View buttons, located in the bottom left corner of the window, let you change how you look at your slides. To learn more about PowerPoint's Views, see Task 5.

How to Use the AutoContent Wizard

The easiest way to create a new presentation is to use the AutoContent Wizard. PowerPoint's AutoContent Wizard walks you through each step in designing and creating a slide presentation. You can select a type of presentation, and PowerPoint builds an outline for it. It's up to you to fill in the text and choose graphics.

AutoContent Wizard taps into the many Presentation templates available. Presentation templates provide a color scheme, formatting, and a basic outline for the slide text.

Begin

1 Start the AutoContent Wizard

From the opening dialog box, click the **AutoContent Wizard** option and click **OK**. If the dialog box no longer appears onscreen, open the **File** menu and select **New**. From the **General** tab, double-click the **AutoContent Wizard** icon.

Click

2 Click Next

When the first AutoContent Wizard dialog box appears, choose **Next** to begin.

Click

3 Choose a Presentation Type

From the next dialog box, click the button that best represents the type of presentation you want to build. For example, if you click the **Sales/Marketing** button, the list box displays several types of presentations geared toward this topic. Select a presentation type, then click **Next**. (To see all the available presentation types, click the **All** button.)

Click

4 Choose a Method

Next, choose the method that best describes how you're going to give your presentation. Click **Next** to continue.

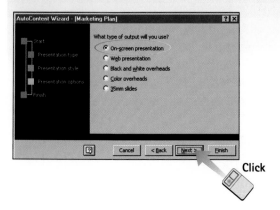

Click

5 Enter a Title

Enter a title for the presentation and choose any footer items you'd like to appear at the bottom of each slide. Click **Next**.

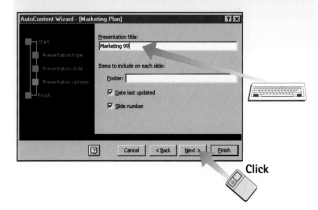

Click

6 Click Finish

The last AutoContent Wizard dialog box appears. Click **Finish** to complete the procedure.

Click

7 The Presentation Opens

PowerPoint opens the presentation in Normal view, which includes the outline for the entire presentation and displays the first slide in the presentation.

End

How to Start a New Presentation Based on a Template

You can also create a slide show by basing it on a PowerPoint template. You can use the same templates offered by AutoContent Wizard (these templates provide a basic color scheme, as well as a basic outline for slide text), or use PowerPoint's Presentation Design templates.

The Design templates offer a single color scheme that you can use for each slide you create. This gives the presentation a consistent look. You provide the slide content. Unlike in AutoContent Wizard (which walks you through the procedure for building a slide show) when you select a Design template, PowerPoint immediately opens a new slide based on your selection.

Begin

1 Select the Template Option

From PowerPoint's opening dialog box, click the **Design Template** option and click **OK**. If the dialog box is unavailable, select **File**, **New** to open the New Presentation dialog box.

Click

2 Preview a Template

Click the **Design Templates** tab to view the available designs. Select a template, and the **Preview** area displays a sample of the design.

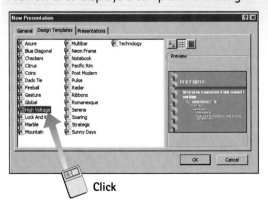

Click

3 Select a Template

To choose a template, double-click its name, or select it and click **OK**.

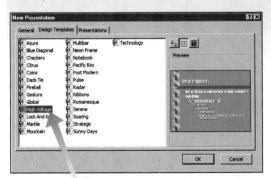

 Double Click

4 Choose a Layout

The New Slide dialog box appears for you to choose a layout for the slide. Click the AutoLayout you want to use and click **OK** (or double-click the layout example).

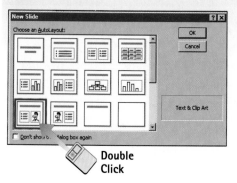

Double Click

5 The Template Opens

PowerPoint opens the template design and layout you selected. Now you're ready to start filling in text or graphics.

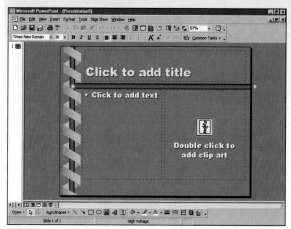

End

How-To Hints

Customize Templates

Create your own design template by making changes (color, font, or so on) to an existing template and saving the file as another template using the **File**, **Save As** command. In the Save As dialog box, name the new design and select **Design Template** in the **Save as Type** drop-down box.

Can't Find a Design You Like?

If you don't like any of the templates (including those used by the AutoContent Wizard), start with a blank slide and design your own presentation from scratch. Task 4, "How to Build a Presentation from Scratch," explains how to start a blank presentation.

How to Build a Presentation from Scratch

If you're the adventurous type, you may prefer creating your own presentations and designs. Rather than relying on a preset color scheme or format, build a blank presentation and add your own touches. After you start a blank presentation, you can add text boxes, attach graphics, and set backgrounds and colors as needed.

Begin

1 Start a Blank Presentation

From PowerPoint's opening dialog box, click the **Blank Presentation** option, click **OK**, and skip to step 4.

Click

2 Or Use the New Dialog Box

If the dialog box is unavailable, open the **File** menu and select **New** to open the New Presentation dialog box.

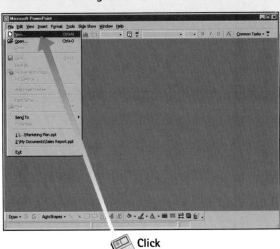

Click

3 Display the General Tab

Click the **General** tab and double-click the **Blank Presentation** icon.

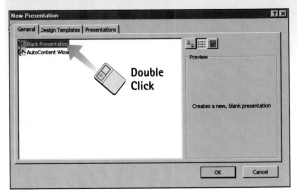

Double Click

4 Choose a Layout

The New Slide dialog box appears for you to choose a layout for the slide. Click the AutoLayout you want to use and click **OK** (or double-click the layout example).

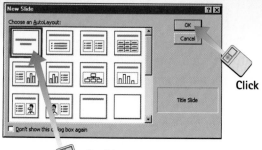

Double Click

Click

5 The Template Opens

PowerPoint opens the template and layout you selected in Slide View. Now you're ready to start filling in text or graphics (see Task 7, "How to Add and Edit Slide Text").

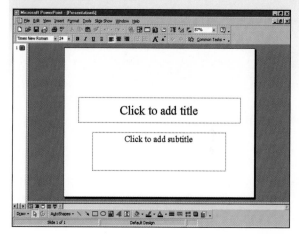

End

How-To Hints

Need Help?

For help with adding text boxes to your blank slide, see Task 10, "How to Add New Text Boxes." For help with adding graphics, see Task 11, "How to Add an Illustration to a Slide."

Choosing a Color Scheme

To change the color scheme for your blank presentation, open the **Format** menu and select **Slide Color Scheme**. Click the **Standard** tab, choose a color scheme, and click **Apply**.

Customizing the Background

To change the background of your blank presentation, open the **Format** menu and select **Background**. Click the **Background fill** drop-down list and select **Fill Effects**. The Fill Effects dialog box opens. Now you can set a gradient effect, add a pattern or texture background, or turn a picture into a background.

How to Use PowerPoint's View Modes

You can display your slide presentation in different views within PowerPoint to help you work with the slides. You can use the View buttons to change your view quickly, or you can open the View menu and select a view. In this task, you will learn about each view.

Begin

1 Using the View Buttons

To change your view, click the appropriate View button located in the bottom left corner of the PowerPoint window.

Normal   Slide
view   view

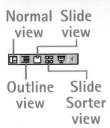

Outline   Slide
view   Sorter
        view

2 Or Use the View Menu

You can also switch views using the View menu. Simply click the **View** menu and make your selection.

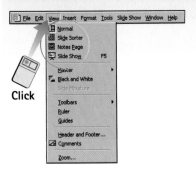

Click

3 Normal View

In Normal view, you see a single slide in the right pane, the presentation outline in the left pane, and the slide notes in the bottom pane. You can work with the various slide elements (such as text boxes and graphics) and move them around the slide, or change the outline and add slide notes as needed. Normal view is the default view.

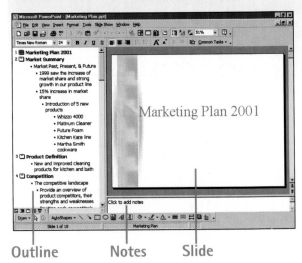

Outline   Notes   Slide

4 Outline View

In Outline view, your slide presentation is shown in outline form, which allows you to see the organization of your presentation's contents. The slide itself appears in miniature in the top right pane, and the slide notes appear in the bottom right pane.

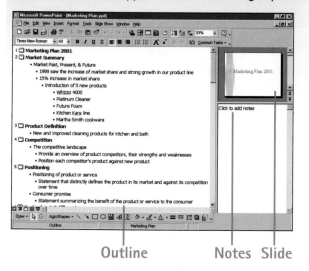

Outline   Notes Slide

5 Slide View

In Slide view, you see a single slide, including its contents and background, and the outline is reduced to a thin pane on the left. You can work with the various slide elements, such as text boxes and graphics, and move them around the slide.

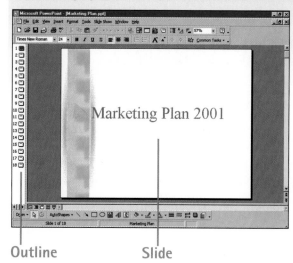

Outline   Slide

6 Slide Sorter View

In Slide Sorter view, you can see a *thumbnail* (or miniaturized version) of each slide in the presentation and the order in which the slides appear. You can easily rearrange the slide order and add or delete slides. (You can't select individual slide elements in Slide Sorter view. You will have to switch to Slide view or Normal view to edit slide objects.)

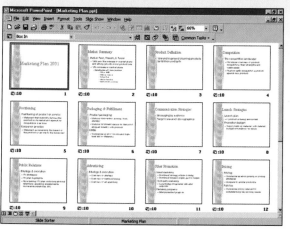

How-To Hints

What About Slide Show View?

PowerPoint has one more View button: Slide Show. It actually runs your slide show presentation. To learn more about this, see Task 6, "How to Run the Slide Show," in Chapter 10, "How to Prepare a Slide Presentation."

Zooming Your View

You can use PowerPoint's Zoom controls to change your perspective in any view. To gain a closer look at a graphic object in Slide view, for example, click the **Zoom** drop-down list on the Standard toolbar and choose a zoom percentage.

End

How to Understand Slide Elements

Slide presentations can include a few slides or many slides, and each slide conveys particular information. Depending on the layout, whether AutoContent Wizard assigned it or you select it, each slide can have one or more slide elements. Those elements include text boxes, clip art, bulleted lists, tables, charts, and more. The slide layout you select will indicate each element type you can use.

Each slide element is treated as an object on the slide, which means that you can move or resize it as needed. The remaining tasks in this chapter will show you how to work with the various types of slide elements. To change a layout at any time, click the **Common Tasks** button and choose **Slide Layout**.

Begin

1 Text Boxes

PowerPoint's text boxes let you enter slide text of your choice. Just about every slide you create in PowerPoint will require text. This figure shows a common title text box and subtitle text box layout. To enter text, click inside the text box and start typing.

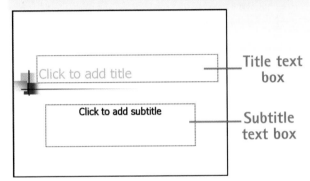

Title text box

Subtitle text box

2 Bulleted Lists

Bulleted lists are quite common among slide presentations. They let you present data succinctly and focus the audience on the points you want to make. Here's an example of a bulleted list text box. To enter text, click inside the box and start typing. Press **Enter** to begin a new bullet item automatically.

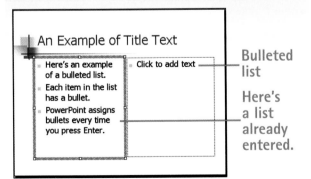

Bulleted list

Here's a list already entered.

3 Clip Art

Artwork can really spruce up your slide's message. Many of the layouts you can choose from preset clip art boxes. To insert clip art, simply double-click the box and locate the clip art you want to use. This figure shows clip art already selected and in place. Learn more about adding clip art in Task 11.

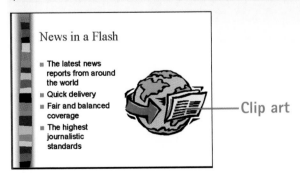

Clip art

4 Tables

If you've already worked with Word and Excel, you know how tables can help organize and present data. Use tables in PowerPoint to do the same. To insert text in a PowerPoint table, click inside the first cell and start typing. Use the Tab key to move from cell to cell. This figure shows a table already filled in.

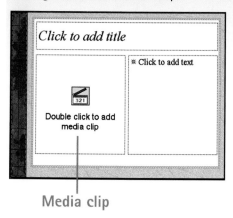

Household Budget

Mortgage	Insurance	Telephone
Car payment	Cable	Trash removal
Water	Sewer	Gas
Groceries	Taxes	Child care
Credit cards		

—Table

5 Charts

Another way to present data is with charts. A few PowerPoint layouts let you insert charts into your slides, even organizational charts, or you can choose to add your own charts to any slide as needed. Here's an example of a chart already inserted and sized to fit.

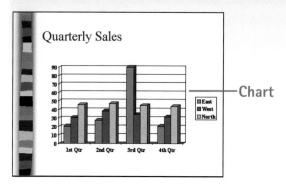

Quarterly Sales

—Chart

6 Objects

In addition to the slide elements already discussed, you can also add other types of objects, such as graphic files created with other programs, media clips, or any other data object. Here's an example of a layout that lets you add a media clip. Double-click to open the Microsoft Clip Gallery for adding a sound or motion clip.

Click to add title

❋ Click to add text

Double click to add media clip

Media clip

End

How to Add and Edit Slide Text

After you have started a presentation, you're ready to start entering text. Your slides will have one or more text boxes, and some may include *placeholder* text. Placeholder text is simply default text included to give you some ideas about content and the overall appearance of the slide.

You can add and edit text in Normal view, Outline view, or Slide view. This task will show you how to edit text in Outline view and directly on the slide. To learn how to add new text boxes, see Task 10.

Begin

1 Select Outline Text

To edit text in the Outline pane, select the placeholder text you want to replace. You can select text in PowerPoint just as you do in Word or Excel: Click your mouse at the beginning of the text, hold down the left mouse button, and drag to select the text.

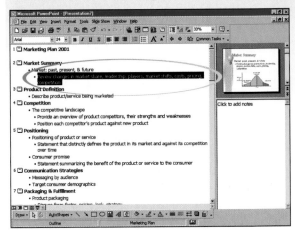

2 Enter Text in Outline View

Type in your new text. Use the **Delete** key to delete characters to the right of the insertion point, or use the **Backspace** key to delete characters to the left.

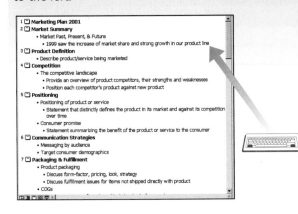

3 Use the Outline Pane

Your presentation is organized in an outline format in the Outline pane. A numbered slide icon represents each slide to the left of the slide title. Each slide's contents are subordinate to the slide title. Some have multiple levels of subordination.

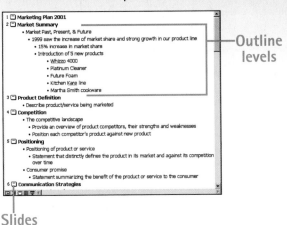

Outline levels

Slides

4 Change Outline Levels

To change the level at any time, select the text and press the **Demote** button on the Formatting toolbar to demote a level or the **Promote** button to promote a level. PowerPoint immediately changes the status of the text to the appropriate level. You can keep clicking the **Demote** or **Promote** buttons as needed to place the text in the level you want.

Promote

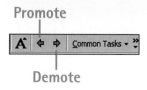

Demote

5 Select Slide Text

You can also enter and edit text directly on the slide. Click the text box you want to edit, and selection handles surround the box.

Selection handles

6 Enter New Slide Text

Select the placeholder text you want to replace and type in the new text. The placeholder text disappears. Use the **Delete** key to delete characters to the right of the insertion point, or use the **Backspace** key to delete characters to the left.

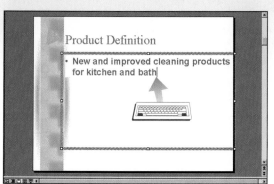

End

How-To Hints

Adding Lots of Text?

If you want to add a lot of text, it's best to work directly on the slide so that you can have a better sense of when the slide is getting too cluttered to be effective. To switch your view, click the **Slide View** or **Normal View** buttons.

Using the Outlining Toolbar

To move a slide up or down in the outline and rearrange the presentation order, use the **Move Up** or **Move Down** buttons on the Outlining toolbar. To display the toolbar, right-click over the Drawing toolbar and choose **Outlining**. Then select the outline text to move and click the **Move Up** button to move up in order, or click **Move Down** to move down in order.

Run a Spelling Check

You can check your spelling, one slide at a time, in PowerPoint. To start the spelling check, open the **Tools** menu and choose **Spelling**.

How to Format and Align Slide Text

You can quickly change the look of your slide text using PowerPoint's formatting commands. You can make text bold, italic, or underlined with a click of a button, or change the alignment to left, right, or center. You can even add a shadow effect to give text a three-dimensional look.

If you learned how to use formatting commands with Word, those same commands come into play with text in PowerPoint. The easiest way to format text in PowerPoint is to use the available buttons on the Formatting toolbar.

Begin

1 Select the Text

Start by opening the slide that contains the text you want to format and selecting the text. (It's easiest to format text in Slide view or Normal view.)

2 Bold, Italic, Underline

To bold text, click the **Bold** button on the Formatting toolbar. To italicize the text, click **Italic**. To add an underline to text, click the **Underline** button.

Bold   Underline

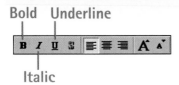

Italic

3 Create a Shadow Effect

To add a shadow effect to the text, click the **Shadow** button on the Formatting toolbar.

Shadow

4 Shadow Is Applied

PowerPoint adds a subtle shadow effect to the text, as shown in this figure.

5 Change the Alignment

To align text to the left in the text box, click the **Left Alignment** button on the Formatting toolbar. To center text, click **Center Alignment**. To align text to the right, click **Right Alignment**.

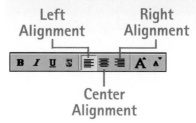

Left Alignment   Right Alignment

Center Alignment

6 Alignment Is Applied

PowerPoint aligns your text in the text box as you specified. The figure below shows examples of each of the alignment options as applied to slide text.

Left-aligned   Centered

Right-aligned

End

How to Change Slide Fonts and Sizes

If you don't like the default font assigned to a slide by AutoContent Wizard or the template you chose, you can change it. You can use the Font button on the Formatting toolbar, or open the Font dialog box.

You can also adjust the font size as needed. Unlike Word or Excel, however, PowerPoint includes an extra feature for adjusting font sizes. You can use the Increase Font Size or Decrease Font Size buttons on the Formatting toolbar to adjust the font size in increments. As you use these buttons, you can clearly see on the slide how the size affects the text.

Begin

1 Change the Font

Select the text you want to change, click the **Font** drop-down arrow on the Formatting toolbar, and choose a new font from the list.

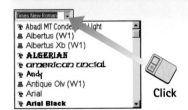

Click

2 Change the Font Size

To choose a specific font size, click the **Font Size** drop-down arrow and select a size.

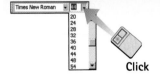

Click

3 The Increase and Decrease Buttons

If you would rather resize the text a little at a time until you reach the desired size, use the Increase and Decrease buttons. To nudge the selected text up a size, click the **Increase Font Size** button. To make the text smaller, click the **Decrease Font Size** button.

Increase Font Size

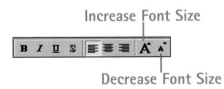

Decrease Font Size

4 PowerPoint Nudges the Font Size

Depending on which direction you're going (enlarging the text or reducing its size), PowerPoint makes the necessary adjustments each time you click the Increase or Decrease buttons. The figure below shows one text box with the default size recommended by PowerPoint, and the text box below it shows the size increased with the Increase Font Size button.

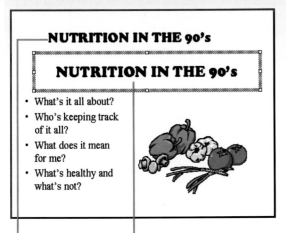

Default size   Increased size

5 Open the Font Dialog Box

If you prefer handling all your formatting needs all at once, open the Font dialog box and select new settings. Open the **Format** menu and choose **Font**.

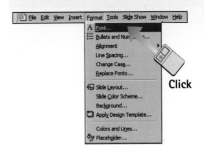

Click

6 Change the Font Settings

In the Font dialog box, make any changes to the formatting settings, click **OK** to exit, and the new settings are applied to the text.

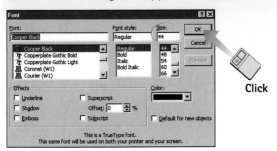

Click

End

How-To Hints

Other Formatting Effects

Notice that the Font dialog box includes other formatting effects that you can apply to your PowerPoint text. You can add an Emboss effect, for example, or choose a color for the text. To preview your selections, click the **Preview** button; however, you will have to drag the Font dialog box out of the way to see how the settings look on your slide.

Replacing Fonts

To change all the fonts for every text box in your slide, use the Replace Fonts command. Open the **Format** menu and select **Replace Fonts**. This opens the Replace Font dialog box. Use the **With** drop-down arrow to select a new font style, click **Replace**, and the font is changed.

How to Add New Text Boxes

At times, you will need to add a new text box to a slide. You may need to add a box for your corporate slogan, for example, or add a caption text box for a graphic. When you add a new text box, you can decide how large to make the box or let PowerPoint create a default size.

In this task you learn how to use a tool from the Drawing toolbar. Make sure you're in Slide view. If the Drawing toolbar is not displayed, right-click over another toolbar and select **Drawing**.

Begin

1 Select the Text Box Tool

From the Drawing toolbar (located at the bottom of the PowerPoint window), click the **Text Box** button.

Click

2 Click in Place

Move the mouse pointer to the area on the slide where you want the new text box inserted and click the mouse button.

Click

3 Start Typing

A text box the size of one character appears. Start typing the text you want to add.

4 The Box Expands

As you type, the size of the text box increases. To start a second line, press **Enter**.

5 Or Drag the Text Box

Another way to insert a text box after clicking the Text Box tool is to drag the size of the box on the slide. Click in the top left corner where you want the text box to start, drag to the desired size, and release.

6 Enter the Text

Release the mouse button and the text box is set. To enter text, click inside the box and start typing.

End

How-To Hints

Resize the Box

You can resize a text box by dragging any of its selection handles. Select the box, position the pointer over a selection handle, hold down the left mouse button, and drag the box to a new size.

Use Rulers

Sometimes it's helpful to display the PowerPoint rulers to assist in placing text boxes on the slide. To display the rulers, open the **View** menu and choose **Ruler**.

Delete a Text Box

To remove a text box, first select it. Click on the box, but don't select any text inside the box. To avoid selecting text inside the box, click on the text box border only. Once you've selected the box, press **Delete**.

Using WordArt Text

Use the WordArt tool to turn ordinary words into graphic objects. To learn more about this feature, check out Task 4, "How to Insert a WordArt Image" in Chapter 16.

How to Add an Illustration to a Slide

Slide shows are meant to be visual, and part of their appeal is graphics—whether it's clip art, a picture you create from a drawing program, or a photo found on the Internet. Illustrations, or graphics, can really spruce up your slides. For that reason, PowerPoint's templates and presentations created with AutoContent Wizard have areas on the slides already designated for graphic elements.

PowerPoint comes with a large collection of clip art that you can use in your own slide shows, or you can use artwork from other files. After you insert a graphic, you can resize it, move it, rotate it, and more (see Task 5, "How to Move and Size an Image," in Chapter 16).

Begin

1 Select a Graphic Placeholder

If your slide already has a placeholder for a graphic, double-click the placeholder to open the Clip Gallery (skip to step 3).

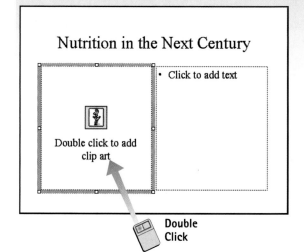

2 Add a New Graphic Object

To add a new object box to hold a piece of clip art, click the **Insert Clip Art** button on the Drawing toolbar.

Click

3 Choose a Category

From the **Pictures** tab, peruse the catalog of available clip art. To choose a category, click it. Use the scrollbar to scroll through and view all the available categories.

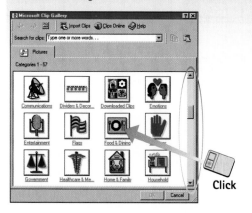

Click

4 Select a Clip

When you find a clip art piece that you want to use, click it to display a bubble menu and click the **Insert Clip** button. The clip art is immediately placed on your slide. Click the **Close** button to close the Clip Gallery dialog box.

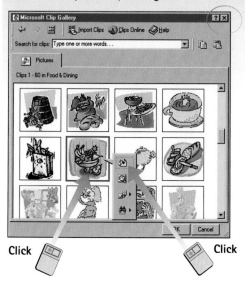

Click   Click

5 Or Use an Image File

If you have a graphic image file stored elsewhere on your computer, you can insert it into a slide. Open the **Insert** menu and select **Picture, From File**. This opens the Insert Picture dialog box.

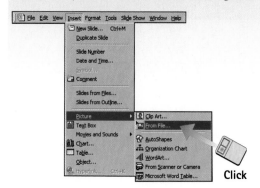

Click

6 Locate the Image

Locate the image file you want to use. When you find the file, double-click it to insert it into your slide.

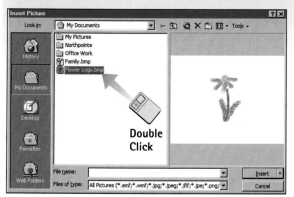

Double Click

End

How-To Hints

Graphics, Illustrations, or Pictures?

The terms *graphic*, *illustration*, and *picture* are used interchangeably to describe artwork that can be inserted into a slide.

Resizing Clip Art

Depending on the clip art you select, you may need to resize it to fit better on your slide. Select the object and drag a selection handle to resize it.

Working with Slide Objects

You can work with clip art and other objects on PowerPoint slides in a variety of ways. Chapter 16 covers inserting objects such as basic shapes and WordArt, how to add shadow effects, how to change the image formatting, and how to layer and group objects on top of each other. Check out Chapter 16 to learn more about these techniques.

How to Add a Chart to a Slide

In addition to adding text boxes and clip art to your slides, you can also add charts. You can add a chart you create with another program, such as Microsoft Excel, using the Copy and Paste commands, or you can create a chart from within PowerPoint. Charts go a long way in illustrating your data, and you can easily create a chart without leaving PowerPoint, as you'll see in this task. Start by displaying the slide in which you want to insert a chart.

Begin

1 Select the Insert Chart Command

To insert a chart, open the **Insert** menu and select **Chart**, or click the **Insert Chart** button on the Standard toolbar. If your layout already has a box for a chart, double-click the box.

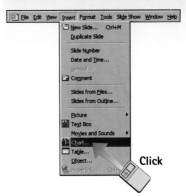

Click

2 A Chart Appears

Immediately, a generic chart appears in your PowerPoint slide, along with a datasheet. Notice the PowerPoint menu bar now has a Chart menu. The menu has commands to help you create or edit your chart.

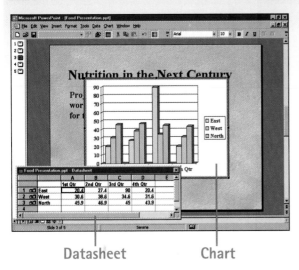

Datasheet   Chart

3 Enter Your Chart Data

Use the datasheet to enter your chart data. Just replace the sample data with your own. For example, if you want to create a simple bar chart as shown in the generic sample, replace the generic chart data with your own column and row labels. You can also choose to delete all the sample data before entering your own. Select the data and press **Delete**.

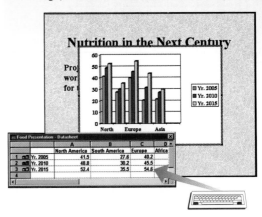

4 Change the Chart Type

By default, the charting tool displays a bar chart, but you can select another chart type. To do so, open the **Chart** menu and choose **Chart Type**.

Click

5 Select a Chart Type

From the Chart Type dialog box, choose a new chart type from the list box and select a subtype from those available. Click **OK** to exit and apply the new chart type.

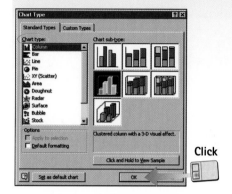

Click

6 Insert the Chart

To insert the chart into your slide, click the **Close** button on the datasheet. The chart is placed in your slide. You may need to resize or move it to fit properly. To edit the chart, double-click the chart object.

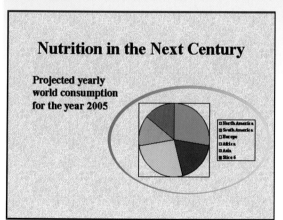

End

How-To Hints

Working with the Datasheet

You can move and resize the datasheet as needed to create your chart. To move it, drag its title bar. To resize it, hover your mouse pointer over any border on the datasheet until the pointer becomes a double-sided arrow and drag to resize. Use the scrollbars to move around the datasheet.

Insert a Chart from Another Program

To insert a chart from Excel, open the Excel file containing the chart and select the chart. Click the **Copy** button or select **Edit**, **Copy**. Switch back to the PowerPoint slide where you want the chart inserted and click the **Paste** button, or select **Edit**, **Paste**. You may have to move or resize the chart to fit in the slide.

Need Help?

For more information on creating and customizing charts, turn to Chapter 8, "How to Use Excel's Chart Tools," to learn more about chart elements and how to build charts.

How to Insert a Table in a Slide

One way to organize and present information in a slide is to use a table. PowerPoint tables work like Word or Excel tables, columns and rows intersect to form cells where you can enter data. Depending on the presentation you're making, some layouts include tables automatically. Other times, you might want to insert a table yourself. In this task, you'll learn how to use both methods to add tables to your presentation.

Begin

1 Use a Table Layout Object

If your slide layout has a preset Table object box, double-click the box. Skip to step 3.

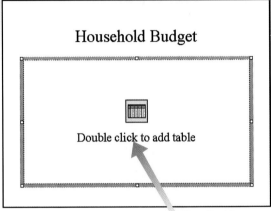

Double Click

2 Insert a New Table

To insert a new table object, open the **Insert** menu and select **Table** or click the **Insert Table** button on the Standard toolbar.

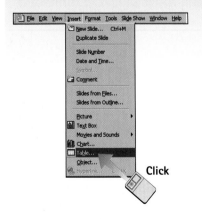

Click

3 Define Columns and Rows

In the Insert Table dialog box that appears, enter the number of columns and rows you want for the table. Click inside each text box and enter a number or use the spin arrows to select a number. Click **OK** to exit the dialog box.

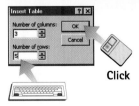

Click

4 The Table Appears

Depending on the number of columns and rows you selected in step 3, the table appears on the slide along with the Table and Borders toolbar. This figure shows an example of a table with three columns and five rows.

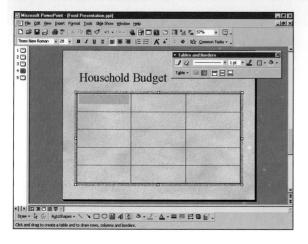

5 Enter Table Text

By default, the cursor waits in the first empty cell ready for you to enter data. Start typing to enter data in the first cell. Press **Tab** to move to the next adjacent cell on the right, or use the keyboard arrow keys to move around the table cells.

6 Finish the Table

When you've filled each cell of the table, click outside the table to see how it looks in the slide.

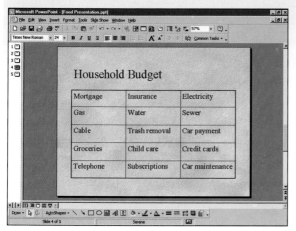

End

How-To Hints

Add Rows or Columns

Right-click inside the cell where you want to add a row above and choose **Insert Rows**. To add a column, select the entire column by clicking above the column where you want to insert a column to the left, then right-click, and choose **Insert Columns**.

Move or Resize the Table

To resize the table, select it first so that it's surrounded by selection handles and drag a handle to resize. To move the table, select it and hover your mouse pointer over the border until it takes the shape of a four-sided pointer. Then drag the table to a new location on the slide.

How to Change the Slide Layout

PowerPoint's AutoLayouts feature enables you to establish a structure for a slide. When you add a new slide, the New Slide dialog box appears with a variety of layout options you can apply. You can also change the layout of an existing slide, using the same dialog box with a different name: the Slide Layout dialog box.

Applying a layout is much easier than adding your own text and graphic boxes. PowerPoint has layouts for just about any kind of slide you want. You will find layouts that offer a combination of title text, bulleted text, charts, and graphics. With AutoLayouts, these slide elements are already positioned in place and ready to go. All you have to do is add your own text or choose a graphic.

Begin

1 Display the Slide

Display the slide you want to change. It's best to switch to Normal or Slide view, so you can clearly see the slide itself.

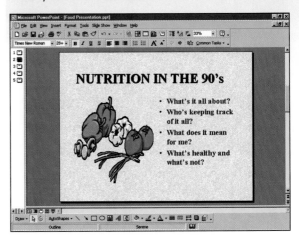

2 Open the Slide Layout Dialog Box

Click the **Common Tasks** button on the Formatting toolbar and choose **Slide Layout** to open the Slide Layout dialog box.

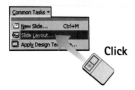

Click

3 Choose a Layout

Use the scrollbar to scroll through and view each layout. To find out what slide elements are on a layout, select the layout and look in the bottom right corner for a description.

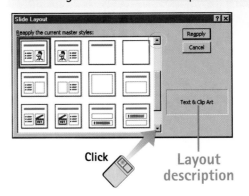

Click

Layout description

4 Select a Layout

When you find a layout you want to use, click it.

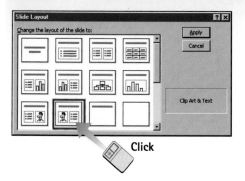

Click

5 Click Apply

To exit the dialog box and apply the layout, click the **Apply** button, or double-click the layout you want to use.

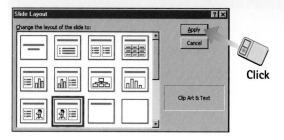

Click

6 The New Layout Applied

PowerPoint applies the new layout. Depending on your slide's contents, you may have to resize or move some slide objects to fit the new layout. In this figure, I applied a layout that switched the placement of the clip art and the bulleted text.

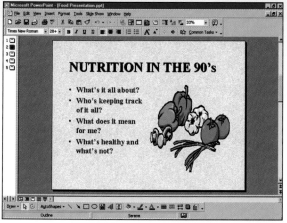

End

How-To Hints

Right-Click

You can also right-click the slide you want to change and choose **Slide Layout** from the shortcut menu to open the Slide Layout dialog box.

How to Change the Slide Background

You can change the background of a single slide for every slide in your presentation. Changing the background will give your slides a new look. You'll find plenty of options: Backgrounds can include color, texture, or patterns. Be sure to explore the options available to find just the right look you need. The Background dialog box lets you change color background or add a fill effect, such as a gradient, pattern, or texture.

Begin

1 Display the Shortcut Menu

Display the slide you want to change (switch to Normal or Slide view so that you can clearly see the slide), right-click on the slide (don't right-click over a slide object), and choose **Background** from the shortcut menu.

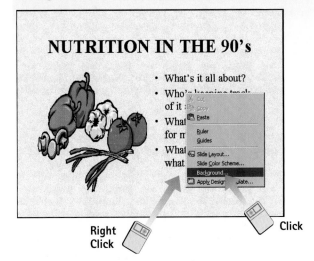

Right Click

Click

2 Open the Background Dialog Box

From the Background dialog box, click the drop-down arrow to display a list of other colors. If the background color you want to use is displayed, click it. If not, click the **More Colors** option. This opens the Colors dialog box.

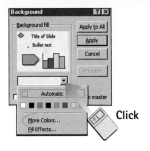

Click

3 Choose a Color

From the Colors dialog box, select a color from the **Standard** tab. Click the color you want to use from the palette and click **OK**.

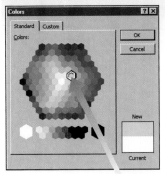

Click

4 Apply the New Color

To apply the color to your background, click **Apply**. To apply the color to every slide in the presentation, click **Apply to All**.

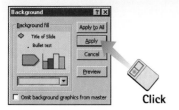

Click

5 Choose Fill Effects

If you'd prefer another type of background besides color, click the **Fill Effects** option in the Background dialog box instead of **More Colors**. This opens the Fill Effects dialog box where you can select from Gradient, Texture, Pattern, or Picture backgrounds. The Texture tab, shown in this figure, contains quite a few interesting texture backgrounds that you can apply. Select the fill effect you want to use and click **OK**.

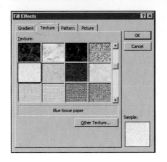

6 Apply a Texture

Click the **Apply** button to apply the fill effect to your slide, or click **Apply to All** to apply the effect to every slide in the presentation. In this figure, I've applied a texture background that looks like beads of water.

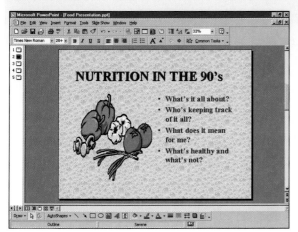

End

How-To Hints

Use the Menu Route

You can also open the **Format** menu and select **Background** to display the Background dialog box.

Change the Color Scheme

For a quick change of color in your slide presentation, consider changing the color scheme. Right-click the slide and select **Slide Color Scheme** to display the Color Scheme dialog box. Use this box to select a different color scheme to apply to the text, background, chart data colors, and more. Make your selection and click **Apply**.

Turn a Picture into a Background

If you have a picture that would make a good slide background, you can use the Picture tab in the Fill Effects dialog box to select and insert the picture. Be careful not to use a picture that competes too much with your slide message text!

Task

CHAPTER 10

How to Prepare a Slide Presentation

As you begin building your slide presentation, you will find that you need to add and delete slides and rearrange their order. In this chapter, you will learn how to view and navigate your slides and complete the necessary steps to assemble your slide show for viewing.

When you finally have every slide just the way you want it, you're ready to start assigning transition effects that control how each slide segues into the next. You will learn how to add animation effects, run the slide show, and create speaker notes to help you with the presentation. You can also create audience handouts based on your slide content.

Last, but not least, you will learn how to use PowerPoint's Pack and Go feature to take your show on the road, or at least use it on another computer.

How to Navigate the Slide Presentation

If your presentation contains more than one slide, you can use PowerPoint's navigation tools to move from slide to slide. You will find navigation buttons at the bottom of the vertical scrollbar. If your slide show contains a large number of slides, use the vertical scrollbar to view various slides.

Begin

1 Move Forward and Back

To advance to the next slide, click the **Next Slide** button on the vertical scrollbar. To display the previous slide, click the **Previous Slide** button.

—Previous Slide
—Next Slide

2 Use the Scrollbar

If your presentation has a lot of slides, clicking the **Next Slide** and **Previous Slide** buttons won't take you to the slide you want to view fast enough. Instead, use the vertical scrollbar. Move your mouse pointer over the scroll box.

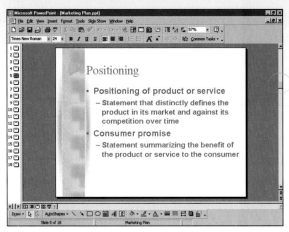

3 Drag the Scroll Box

Hold down the left mouse button and drag the scroll box up or down, depending on which direction you want to go. As you drag, PowerPoint displays each slide number and the slide title text in a ScreenTip box. Use this feature to help you locate a specific slide.

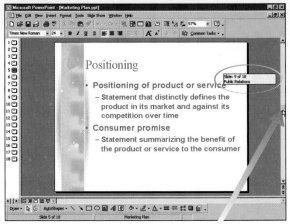

Click & Drag

4 Release the Mouse Button

When you scroll to the slide you want to see, release the mouse button and the slide appears in the presentation window.

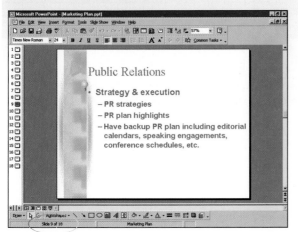

5 Keyboard Shortcut

If you prefer using the keyboard to navigate slides, use the **Page Up** and **Page Down** keys to move from slide to slide. Press **Ctrl+Home** to move to the first slide, or press **Ctrl+End** to move to the last slide.

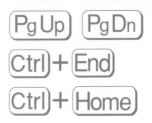

End

How-To Hints

Use Slide Sorter View to Navigate

You can also move from slide to slide using Slide Sorter view. Switch to Slide Sorter view and double-click the slide you want to view. This displays the slide in Slide or Normal view.

Running the Show

You have another way to view slides: actually running the slide show. To learn more about running a PowerPoint slide show, turn to Task 6, "How to Run the Slide Show," in this chapter. When you run the actual show, you won't see the menu bar, toolbar, or other screen elements. You will see only each slide, one at a time.

Check the Status Bar

One way to find out which slide you're viewing is to check the status bar. It always tells you the slide number.

How to Insert and Delete Slides

Need to add a new slide to your presentation? Or, perhaps you want to delete a slide that you no longer need? PowerPoint makes it easy to add and delete slides. You can add or delete slides in Slide view, Normal view, or Slide Sorter view.

Begin

1 Insert a New Slide

Display the slide that precedes the place where you want to add a new slide and click the **Insert New Slide** button on the Standard toolbar.

Click

2 New Slide Dialog Box

From the New Slide dialog box, use the scroll arrows to view the various slide layouts.

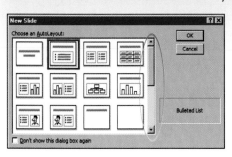

3 Click OK

When you find a layout you want, select it, click **OK**, and the slide is added. You can now fill it with text or graphics.

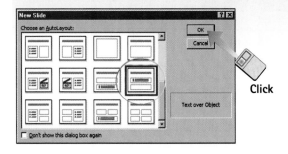

Click

4 Delete a Slide

To delete a slide, display it, open the **Edit** menu, and choose **Delete Slide**.

Click

5 Slides from Other Presentations

Use PowerPoint's Slide Finder feature to insert slides from other presentations into your current slide show. Open the **Insert** menu and select **Slides from Files**.

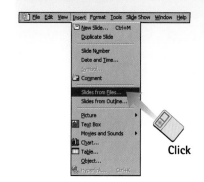

Click

6 Use the Slide Finder Dialog Box

From the Slide Finder dialog box, locate the presentation from where you want to borrow slides (use the **Browse** button, if needed, to find the file) and click the **Display** button to view the slides. Then select the slide or slides you want to insert and click the **Insert** button. (Click **Close** to exit the Slide Finder dialog box when you're finished.)

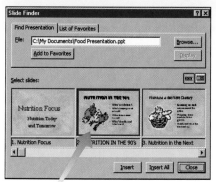

 Click

How-To Hints

Keyboard Shortcut

To insert a new slide using the keyboard, press **Ctrl+M**. This opens the New Slide dialog box where you can choose a layout.

Delete Slides in Slide Sorter View

To remove a slide in Slide Sorter view, click the slide and press **Delete** on the keyboard.

Oops!

If you accidentally delete the wrong slide, click the **Undo** button on the Standard toolbar.

End

How to Reorder Slides

Inevitably, you will need to rearrange the order of slides in your presentation. This is especially true after you have added new slides and deleted others. The easiest way to rearrange slides is in Slide Sorter view, where you can see all the slides at once. In Slide Sorter view, you can drag a slide from one location to another.

Begin

1 Switch to Slide Sorter View

Click the **Slide Sorter View** button located in the bottom left corner of the PowerPoint window to switch to Slide Sorter view.

Slide
Sorter
View

2 Select the Slide to Move

Click the slide you want to move to a new location.

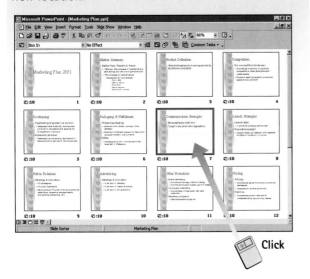

Click

3 Drag the Slide

Hold down the left mouse button and drag the slide to its new destination. As you drag, a line appears showing you where you're moving the slide.

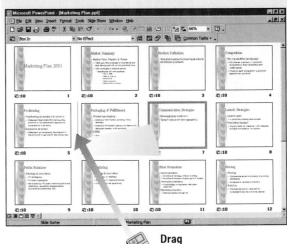

Drag

4 Release the Mouse Button

When the slide is positioned where you want it, release the mouse button. PowerPoint scoots the other slides over and places the moved slide in the new location.

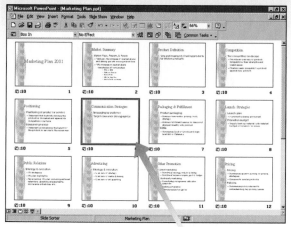

Release

5 Scrolling and Dragging

Slide Sorter view shows only six slides at a time. If you want to move the selected slide beyond the slides in view, drag in the direction you want to go. The display will scroll in that direction.

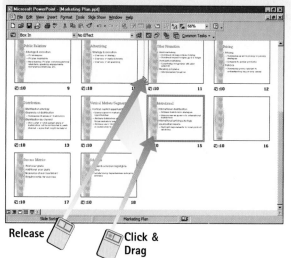

Release   **Click & Drag**

End

How-To Hints

Quick Switch

To view any slide in Normal or Slide view quickly, double-click the slide in Slide Sorter view.

Slide Sorter Toolbar

When you switch to Slide Sorter view, the Slide Sorter toolbar appears at the top of the presentation window. The toolbar contains buttons for setting slide transitions, rehearsing timings, and setting other special effects.

Select Multiple Slides

To select two or more slides at the same time, press the **Shift** key while you select each slide. To select slides that aren't next to each other, press the **Ctrl** key while selecting slides.

Copy a Slide

To copy a slide quickly, hold down the **Ctrl** key, drag the slide you want to copy, and release it in a new location. Now you have a copy of the original slide.

How to Define the Slide Transition

To make your slide show more professional, add *slide transitions*. Slide transitions determine how one slide advances to the next. PowerPoint includes numerous transition effects that you can use: including dissolves, tiling effects, fades, and split screens. You can assign a different transition to each slide or the same transitions to the entire slide show.

Begin

1 Switch to Slide Sorter View

Click the **Slide Sorter View** button to switch to Slide Sorter view and choose the slide for which you want to set a transition. If you want the same transition for all the slides, select the first slide.

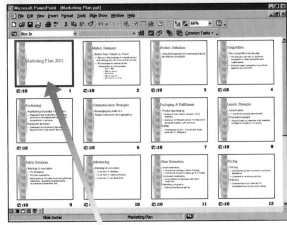

Click

2 Click Slide Transition

From the Slide Sorter toolbar, click the **Slide Transition** button.

Click

3 Choose an Effect

The Slide Transition dialog box opens. From the **Effect** drop-down list, choose a transition effect. When you make a selection, you can preview the transition effect in the picture area above the drop-down box.

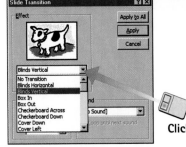

Click

4 Choose a Speed

Beneath the Effect drop-down box, choose a speed option for the speed of the transition: **Slow**, **Medium**, or **Fast**.

Click

5 Choose How to Advance

Use the **Advance** options to control how the slides will advance: either by mouse click or automatic advance. If you select the **Automatically After** option, you must specify an amount of time, in seconds, for the advance. Enter a time or use the spin arrows to set the time. You can set the advance at 10 seconds, for example, and PowerPoint automatically advances the slide after 10 seconds.

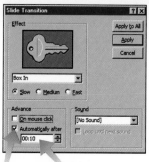

Click

6 Apply the Transition

Click the **Apply** button to apply the transition effects to the one slide. Click **Apply to All** to apply the transition to every slide in your presentation.

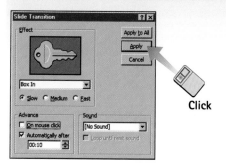

Click

End

How-To Hints

Viewing Transition Icons

When you return to Slide Sorter view after setting a transition, you will notice a transition icon under the slide (or slides). You can click any transition icon to see a demonstration of the transition effect.

Advancing with Sounds

Use the Sound options in the Slide Transition dialog box to add sound effects to the slide transition. Click the **Sound** drop-down list and select a sound effect. The sound will play while the slide transition occurs.

Advancing Tips

When setting an advance time, make sure you practice viewing your slide show first to see how long it takes to read everything in the slide or read from your presentation notes. Learn how to run your slide show in Task 6.

How to Add Animation Effects

You can apply PowerPoint's build and animation effects to slide objects. You can make a bulleted list appear on the slide, for example, and one bulleted item at a time during the presentation. You can control exactly when each item appears, which prevents your audience from reading ahead of you during the presentation. You can also make each list item fly in from the side of the screen or fade in slowly.

Many effects are possible, so be sure to test each one to see what it does. You can apply animation effects to any slide object.

Begin

1 Display Animation Effects Buttons

From Slide view or Normal view, select the slide object you want to animate and click the **Animation Effects** button on the Formatting toolbar to display a floating toolbar of animation buttons. To find out what a button does, hover your mouse pointer over the button to display its ScreenTip name. Click a button to assign the effect to the object.

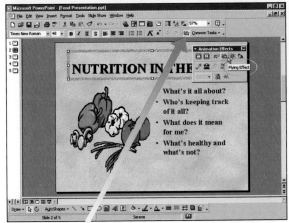

Click

2 Open Custom Animation Dialog Box

For more control over animation and build effects, select the object and then open the Custom Animation dialog box. From the Animation Effects floating toolbar, click the **Custom Animation** button. (You can also open the dialog box by displaying the **Slide Show** menu and choosing **Custom Animation**.)

Click

3 Choose Your Objects

In the top list box, select the slide objects you want to animate. Click to place a check mark beside each object to be animated.

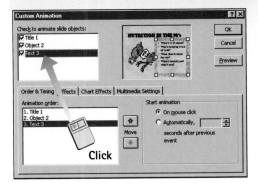

Click

4 Animation Order and Timing

Click the **Order & Timing** tab and choose the animation order and timing. Select a slide object in the **Animation Order** list box, click **Automatically**, and set a timing for the animation. Repeat this for every object you wish to animate. If you leave the **On Mouse Click** option selected, you'll have to click during the slide show to animate the object.

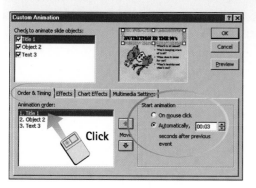
Click

5 Assign an Animation Effect

Click the **Effects** tab to assign an animation effect. Select the object from the top list box to animate, click the animation drop-down list, and choose an effect. With some effects, you can also choose a direction, such as **Across** or **Down**.

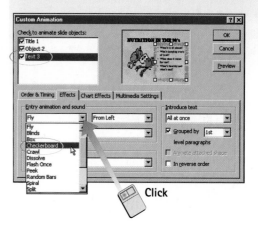
Click

6 Preview the Effect

Click the **Preview** button to see a preview of the effect. When finished assigning animation effects to your objects, click **OK** to exit the dialog box.

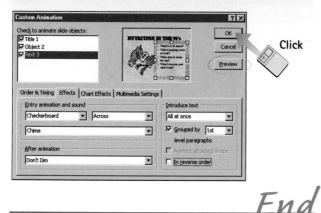
Click

End

How-To Hints

Testing Effects

You have numerous animation effects from which to choose, so be sure to preview them all to find exactly what you want.

Setting Sound Effects

To add a sound effect, click the sound drop-down list in the Custom Animation dialog box (located directly below the effect drop-down list on the Effects tab).

After Animation Effects

Use the After Animation drop-down list in the Effects tab to control what happens after the effect. For example, you can choose to hide the object briefly after it's animated, or hide it until you click the mouse. Be sure to check out all the options.

How to Run the Slide Show

After you complete building and preparing your presentation, you're ready to run the show. It's a good idea to run the show several times while preparing your presentation so that you have some idea of how the slides will look, how long you want each slide to display, and how transitions and animation effects will be used.

You can set up a slide show to run manually so that you click the mouse or press a keyboard key to advance each slide (or have each slide advance automatically) so that PowerPoint displays each slide for the amount of time you preset. You can even set the show to loop continuously.

Begin

1 Open the Set Up Show Dialog Box

Open the presentation you want to view, open the **Slide Show** menu, and select **Set Up Show**. This displays the Set Up Show dialog box.

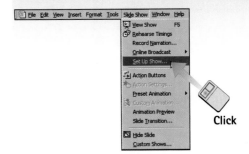

Click

2 Choose Show Type Options

From the **Show Type** options, select the option that best suits your situation. If you plan to run the presentation with yourself as speaker, for example, select the **Presented by a Speaker** option. If another user, such as a trainee, browses the presentation, select the **Browsed by an Individual** option. If the presentation will run at a kiosk, select the **Browsed at a Kiosk** option.

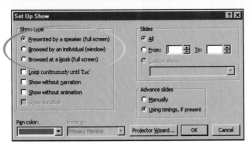

3 The Show Type Check Boxes

Use the **Show Type** check boxes to indicate how the presentation should appear. You can choose to loop the show continuously and whether to run the show without animation or narration.

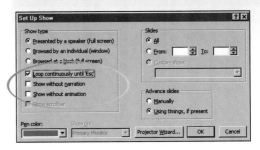

4 Choose Advance Options

From the **Advance Slides** options, choose to advance your presentation manually or use preset timings. Click **OK** to exit the Set Up Show dialog box.

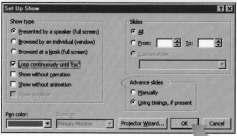

Click

5 Run the Show

To start the slide show, display the first slide (or click the first slide in Slide Sorter view) and then click the **Slide Show** button.

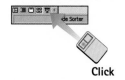

Click

6 Stop the Show

PowerPoint starts your presentation. Each slide appears full screen, without toolbars or menu bars. To stop the show at any time, press **Esc**.

End

How-To Hints

Slide Show Controls

During the course of the slide show, you can use manual controls to advance slides, to return to previous slides, or to pause the show. Click the mouse or press the right arrow key on the keyboard to advance to the next slide. Press **Backspace** to return to the previous slide. Press the **S** key to pause or resume the show.

Rehearse Your Timings

You can automate your slide show to advance each slide based on slide timings you set. One way to set timings is with the Rehearse Timings feature. Open the **Slide Show** menu and select **Rehearse Timings**. You can then time each slide. At the end, PowerPoint tells you the total time for the presentation.

Take the Show on the Road

To learn how to save your presentation on disk to use with another computer, turn to Task 9, "How to Use Pack and Go."

Use the Pen Feature

PowerPoint includes a pen tool that you can use during the course of your presentation to draw on the slides in Slide Show view. To open the pen, right-click on the slide and choose **Pointer Options, Pen**. Now you can draw or write on the slide.

How to Create Speaker Notes

To make your presentation professional, polished, and organized, you can make speaker notes to assist you with the slide show. Speaker notes can help you organize your thoughts, make sure you cover all the important points, and ensure a cohesive presentation.

You can add notes in Normal view, or switch to Notes Pages view. In Notes Pages view, speaker notes include a picture of the slide and an area for typing in your own notes. After you complete notes for the entire presentation, you can print them out. In this task, you will learn how to add notes in either view.

Begin

1 Add Notes in Normal View

Click the **Normal View** button and display the first slide in your presentation. Click inside the **Notes** pane in the lower half of the window and start typing in your notes for that particular slide. To print your notes, skip to step 5.

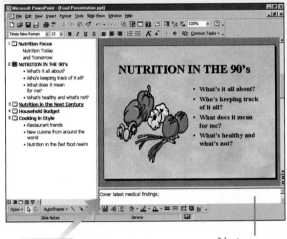

Notes pane

2 Add Notes in Notes Pages View

To switch to Notes Pages view, open the **View** menu and select **Notes Pages**.

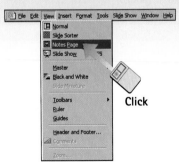

Click

3 Enter Note Text

Click inside the **Notes** text box in the lower half of the window and start typing in your notes for that particular slide.

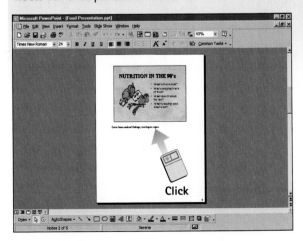

Click

4 Use the Zoom Tools

If you're having trouble seeing what you type, use the **Zoom** drop-down list on the Standard toolbar to zoom in closer: Try **100%**.

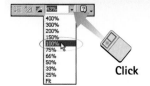

Click

5 Next Slide

When you finish your notes for the slide, click the **Next Slide** button to continue to the next slide in the presentation.

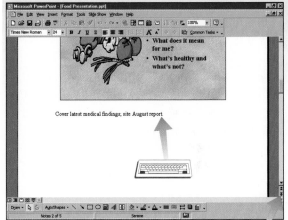

Click

6 Prepare to Print

Continue entering notes for each slide in the presentation. When you're ready to print the notes, open the **File** menu and select **Print**.

Click

7 Select Notes Pages

In the Print dialog box, click the **Print What** drop-down list box and choose **Notes Pages**. Click **OK** to print.

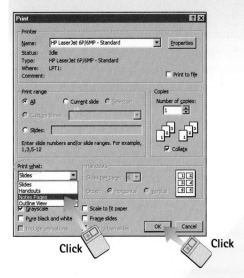

Click   Click

End

How to Create Audience Handouts

To make your presentations more memorable, consider distributing handouts to your audience based on your slide show content. Handouts will help them recall the points you covered. PowerPoint makes it easy to create handouts: All you have to do is print them out.

Begin

1 Open the Presentation

Start by opening the presentation for which you want to create handouts.

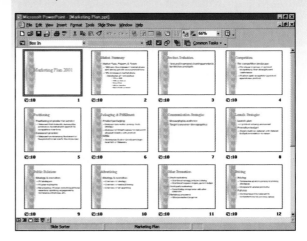

2 Open the Print Dialog Box

Display the **File** menu and select the **Print** command. This opens the Print dialog box.

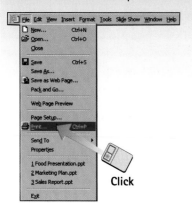

Click

3 Set Up for Handouts

Click the **Print What** drop-down arrow to display a list of print options, and select **Handouts**. Notice the three layout styles: two, three, or six slides per page. Select the layout that best suits your presentation or paper needs.

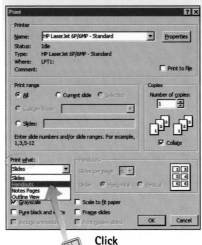

Click

4 Change Other Print Options

Set any additional options in the Print dialog box before printing. Click the Printer **Name** drop-down box, for example, to choose which printer to use, or choose to print Grayscale or Pure black and white.

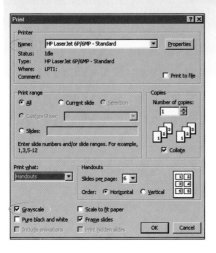

5 Print the Handouts

If you want to collate the pages, make sure the **Collate** check box is selected. Use the **Number of Copies** box to set how many copies of each page you want to print, which is handy if you're only printing a small number of handouts for a small number of slides.

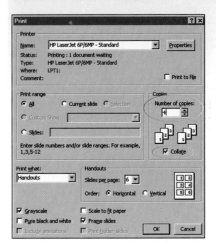

6 Print the Handouts

Click **OK** to print the handouts.

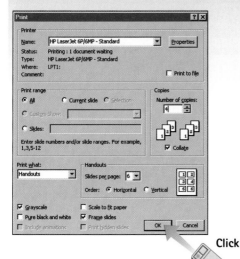

Click

End

How to Use Pack and Go

To take your show on the road, you can package the presentation on disk to use at another computer. For example, you may need to take the presentation to a client across town or across the country. Use the Pack and Go Wizard to help you store the complete presentation on disk, including a PowerPoint viewer to use in case the client doesn't have PowerPoint.

Begin

1 Open the File Menu

Start by opening the presentation that you want to store on disk and insert an empty disk into your floppy disk drive. Then, open the **File** menu and select **Pack and Go**.

Click

2 The Wizard Opens

The first wizard box appears. Click **Next** to continue.

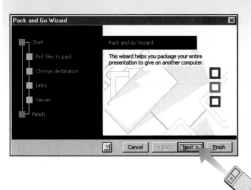

Click

3 Choose a Presentation

If you have already opened the presentation that you want to pack, leave the **Active Presentation** check box selected and click **Next**. If you want to pack a different presentation, click the **Other Presentation(s)** check box and use the **Browse** button to locate the file.

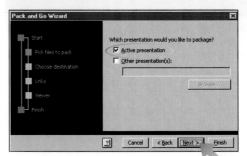

Click

4 Choose a Drive

In the next wizard dialog box, select the drive you want to save the presentation to and click **Next** to continue.

Click

5 More Options

The next wizard box presents you with options for saving linked files that you may have used with the presentation and fonts used exclusively in your presentation. The computer you might use later to run the show might not have all the fonts you carefully selected, so use the **Embed TrueType Fonts** option to make sure the same fonts are used. Select the options you want and click **Next**.

Click

6 Pack the Viewer

If the computer on which you're going to run the slide show doesn't have PowerPoint installed, select the **Viewer for Windows 95 or NT** option. If you know the computer has PowerPoint, select the **Don't Include the Viewer** option. Click **Next**.

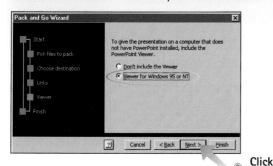

Click

7 Finish

In the final wizard box, click **Finish**. PowerPoint starts copying the files to the disk. If it's a particularly large presentation, you may need to use additional disks. A prompt box appears when the packing is complete; click **OK**.

Click

End

Task

11

How to Use Access

*A*ccess is a computerized database program that enables you to you store, manipulate, manage, and retrieve data. If you're new to the world of databases, this may sound a bit intimidating. You work with databases each day, though, so you probably know more about them than you think. Your local telephone directory, for example, is a database. Do you have a Rolodex file on your desk? That's a database, too. And so is the card catalog at your nearby library. In its strictest sense, a database is simply a collection of information.

You can use an Access database to store information, just as directories or Rolodex cards do. In addition to storing the data, you can manipulate it in many ways. If you keep a database of your customers in Access, for example, you can sort them by ZIP code, print out a list of all the customers who haven't ordered from you in the past six months, and create an order entry form your employees can use to process phone orders. That's only the tip of the iceberg; you can manage and manipulate your data for many purposes.

In this chapter, you will learn the basics for using Access. After you master these fundamental skills, you can tap into the power of Access to work with your own computerized databases. ●

How to Understand Database Basics

The basic components of a database are tables, records, fields, forms, reports, and queries. All these components compose an Access database file. Before you can begin building your own databases, you must first understand these basic elements and how they fit together.

Begin

1 Tables

The root of any database is *tables*. Access tables are a lot like Excel spreadsheets. Information is organized into columns and rows. You can have many tables in each database file. You might have one table listing customers and addresses, for example, and another table listing products you sell.

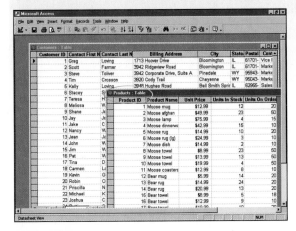

2 Records

Each entry in a database is called a *record*. Records appear as rows in a database table; each row represents one record.

Records

3 Fields

The detailed information that makes up a single record is broken into categories, called *fields*. When you're planning a database, think about what fields you need for each record. An address database, for example, needs fields for Name, Address, City, ZIP code, and Phone number.

Fields

4 Forms

Entering data into tables can be awkward as you try to keep track of which column represents which field. To make things easier, use a *form*. A form is an onscreen fill-in-the-blanks sheet for completing a record. The form comprises all the fields needed to create a record. With forms, you enter data one record at a time.

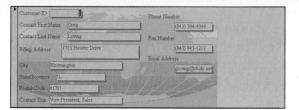

5 Reports

After you build a database, you will probably want to organize certain aspects of the information and create specialized *reports*. Reports summarize and organize the data. Typically, they are printed out. You might generate a report, for example, listing your top 20 clients based on sales.

Customers, Sales and Marketing

ContactLast	Contact First	Phone Numb	Billing Address	City	State/Pr	Postal Co
Cannon						
	Jake	(768) 585-45	3948 Prairie Way	Denver	CO	39483-
	Joshua	(438) 483-82	5577 South Wainwright	New York	NY	30202-
Crabtree						
	Patti	(233) 939-39	8038 Main Street	Charleston	SC	21211-
Crosson						
	Tim	(432) 432-34	3920 Cody Trail	Cheyenne	WY	95043-
Daniels						
	Tina	(773) 928-39	39788 Corporate Way	Dallas	TX	39402-
Farmer						
	Scott	(843) 941-22	3942 Ridgeview Road	Bloomington	IL	61701-
Gray						
	Kevin	(283) 203-02	392 Alicia Way	Kansas City	KS	20303-
Howell						

6 Queries

Queries are a formal way of sorting and filtering your data to produce specific results. With queries, you can specify which fields you want to see, the order in which you want to view them, filter criteria for each field, and more.

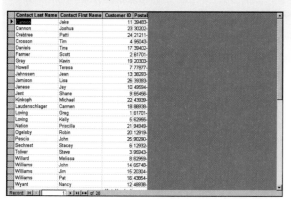

End

How-To Hints

Planning Is Everything

Before you build a database, spend a few minutes planning it. What kind of data do you want to store, and how should it be organized? Each table should have a topic, such as Customer Transactions. Determine what actions you want to perform on the data to help you know what kind of forms to create. Think about what information you want to extract from the data to help you know what kind of reports to generate. Try to break down your data as much as possible. For example, when compiling an address database, you need a separate field for each part. Don't combine fields, such as City and State, but instead break out the information into separate fields.

How to Use the Database Wizard

When you first open Access, you have the option of creating a blank database, using a database wizard, or opening an existing database. The easiest way to create a database is with a database wizard. Access includes several different database wizards that you can use to help you create the tables, forms, and reports you will need. Choose the kind of database you want to build and follow each wizard step for completing the database structure.

To begin, click the **Access Database Wizards, Pages, and Projects** option on the opening Access dialog box and click **OK** to begin. (If Access is already open, display the **File** menu and select **New**.)

Begin

1 Choose a Database

From the New dialog box, look through the wizards on the **Databases** tab to find the type of database you want to create and double-click the wizard name. To create an asset tracking database, for example, double-click **Asset Tracking**.

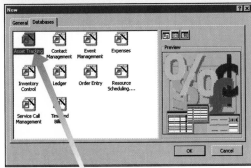

Double Click

2 Name the Database

Next, name your new database file. Either accept the name supplied by Access or type your own in the **File Name** text box. Make it something that will be easy to identify the next time you want to use the database. Click **Create** to continue.

Click

3 Determine the Structure

The first wizard dialog box tells you that you are creating a database. Click **Next**. The next box has options for the actual structure of your database, including the tables that will be created and the fields to be included. Choose the table from the left and select (or deselect) the fields to use in the right. Click **Next**.

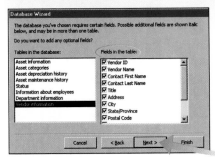

Click

4 Choose a Screen Display

The next dialog box offers you several choices of backgrounds for screen displays and forms in the database. Click each name in the list to display the sample background. Choose a background and click **Next**.

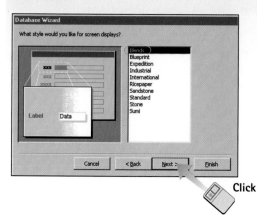

Click

5 Choose a Style for Reports

From the next dialog box, choose the style for your printed reports and click **Next** to continue.

Click

6 Enter a Title

Enter a title for your database (it can be the same or different from the file name used in step 2). Indicate whether to include a picture on all reports. (If you choose to include a picture, you will have to locate the picture file you want to use by clicking the **Picture** button.) Click **Next**.

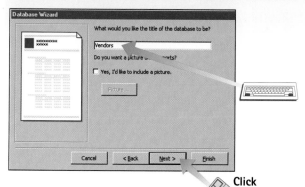

Click

7 Last Dialog Box

In the final dialog box, you can choose to start the database immediately. Click **Finish** to create your new database.

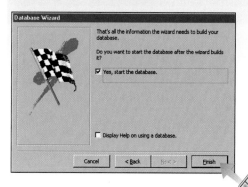

Click

End

How to Navigate the Access Window

Familiarize yourself with the elements of the Access program window before you start to use your database file. Most of the onscreen elements are the same as those in the other Office programs. You will also work with the Database window and various other report and query windows.

After you create a new database, the Database window or the Main Switchboard window might appear. Your database includes tables, forms, reports, and queries. Use the Database window to switch among the various elements of your database. Use the Main Switchboard window as another method for viewing and working with your database (see Task 4, "How to Use the Switchboard Window").

Begin

1 View the Access Window

The Access program window consists of a title bar, a menu bar, a Database toolbar, and a status bar. Each of these elements works the same as it does in the other Office programs.

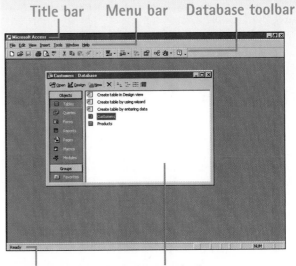

Title bar   Menu bar   Database toolbar

Status bar   Database window

2 Use the Program Window Controls

The program window includes controls for resizing and closing the window. When maximized, the **Restore** button is displayed in the set of buttons in the top right corner of the window's screen. If your program window isn't maximized, click its **Maximize** button. To minimize the program window to a button on the Windows taskbar, click the **Minimize** button.

Minimize   Close

Restore

3 Use the Database Window

When the Database window is maximized or shown at its default size, you will notice it has a bar, called the Objects bar, that organizes the elements of your database file. Click an object to see its contents. To open any item in the Database window list box, double-click the item's name.

Objects bar   List box

4 Minimize and Maximize

When you're using different parts of your database, the Database window is often minimized onscreen. To restore the window to its default size, click the **Restore** button. To maximize it, click its **Maximize** button. To minimize the window again, click its **Minimize** button. To close the database file completely, click the **Close** button.

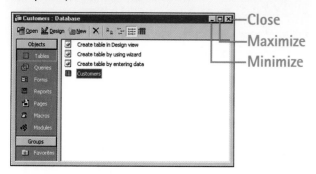

—Close
—Maximize
—Minimize

5 The Database Buttons

The Database window has a toolbar of buttons. Click the **Open** button to open the selected item (or double-click the item's name). Click the **Design** button to open the selected item in Design view. Click the **New** button to start a new item in your database.

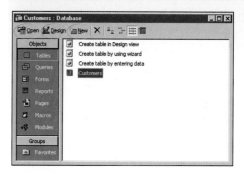

6 Close Feature Windows

Every object you open in your database file—whether it's a table or a Web page—will appear as its own window in the Access program window. Like the Database window, each feature window has its own set of controls for resizing or closing the window. To close a window, click its **Close** button.

Click

End

How-To Hints

More About Buttons

To delete an Access item in the Database window, select the item in the list box and click the **Delete** button on the Database window toolbar. The remaining four buttons on the toolbar can change how the items are displayed in the list box.

Ever-changing Toolbar Buttons

As you use different features in Access, the toolbar buttons change to reflect the task you're trying to accomplish. In addition, with some tasks (such as changing items in Form view) a second toolbar is displayed. To learn about any toolbar button, hover your mouse pointer over the button to display the ScreenTip name.

How to Use the Switchboard Window

When you construct a database using the Database Wizard, a Switchboard is created for you. The Switchboard window appears automatically after you create a database. You can begin entering data using the Switchboard, or you can use the Database window to do the same things. The Main Switchboard is a handy menu system for entering, viewing, and modifying information in your database. Some users find it easier to use the Switchboard to switch between Access tasks, while others prefer the Database window (refer to Task 3). You can decide which method you prefer. The rest of this chapter focuses on using the Database window; however, this task shows how to use the Switchboard. Just remember, either window can be used to perform Access tasks.

Begin

1 View the Switchboard Window

The Main Switchboard window has buttons for performing specific database tasks. The buttons will vary based on the type of database you created. This figure shows a Contact Management database. To activate a button, such as **Enter/View Contacts**, click the button.

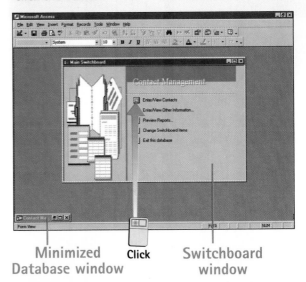

Minimized   Click   Switchboard
Database window   window

2 A Form Opens

Depending on which Switchboard button you select in step 1, a form or other database task window will appear. In this example, I selected the **Enter/View Contacts** button in step 1, so the Contact form opens onscreen, as shown in this figure. To learn how to enter data into forms, see Task 5. To return to the Switchboard, click the form's **Close** button.

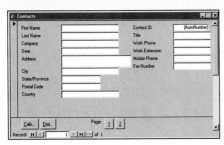

3 Close Only the Switchboard

To close the Switchboard window, click the window's **Close** button. This closes only the Switchboard window, not the database you were working on.

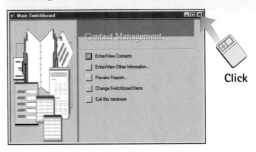

Click

4 View the Database Window

You can choose to use the Database window at any time, whether the Switchboard window is closed or opened. To maximize the Database window, click the **Restore** button on the minimized Database button.

Click

5 The Database Window Restored

The Database window opens. If the Switchboard window is still open, the Database window appears on top of the Switchboard window. To learn more about the Database window, refer to Task 3.

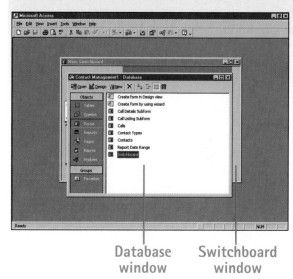

Database   Switchboard
window   window

6 Exit with the Switchboard

If you're using the Switchboard to perform database tasks, you can also close your database using the Switchboard window. Simply click the **Exit This Database** button.

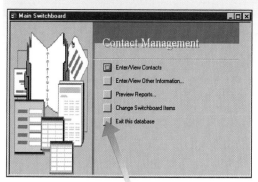

Click

End

How-To Hints

Customize the Switchboard

You can customize which database tasks appear on your Switchboard. Click the **Change Switchboard Items** button on the Switchboard, then click the **Edit** button to edit the Main (default) Switchboard. This opens the Edit Switchboard Page dialog box. From here you can add new items, delete existing items, or move the arrangement around. Use the Help system to learn more about editing Switchboards.

Don't Have a Switchboard?

If you didn't use the Database Wizard to create your database, you may not have a Switchboard. If you decide you like the feature, you can easily add one at any time. Open the **Tools** menu and select **Database Utilities, Switchboard Manager**. Click **Yes** to open the Switchboard Manager and use the buttons to add items to the switchboard.

How to Enter Data into the Database

You can enter data in your database several ways. Although you can enter data directly into a table, it's much easier to use a form. Forms are more attractive and simpler to use. Form view shows fields as boxes with labels.

If you prefer the plainness of the table format with endless columns and rows, you can also use Datasheet view. This task will illustrate both methods.

Begin

1 Open the Form

From the Database window, click the **Forms** object in the Objects bar and double-click the form you want to use in the list box. You can also select the form and click the **Open** button.

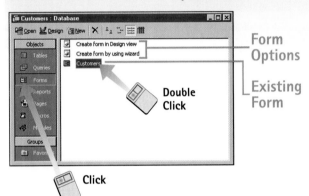

Form Options

Existing Form

Double Click

Click

2 Enter the Data

By default, you start out in Form view. Begin filling out a record. Click inside a field and start entering text, or use the **Tab** key to move from field to field.

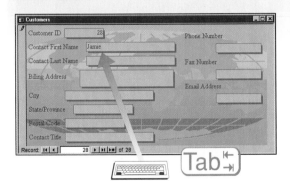

Tab

3 Start a New Record

After you complete a record, click the **New Record** button at the bottom of the form to open another record to fill out.

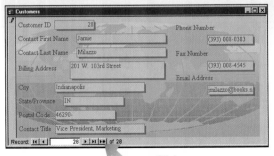

Click

4 Switch to Datasheet View

To enter data using Datasheet view, click the **View** drop-down arrow on the Database toolbar and choose **Datasheet View**. You can also open the **View** menu and select **Datasheet View**.

Click

5 Enter the Data

Your form now appears as a table. Field names appear in the column headers, and each row represents a record. Click inside the first empty cell in the first column and enter data for that field. Press **Tab** to move from field to field. Press **Enter** to start a new record.

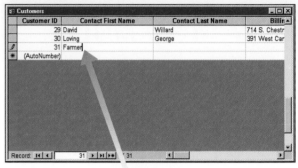

6 Exit the Form

To exit the form in Form view or Datasheet view, click the window's **Close** button. (Don't confuse the form window's Close button with the program window's Close button or you will exit Access entirely.)

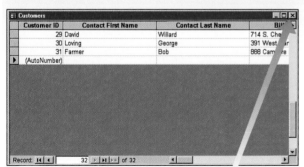

Click

End

How-To Hints

I Don't Have a Form

If you haven't started a new form yet, use the **Create Form by Using Wizard** option in the Database window list box. Double-click the item and follow the wizard prompts for creating a form. When you're finished with the wizard, follow step 1 in this task to open and start using the new form.

Navigate Forms

Use the Record arrow buttons at the bottom of the form to navigate back and forth to view your records. Click the **New Record** button (the right-pointing arrow with an asterisk) to start a new record.

Repeat Your Entries

You can repeat an entry for a field in Datasheet view. Press **Ctrl+'** to copy the contents of the cell above to the current cell. This only works in Datasheet view.

How to Open New or Existing Databases

When you first start Access, an opening dialog box appears with options for creating a blank database, using the database wizards, or opening an existing database you have already created and saved. If you're a new Access user, it's easiest to start a new database with a database wizard, as explained in Task 2, "How to Use the Database Wizard." If you're a bit more seasoned, you can create a blank database from scratch, as explained in this task.

If you've already created one or more databases, you can just open them up to work on them again. I'll also show you how to retrieve saved databases in this task.

Begin

1 Open an Existing Database

From the opening dialog box, click the **Open an Existing File** option.

Click

2 Locate the File

Use the list box to locate the file you want to open. Select the file from the list and click **OK**, or simply double-click the filename.

Click

3 Use the Open Dialog Box

If the file you want to open isn't listed, double-click **More Files** to open the Open dialog box. Locate the file you're looking for and double-click the filename. (For more information about using the Open dialog box, see Task 6, "How to Open and Close Files," in Chapter 1, "How to Use Common Office Features.")

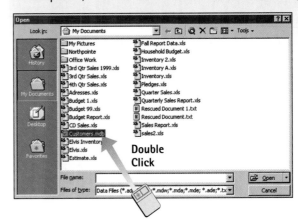

Double Click

4 Start a Blank Database

To build your own database, click the **Blank Access Database** option in the opening dialog box and click **OK**.

Click

5 Assign a Name

From the File New Database dialog box, enter a name for the database in the **File Name** text box and click the **Create** button.

Click

6 The Database Is Created

A Database window opens. You can now enter and edit data as needed. Turn to Task 3, "How to Navigate the Access Window," to learn how to use the Database window. Turn to Task 5, "How to Enter Data into the Database," to learn how to enter data.

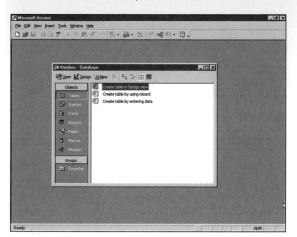

End

How-To Hints

Edit the Table

To learn more about editing a table and changing table elements, turn to Task 8, "How to Modify a Table in Design View."

Tables or Forms?

You can enter data into your database in several ways. You can use a form, as explained in Task 5. You can also enter data into tables, which, by default, display in Datasheet view. You can learn more about using Access tables in the next task, "How to Add New Tables."

Need Wider Columns?

If you need wider columns for your field labels, you can click and drag the border between the column labels. When you hover your mouse pointer over the border between two labels, the pointer becomes a two-sided arrow pointer. Click and drag to resize the column.

Exit the Table

To exit the table and return to the Database window, click the table window's **Close** button.

How to Add New Tables

Access tables organize and present your data in an easy-to-read manner. You can create many different tables in each Access file, and each table may vary in its focus from other tables. For example, you might have one table consisting of customer data, such as name and address, and another table detailing your inventory, such as item number and price.

You have several ways of creating new tables. You can use the Table Wizard, you can design your own table from scratch, or you can use a default blank table and fill in your own fields. Regardless of how you create a table, all tables work the same way. Fields are listed in columns, and records are listed in rows.

1 Select the Table Object

To work with database tables, click the **Tables** object in the Objects bar of the Database window. You'll see three options for working with tables. Use the **Create Table in Design View** option to custom-design a table. Use the **Create Table by Using Wizard** option to open the Table Wizard that walks you through steps for creating a table. To create a default blank table, use the **Create Table by Entering Data** option.

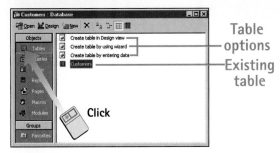

Table options

Existing table

Click

2 Start a Blank Table

To start a blank table, double-click the **Create Table by Entering Data** option. This opens a default table in Datasheet view, as shown in this figure. To rename the fields, double-click the field label and enter your own text. To fill out a record, click the first empty cell in the first column and start entering data.

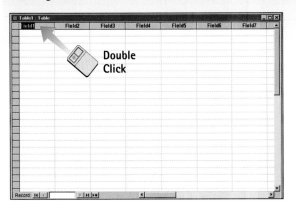

Double Click

3 Use the Table Wizard

Another way to start a table is to use the Table Wizard, which does all the design work for you. From the Database window, double-click the **Create Table by Using Wizard** option. This opens the Table Wizard, as shown in this figure. You can view two separate table lists, Business or Personal. Select the one you want.

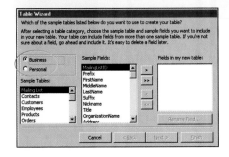

4 Add Fields

You can build your table using fields from different sample tables; just mix and match what you need from the samples. Select a table from the **Sample Tables** list and the **Sample Fields** list box displays the available fields. To add a field, select the field and click the > button. When you have finished adding fields, click **Next** to continue.

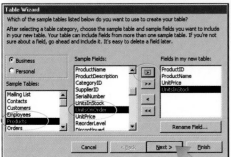

Click

5 Assign a Name

In the next dialog box, enter a descriptive name for the table and let the wizard determine the primary key. Click **Next** to continue.

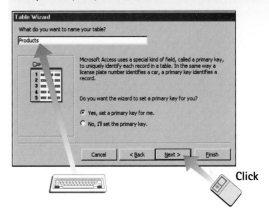

Click

6 Create the Table

If your database already has at least one table, the next dialog box that appears asks about the relationship between tables. Click **Next** for now to open the final dialog box. Indicate whether you want to change the table design, enter data directly, or have the wizard create a data entry form for you. Click **Finish**.

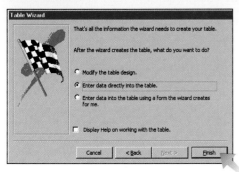

Click

End

How-To Hints

Rename Your Fields

You can select fields that are similar to ones you need and then rename them using the **Rename Field** button in the Table Wizard.

Enter Table Data

After you create a table, you can start entering data into it at any time. Open the table, click in the first empty cell in the first empty column, and type in the data for that field. Be sure to use the correct data type. If it's a text field, use text; if it's a number field, use numbers. Press **Tab** to move to the next field and continue filling out a complete record for the table. When you get to the last field, press **Enter** to start a new record.

Design a Table from Scratch

Use Design view to build a table from scratch. Learn more about using Design view in the next task, "How to Modify a Table in Design View."

How to Modify a Table in Design View

Access databases are flexible in their design. You may find that you have a field that is almost always blank, for example, indicating that it is unnecessary and should be removed. You may also want to enter information for a field that you forgot to create. In either case, you can open the appropriate table and make the necessary change.

Access makes it easy to change the various elements in your tables. You can change the look and design of any table, form, report, or query in Design view.

Begin

1 Open the Table

With your Database window open, click **Tables** on the Objects bar and select the table you want to change in the list box. Click the **Design** button to open the table in Design view.

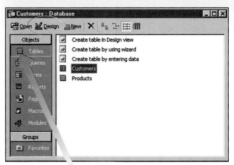

Click

2 Add a Field

To add a new field to the table, click inside the first blank line of the **Field Name** column and enter the new field name.

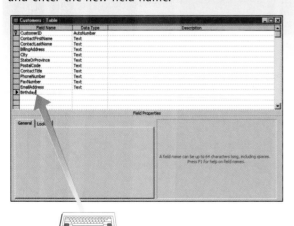

3 Select the Field Type

Tab to the **Data Type** column, click the down arrow to view the list of data type choices, and select a type. If the field will contain text entries, for example, select **Text**; if it requires number entries, select **Numbers**. (Note that the Field Properties sheet appears at the bottom of the window based on the data type.)

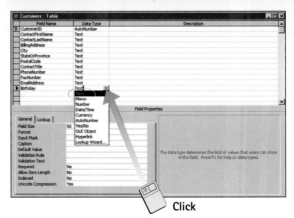

Click

4 Remove a Field

To remove a field, click the row selector to the left of the field name to highlight the entire row. Click the **Delete Rows** button on the Database toolbar to remove the highlighted row. Click **Yes** when asked if you want to delete the selected field permanently.

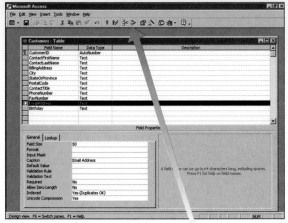

 Click

5 Edit a Field Name

To change a field name, click the field name and make your changes. You can edit existing text or enter a brand new name.

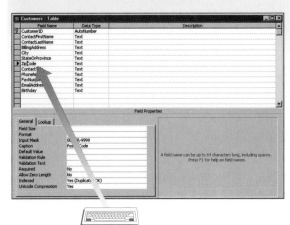

6 Close the Table

Click the **Close** button to close the table and return to the Database window. Click **Yes** in the dialog box that asks whether you want to save your changes.

Click

End

How-To Hints

Reorder Fields

To move the field to a new location in the table, select the field row in Design view and drag it to a new location in the table.

Use Field Properties

Use the field properties sheet in the Table Design view to change things such as the default size of the field, whether the field can be left blank when entering data, how many decimal places you want (number fields only), and more. To change a property, click its line and make the necessary changes.

Quick Delete

You can also delete rows by highlighting them, right-clicking, and selecting **Delete Rows** from the shortcut menu that appears.

How to Create a New Form with the Form Wizard

To make data entry easy, use a form. You can use two types of forms: data entry forms or dialog box forms. Data entry forms are fairly self-explanatory. They're designed like a regular old form you fill out, with empty boxes where you type in your data. Dialog box forms enable you to provide a vehicle for user input and a follow-up action based on the input.

This task will focus on the data entry form, which can be produced with the Form Wizard. To begin, open the database you want to use.

Begin

1 Open the New Form Dialog Box

From the Database window, click **Forms**. Click the **New** button to open the New Form dialog box. Notice the list box has several different form options you can select. In this task, we'll focus on the Form Wizard.

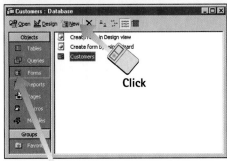

Click

Click

2 Start the Form Wizard

From the New Form dialog box, select **Form Wizard** from the list of form options and click **OK** to start the wizard.

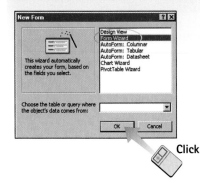

Click

3 Choose a Table

From the **Tables/Queries** drop-down list, select the table that contains the fields you want to include on the form. Then select a field and click the > button to add the field to the new form. (To add all the fields at once, click the >> button.) When you're finished adding fields, click **Next**.

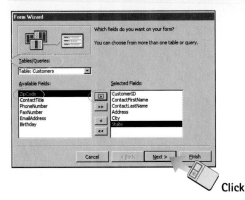

Click

4 Choose a Layout

The next wizard dialog box asks you to choose a layout for the form. Click each option to see an example of each of the layouts. When you find the one you want, click **Next** to continue.

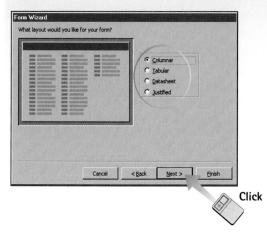

Click

5 Select a Style

Choose a style to use for the form. As you click each style, its sample appears to the left. Select the one you want and click **Next** to continue.

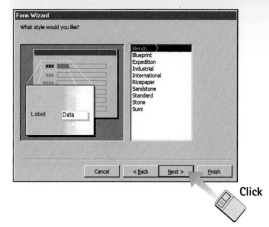

Click

6 Name the Form

The final Form Wizard dialog opens and asks for a title for the form. Enter a descriptive name in the text box and click **Finish**.

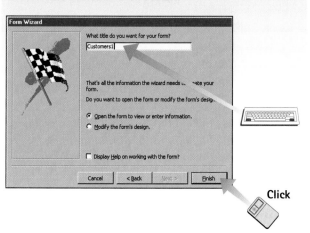

Click

End

How-To Hints

Mix and Match Fields

If you have more than one table in your database, you can select fields from different tables to appear in a single form. In step 3, change the table that appears in the **Tables/Queries** drop-down list and add fields as needed.

Or Use AutoForm

If you want a generic form based on the fields in your table, use AutoForm. From the New Form dialog box, select **AutoForm: Columnar** to create a single column of fields in a form, select **AutoForm: Tabular** to create a form that looks like a table, or select **AutoForm: Datasheet** to make a form that looks like a datasheet. At the bottom of the New Form dialog box, use the drop-down arrow to select the table you want to associate with the form, then click **OK**. A simple form is made.

How to Make Changes to a Form in Design View

The Form Wizard is great for producing a quick form (see Task 8). You will frequently find that after you have your form, you want to change the layout or the fields. You can easily customize the form in Design view.

After you open a form in Design view, you can move the form elements around, add new titles, or change the field size. Design view is rather like an electronic paste-up board that enables you to move items around until they're exactly where you want them.

Begin

1 Open the Form

Open the database you want to use if it's not already open. From the Database window, click Forms. Select the form you want to modify from the list box and click the **Design** button. This opens the form in Design view along with the floating Field List box.

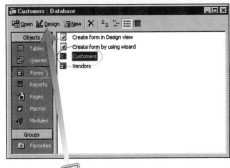

Click

2 Use Form Design

In Design view, you can place various elements into the form and move them about. The form is divided into *Form Header* (which holds title information), *Detail* (which holds the form fields), and *Form Footer* (which holds information placed at the bottom of each record). The Detail area is displayed by default.

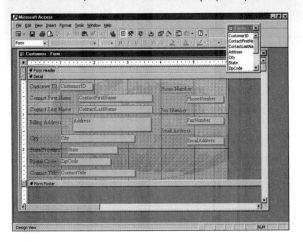

3 Delete a Field

To remove a field and its label, click the field and press **Delete**. Depending on the background design, it's not always easy to tell what's a field and what's a label. In most instances, fields appear larger than text labels. When you click a field, its label is also selected. Selection handles appear around a selected item.

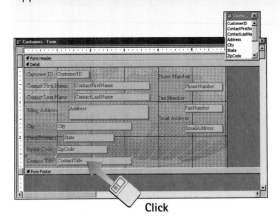

Click

4 Add a Field

To add a field, drag a field from the **Field List** box onto the **Detail** area where you want the new field. Release the mouse button and the field, and its text label is added. Repeat this step to add as many fields as you like.

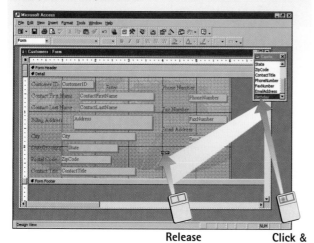

Release

Click & Drag

5 Move a Field

To move a field, click a field to select it, and selection handles surround it. Position the mouse pointer over the field until it takes the shape of a hand icon. Hold down the left mouse button and drag the field to a new position. To resize a field, drag any of the field's selection handles.

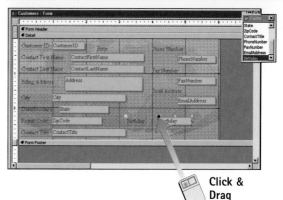

Click & Drag

6 Use the Toolbox

You can use all kinds of editing tools to change your form design. You'll find them all on the floating Toolbox. (If the Toolbox isn't displayed, open the **View** menu and select **Toolbox**.) Use the Toolbox buttons to add additional text to the form, such as subtitles or directions, add pictures to the form, and more.

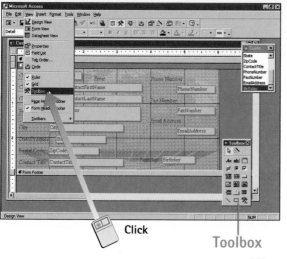

Click

Toolbox

How-To Hints

No Field List?

If the Field List box doesn't appear on your screen, open the **View** menu and select **Field List**.

Save Your Changes

After moving around the form elements and adding or deleting fields and labels, click the form's **Close** button or press **Ctrl+F4**. In the prompt box that appears, click **Yes** to save your changes.

View Headers and Footers

To work with the header or footer area of your form, open the **View** menu and select **Form Header/Footer**. You can add text to a header or footer area the same as you add text to a form.

End

How to Sort Records

After you have entered data into a database, you're ready to start manipulating it. One of the most important ways in which a database manipulates data is by *sorting* it: putting it in a logical order according to criteria you specify.

You may want to sort your address database, for example, by city, ZIP code, or last name. The Sort command is the tool to use. You can sort by *ascending order* (A to Z or 1 to 10) or *descending order* (Z to A or 10 to 1). To begin, open the database you want to sort.

Begin

1 Open the Table

From the Database window, click **Tables** from the Objects bar and open the table you want to sort (double-click the table name or select it and click the **Open** button).

Double Click

2 Choose the Sort Field

Click the column header for the field you want to sort, or place your cursor anywhere in the column you want to use for the sort.

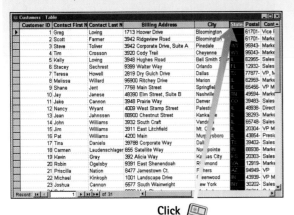

Click

3 Use the Sort Buttons

To sort the table in ascending (A-Z) order, click the **Sort Ascending** button on the toolbar. To sort by descending order (Z-A), click the **Sort Descending** button.

Sort Ascending

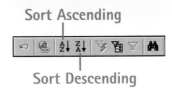

Sort Descending

4 The Data Is Sorted

The table is immediately sorted. Continue sorting the table fields as needed. When you exit the table after sorting, a prompt box asks you whether you want to save the changes. Click **Yes** if you do, or **No** if you don't want the sort to be permanent.

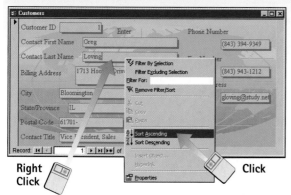

5 Sort by Form Fields

You can also sort your records using a form. From the Database window, select **Forms** and open a form. Place your cursor in the field by which you want to sort.

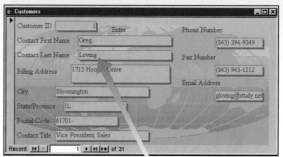

Click

6 Use the Shortcut Menu

This time, perform a sort using the shortcut menu. Right-click to display the menu and select **Sort Ascending** or **Sort Descending** to sort the form by the selected field. As you cycle through the records using the arrow buttons at the bottom of the form, the records appear in the new sort order.

Right Click

Click

End

How-To Hints

What About Empty Records?

If you sort by a field that contains no information in some records, those records are automatically sorted first (ascending order) or last (descending order).

Sort Tip

Changing the sort order of a table does not cause a related sort order change in an existing form. If you create a form using a table with an established sort order, however, the form automatically takes on the sort order of the table.

Sort in Datasheet View

You can also sort a form in the Datasheet view. Open the **View** menu and choose **Datasheet View**. The Datasheet view of the form not only looks the same as the table in step 2, it also sorts the same. After you select the column to sort by, you can use the **Sort Ascending** or **Sort Descending** buttons to perform the sort.

How to Filter Records

You can filter out specific records in your database. Perhaps you want to see information only about a certain vendor or group of vendors, or you may want to find everyone in your address book whose birthday is in the month of May. You can temporarily filter out all the records except those you need to see.

Access enables you to apply a filter in three ways: Filter by Selection, Filter by Form, and Advanced Filters. You can apply any of the filters in a form, datasheet, or query. In this task, I will demonstrate the first two methods.

Begin

1 Filter by Selection

Open the form you want to use and click the field that contains the criteria you want to filter, If you want to search for all the records using the same ZIP code, for example, first locate a record containing that ZIP code and click in the ZIP code field. To begin the filter, click the **Filter By Selection** button on the toolbar.

Click

2 The Records Are Filtered

Any records with matching information in the field selected have been retained, but all others have been hidden (filtered out). Use the form's arrow buttons to view the filtered records.

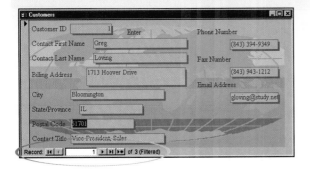

3 Remove a Filter

To remove the filter, click the **Remove Filter** button on the toolbar. (When no filter has been applied, the **Remove Filter** button does double duty as the **Apply Filter** button.)

Click

4 Filter by Form

You can also apply a filter while in Datasheet view. To switch to Datasheet view, open the **View** menu and select **Datasheet View**. Click the **Filter by Form** button on the toolbar to enter your own criteria for the filter. A blank form appears as a single record in a datasheet.

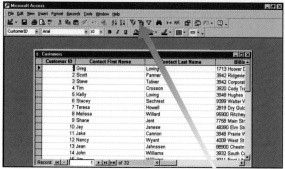

 Click

5 Enter Your Filter Criteria

Type your search criteria in the field of your choice or use the field's drop-down arrow to select a value. (To search for all customers with a billing address in Illinois, for example, type **IL** in the **State/Province** field. You can enter criteria in more than one field, but Access will find only records that match both entries.

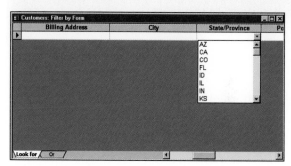

6 Filter the Records

To begin the filter, click the **Apply Filter** button on the toolbar. Access filters your database and displays any records matching your criteria. (Use the arrow buttons to scroll through each record.)

End

How-To Hints

Quick Filter

For a quick search based on input for a certain field, place your cursor in the desired field and right-click. Enter the search criteria in the **Filter For** text box on the shortcut menu and press **Enter** to apply the filter.

Filter by Exclusion

You can also filter out records that contain certain criteria. The regular filter finds records that contain the search criteria and filters out those that don't. The Filter by Excluding Selection returns all records that do not contain the search criteria you specify.

Use an Or Filter

Another way you can filter is to use an Or filter, which means you filter for either one criteria or another. Any records that match one or the other are displayed. Click the **Or** tab in Datasheet view, specify your Or criteria, and click the **Apply Filter** button.

How to Perform a Simple Query

Queries are similar to filters in that they extract information based on criteria that you specify. Queries can be used for editing and viewing your data, as well as furnishing the material for forms and reports.

The easiest way to create a query is to use the Simple Query Wizard. It enables you to select which fields you want to display. You can weed out fields you don't need and still see every record.

Begin

1 Open the New Query Dialog Box

From the Database window, select **Queries** in the Objects bar and click **New** to open the New Query dialog box.

Click

2 Start the Simple Query Wizard

Choose **Simple Query Wizard** and click **OK** to open the first Simple Query Wizard dialog box.

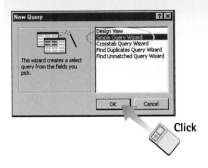

Click

3 Choose a Table

Open the **Tables/Queries** drop-down list and select the first table from which to choose a field.

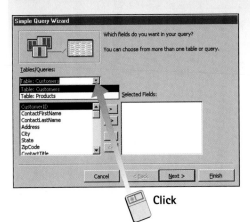

Click

4 Select Fields

Select a field you can include in the query table results and click the > button to add it to your query. Select as many fields from as many different tables as you want and click **Next** when you're ready to continue.

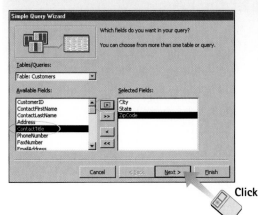

Click

5 Give the Query a Name

The next dialog box asks you whether you want a detail query (which shows every record) or summary query (which is used for totaling values). Detail is the default, so click **Next** to continue. Then enter a name for the query and click **Finish** to create your query, which appears in table form.

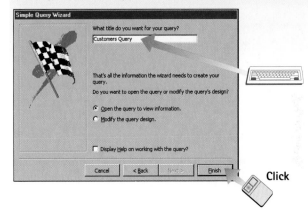

Click

6 Query Results

Access displays the records showing only the fields you specified in Datasheet view. To close the query, click the window's **Close** button.

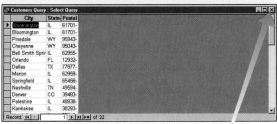

Click

End

How-To Hints

Searching for Blanks

In addition to finding records that contain fields with information, you can also use a query to find records that contain blank fields. To search for blank numeric fields, use **Is Null** for the search criteria. For blank text fields use double quotes ("").

Searching for Wildcards

Another way to conduct a search is to use *wildcards*, symbols (* for multiple characters, ? for single characters) that stand for other characters. For example, to search for all the last names in your address database that start with CAN, you might enter **CAN***, and the results would produce names like *CANNON* or *CANTON*.

How to Create a Report

You can choose to print any table, form, or query at any time; however, using the Report tool can make the data appear more professional and polished. With the Report Wizard, the task of creating a meaningful report becomes simple and effortless.

Open the database you want to use and click **Reports** from the Objects bar of the Database window and click **New** to open the New Report dialog box.

Begin

1 Open the Report Wizard

Select **Report Wizard** from the list of options and click **OK** to open the Report Wizard window.

Click

2 Choose a Table or Query

From the **Tables/Queries** drop-down list, select the table or query to use in your report. Select a field and click the > button to add it to your list. Select as many fields from as many different tables or queries as you wish and click **Next** when you're ready to continue.

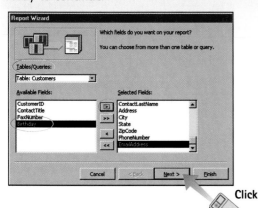

Click

3 Choose a Grouping Category

A report that groups information by relevant categories is much more useful than one that simply lists information alphabetically. From the left display window, choose a field to use as a grouping category and click the > button. Click **Next** to continue.

Click

4 Choose a Sort

You can sort by as many as four fields, in either ascending or descending order. From the first drop-down list, select the field to use for the primary sort and continue until you have chosen as many sort fields as needed. Click **Next** to continue.

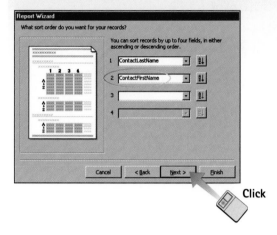

Click

5 Select a Layout

Select a layout option to see an example of how it will look. When you have decided on the layout options, you're ready to move on. Click **Next**.

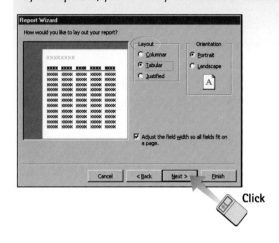

Click

6 Select a Style

As with the layout options, you can see examples of the different styles by clicking the options. Choose a style for your report and click **Next**.

Click

7 Assign a Title

In the final wizard dialog box, enter a report title and click **Finish**. Your new report is created and displayed as its own separate window on-screen.

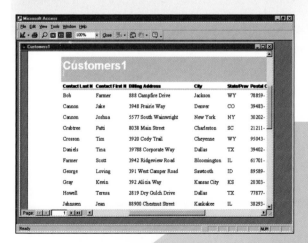

End

Task

CHAPTER 12

How to Use Outlook

*O*utlook is a desktop information manager you can use to organize and manage your daily activities at home or at the office. Outlook is extremely versatile; you can schedule and keep track of your daily appointments, build and maintain a database of people you contact the most, create "to do" lists for projects or events and track each item's status, jot down electronic notes, and more. In addition to managing your daily commitments, you can track and manage your email correspondence. You can send and receive email from the Outlook window, whether it's messages sent to Internet users or colleagues on your company LAN, WAN, or intranet.

This chapter covers the basic features of using Outlook, including how to use the new Outlook Today view, and the basics for using each of Outlook's components, such as Calendar, Contacts, Tasks, and Notes. ●

How to Get Around the Outlook Window

The Outlook window features the familiar title bar, menu bar, toolbar, and status bar used in other Office programs. In addition, you see the Outlook Bar on the left side of the window. Use the Outlook Bar to access each Outlook component. Outlook's components are organized into folders, represented by icons on the Outlook Bar. When you click a component, such as Inbox, the appropriate folder opens in the work area.

Because the Outlook window differs in appearance from the other Office program windows, take a few minutes to acclimate yourself to the window elements.

Begin

1 View the Outlook Window

The Outlook window contains many of the same program elements used in other Office programs. This figure points out the various onscreen elements. Some of them are unique to Outlook; others are common throughout the Office suite.

2 Use the Program Window Controls

Use the Minimize, Maximize, and Close buttons at the far right end of the title bar to manipulate the Outlook window. For example, to make the Outlook program window fill the screen space, click the **Maximize** button.

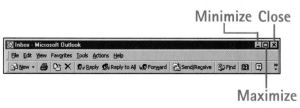

3 Use the Menu Bar

To display an Outlook menu, click the menu name. The menu drops down to reveal a list of commands. Select the command you want to use.

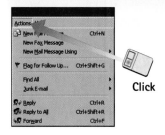

4 Use the Toolbar

Outlook's toolbar buttons change to reflect the component or task on which you're working. To activate a toolbar button, just click on it. To learn more about what a button does, hover your mouse pointer over the button to reveal a ScreenTip.

5 Use Group Buttons

The Outlook Bar has three group buttons for organizing your folders and shortcuts: Outlook Shortcuts (which holds all of the Outlook components), My Shortcuts (which holds various mail folders for sent messages, drafts, and more), and Other Shortcuts (so you can access My Computer and the My Documents and Favorites folders). To display a new folder group, click the appropriate group button.

—Group buttons

6 Change Folders

Each Outlook component has its own folder, represented by an icon on the Outlook Bar in the Outlook Shortcuts group. To open another Outlook component, click the appropriate icon in the Outlook Bar. To open the Contacts feature, for example, click the **Contacts** icon. Use the Scroll button to view more icons on the Outlook Bar.

—Outlook features

Click

—Scroll button

7 Display the Folder List

Another way to view Outlook's components is with the Folder List. Open the **View** menu and select **Folder List**, or click the **Folder** drop-down arrow in the work area. The Folder List displays each Outlook folder, including any you add to organize Outlook items you create. (Click the **Pushpin** icon to keep the Folder List open onscreen.)

Folder List Pushpin

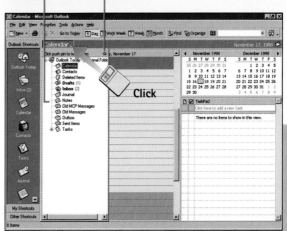

Click

Continues

8 Change Views

Some of the Outlook components enable you to change your view of the information presented. With the Calendar, for example, you can see your schedule by Day, Work Week, Week, and Month. To change a view, use the **View** menu or click the appropriate view button on the toolbar.

View buttons

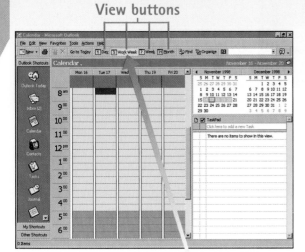

Click

9 Use Outlook Today View

Click the **Outlook Today** icon on the Outlook Bar to see your day's schedule and projects at a glance. The items displayed are actually hyperlinks to other Outlook items. Click an appointment, for example, to open the Appointment window that has details about the appointment.

Click

Link

10 Find Outlook Contacts

Use the **Find a Contact** tool on the toolbar to quickly look up a name in your Contacts database (learn more about adding contacts in Task 9, "How to Phone a Contact"). Click inside the text box and type in the person's name, first or last. Press **Enter**, and Outlook displays the Contact form with details about the person.

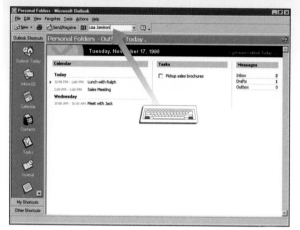

End

Customize Outlook Today

By default, Outlook opens with the Inbox displayed; however, you might want to customize Outlook to start with the Outlook Today feature displayed so you can always see your day's events and tasks at a glance. To do this, click the **Customize Outlook Today** button on the Outlook Today display. This opens another display page with several options. Click the **When Starting, Go Directly to Outlook Today** check box. You can also customize how appointments and tasks appear. Click the **Save Changes** button to return to the previous display page.

How to Schedule an Appointment

Use Outlook's Calendar feature to keep track of appointments, events, and any other special engagements. When you open the Calendar folder, Outlook displays your daily schedule in the schedule pane, along with a monthly calendar pane and a miniaturized version of your TaskPad (learn more about creating Outlook tasks in Task 6, "How to Create a New Task").

You can easily add appointments to your calendar and set reminder alarms to let you know of imminent appointments. To open Calendar, click the **Calendar** icon on the Outlook Bar.

Begin

1 Choose a Date

In the monthly calendar pane, select the month and date for the appointment. When you click the date, the schedule pane changes to reflect that date. Notice the current date is always highlighted with a red border.

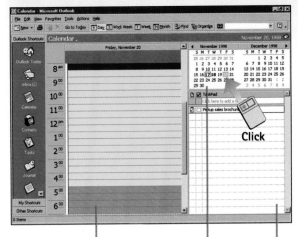

Schedule pane   Monthly pane   TaskPad

2 Choose a Time

On the schedule pane, double-click the time slot for which you want to schedule an appointment. This opens the Appointment window.

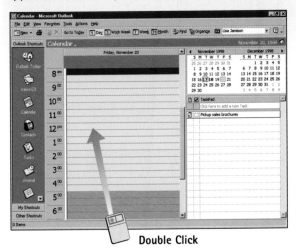

Double Click

3 Fill Out the Form

The Appointment window is actually a form you can use to enter details about the appointment. Fill out the **Subject** and **Location** text boxes. For example, enter the name of the person you're meeting with and the place where you're meeting. Click inside the text boxes or use the Tab key to move from field to field.

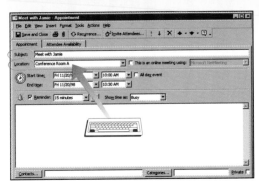

4 Enter Appointment Details

Use the **Start Time** and **End Time** drop-down arrows to set or change the date and time of the appointment. By default, Outlook schedules your appointments in 30-minute increments, but you can easily set a longer time increment.

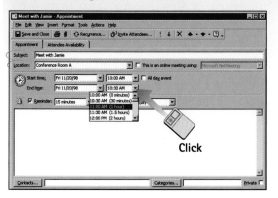

Click

5 Need a Reminder?

Select the **Reminder** check box if you want Outlook to remind you about the appointment with a prompt box and an audible beep. Specify how long before the appointment you want to be reminded.

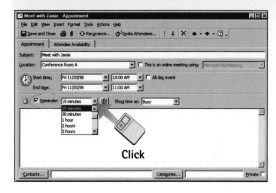

Click

6 Save and Close

When you have finished filling in all of the details you want to include with the appointment, click the **Save and Close** button on the Appointment window's toolbar to exit the form and return to Calendar.

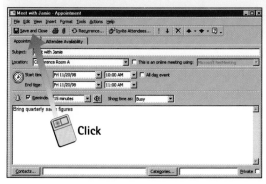

Click

End

How-To Hints

Reminder Prompt

If you select the **Reminder** check box, Outlook reminds you about the appointment with a prompt box and a beep; however, this works only if Outlook is running at the time of the reminder prompt. If you minimize Outlook so it's a button on the Windows taskbar, you can work with other programs, but Outlook can still remind you of imminent appointments.

Block Your Time

If you're using Outlook on a network, use the **Show Time As** drop-down list on the Appointment form to determine how others see the appointment on your calendar. If you don't want others on the network to see the appointment, click the **Private** check box. You might have to enlarge the Appointment dialog box to see the option (drag the bottom right corner to resize the form).

How to Set a Recurring Appointment

If your schedule is prone to recurring appointments, Outlook's Recurring Appointment features can help. For example, perhaps you have a weekly staff meeting. Rather than schedule each meeting separately, set the meeting as a recurring appointment. Outlook adds the meeting to each week's calendar for you automatically.

With the Recurring Appointment feature, you can indicate the recurrence pattern to tell Outlook how often the meeting occurs (Daily, Weekly, Monthly, or Yearly), on which day of the week it falls, and other related options.

Begin

1 Schedule a Recurring Appointment

To schedule a recurring appointment from the Calendar folder, first open the Appointment Recurrence dialog box. Display the **Actions** menu and select **New Recurring Appointment**.

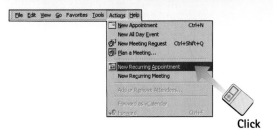

Click

2 Enter a Time

Use the **Start**, **End**, or **Duration** drop-down lists to set the appointment start and end times or designate how long the appointment lasts.

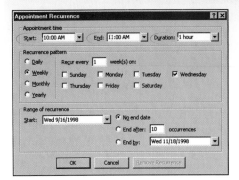

3 Enter a Recurrence Pattern

Under **Recurrence Pattern**, select the frequency of the appointment and the day on which the appointment falls. Depending on your selection, the remaining recurrence options will vary. If you select **Weekly**, for example, you can specify every week or every other week.

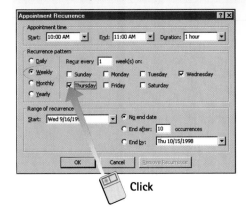

Click

4 Range of Recurrence

Use the **Range of Recurrence** options to enter any limits to the recurring appointment. Suppose you need to schedule five doctor visits over the next five months but will no longer need the appointment after that. Use the **End After** option to set such a range.

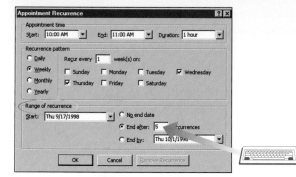

5 Fill In the Details

Click **OK** to close the Appointment Recurrence window and display the Appointment form. Now you can fill in any details about the appointment. Click the **Save and Close** button when you're finished.

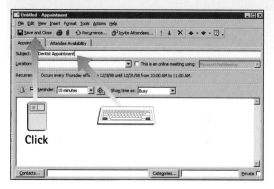

6 The Appointment Is Set

The recurring appointment now appears on your calendar with a double-arrow icon to indicate it's a recurring appointment.

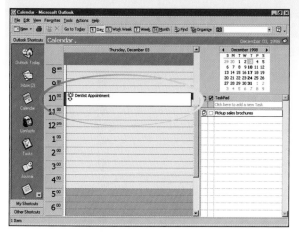

End

How-To Hints

Add a Reminder

Click the **Reminder** check box in the Appointment form to add a reminder alarm to your recurring appointment.

Edit Appointments

To edit a recurring appointment or any other appointment, double-click the appointment in your schedule. Outlook asks if you want to edit just the one occurrence or the series. Select the appropriate option and click **OK**. This opens the Appointment form, where you can make any changes.

Other Recurring Ideas

Recurring appointments are great for marking your kids' athletic practices throughout a season, personal tasks (such as haircuts), staff meetings, community meetings, and so on.

How to Schedule an Event

Not all items you add to your schedule are appointments—some are events. A *calendar event* is any activity that lasts the entire day, such as an anniversary, a conference, a trade show, or a birthday. Use events in your daily calendar to block off larger time slots than appointments. An event appears as a banner at the top of the schedule date.

Begin

1 Open the Event Window

To schedule an event, open the **Actions** menu and choose **New All Day Event**. This opens the Event window.

Click

2 Enter the Event Title

The Event window looks like the Appointment window. Fill in the details pertaining to the event. Start by filling in a title for the event in the **Subject** text box and entering a location in the **Location** text box.

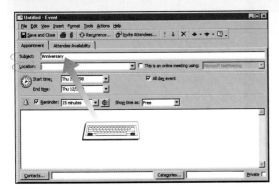

3 Enter Start and End Times

Use the **Start Time** and **End Time** drop-down lists to specify a time frame for the event.

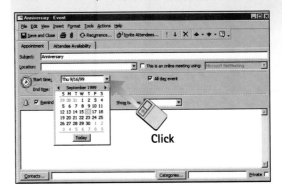

Click

4 Set the All Day Event Option

Be sure to select the **All Day Event** check box. This option is what makes an event different from a regular appointment—as soon as you select it, the hourly drop-down boxes no longer appear on the form.

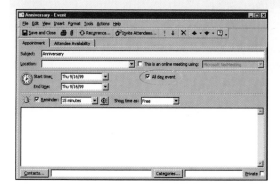

5 Save and Close

When you have finished filling in the Event details, click the **Save and Close** button to exit the Event window.

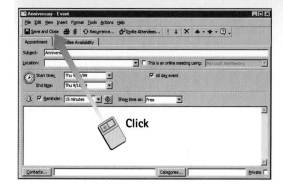

Click

6 The Event Is Saved

The event now appears as a banner at the beginning of the day in the schedule pane (use Day view to see it clearly).

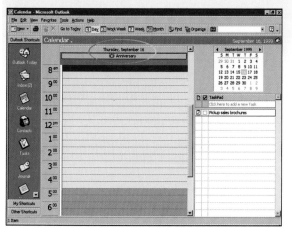

End

How-To Hints

Edit Events

To edit an event, double-click the event on your calendar. This reopens the Event form so you can make the necessary changes.

Event Reminder

Click the **Reminder** check box to assign a reminder alarm to alert you about the event. You can assign a reminder up to two days before the event; if you need a more advanced setting, just type the number in the text box.

Recurring Events

To schedule a recurring event on your calendar, click the **Recurrence** button on the Event window's toolbar.

Turn an Appointment into an Event

You can also turn an appointment into an event by clicking the **All Day Event** check box in the Appointment form.

How to Plan a Meeting

If you're using Outlook on a network, you can use the Plan a Meeting feature to schedule meetings with others. The feature also enables you to designate any resources needed for the meeting, such as a conference room or equipment.

You can use the Plan a Meeting feature to invite attendees via email messages and track their responses. To get started, open the Calendar folder by clicking the **Calendar** icon on the Outlook Bar.

Begin

1 Open the Plan a Meeting Feature

From the Calendar folder, open the **Actions** menu and select **Plan a Meeting**. This opens the Plan a Meeting window.

Click

2 Enter the Attendees

Enter the names of the attendees in the **All Attendees** list. Click **Type Attendee Name Here** and enter the first person's name. Continue entering names on each line, as many as you need.

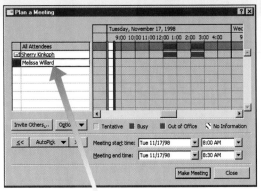

 Click

3 Set a Date...

Click the **Meeting Start Time** drop-down arrow and choose a date and time for the meeting. Use the **Meeting End Time** drop-down arrows to specify an end time for the meeting.

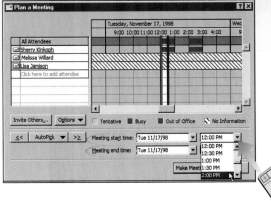

Click

4 ...Or Drag a Time

Alternatively, you can drag the green bar in the schedule area to set a start time for the meeting and drag the red bar to set an end time. (It's difficult to distinguish the colors on some monitors; just remember the bar to the left of the time increment starts the time and the bar to the right sets an end time.)

Start Time bar   End Time bar

Click & Drag

5 Fill In Meeting Details

When you have finished planning the meeting attendees and times, click the **Make Meeting** button. This opens the Meeting window, which resembles the Appointment form. Refine the meeting details as needed.

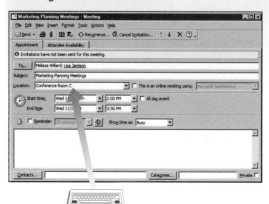

6 Send the Invitations

When you have finished filling out the meeting details, click **Send** to send email invitations to the attendees. Click the **Close** button to exit the Meeting window.

Click

End

How-To Hints

Track Your Responses

To see how the attendees are responding to your meeting invitation, click the **Show Attendee Status** option on the **Attendee Availability** tab of the Meeting window.

Check Others' Schedules

Another way to check the availability of someone on the network you want to invite is to click the **Attendee Availability** tab in the Plan a Meeting form.

How to Create a New Task

Use Outlook's Tasks folder to keep track of things you need to do, such as steps for completing a project or arranging an event. Tasks can be as complex as a year-long project or as simple as a shopping list you need to fill on the way home. A task list can include such things as writing a letter, making a phone call, or distributing a memo.

After you create a task list, you can keep track of the tasks and check them off as you complete them. You can choose to view your task list in the Tasks folder or in the Calendar folder. To open the Tasks folder, click the **Tasks** icon in the Outlook Bar.

Begin

1 Open the Task Dialog Box

From the Tasks folder, open the **Actions** menu and select **New Task**, or click the **New Task** button on the toolbar.

2 Enter a Title

The Task window, like the Appointment window, is a form you can fill out, detailing the task. With the **Task** tab displayed, enter the subject or title of the task in the **Subject** text box.

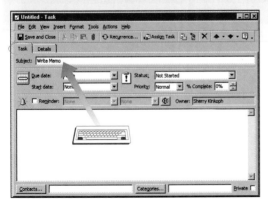

3 Enter a Due Date

If the task has a due date, click the **Due Date** drop-down arrow and choose a due date from the calendar. (You can also enter a start date, if needed.)

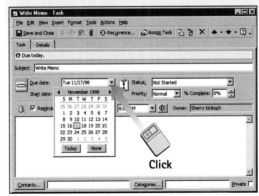

4 Select a Status Setting

Use the **Status** drop-down list to select a status setting for the project: **Not Started**, **In Progress**, **Completed**, **Waiting on Someone Else**, or **Deferred**. As you manage your task list, you can update the status as needed.

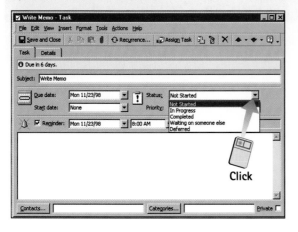

5 Set a Priority

Use the **Priority** drop-down list to give the task a priority level: **Normal**, **Low**, or **High**. Use the **% Complete** box if you want to specify a percentage of completeness.

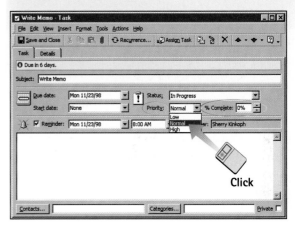

6 Enter Notes

Use the **Notes** box to enter any notes about the task. When you have finished filling out the Task form, click the **Save and Close** button. The task is now added to your Tasks folder's task list, as shown in this figure.

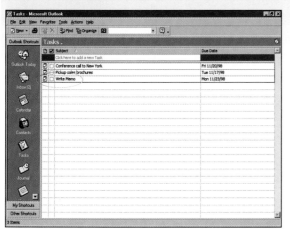

End

How-To Hints

Managing Tasks

To edit a task, double-click the task in the task list. To mark a task as complete, right-click the task and choose **Mark Complete**. The task appears in strikethrough on the list. To delete a task, right-click the task and choose **Delete**.

Recording Statistics

To record statistics about a task, such as billable time, contacts, or mileage, double-click the task and display the **Details** tab of the Task form.

Working with the TaskPad

The TaskPad that appears in Calendar shows your current tasks. To quickly open a task from the TaskPad, double-click the task name.

How to Create a New Contact

Use Outlook's Contacts folder to build a database of people you contact the most. A contact can be any person you communicate with, such as a coworker, relative, vendor, or client. You can enter all kinds of information about your contacts, including addresses, phone numbers, email addresses, birthdays, and Web pages.

After you enter a contact, you will always have access to information about that person. You can quickly fire off an email message, for example, or have your modem dial the phone number for you. To begin entering contacts, first open the Contacts folder by clicking the **Contacts** icon on the Outlook Bar.

Begin

1 Open the Contact Form

From the Contacts folder, open the **Actions** menu and select **New Contact**, or click the **New Contact** button on the toolbar. This opens the Contact window.

Click

2 Use the General Tab

From the **General** tab in the Contact form, you can begin filling in information about the contact. Click inside each text box and fill in the appropriate information. To move from field to field, press the **Tab** key.

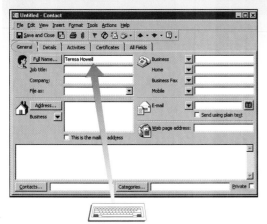

3 The File As List

Click the **File As** drop-down arrow and choose how you want to file your contact—by last name or first name. The default setting is to file the contacts by last name.

Click

4 Enter Phone Numbers

Outlook gives you the option of entering numerous phone numbers for the contact, including business and home numbers, fax numbers, and cell phone numbers.

5 Enter an Address

Enter the contact's address in the **Address** box. Use the drop-down arrow to designate a **Business**, **Home**, or **Other** address. (Use the **Address** button to enter address information in separate fields.)

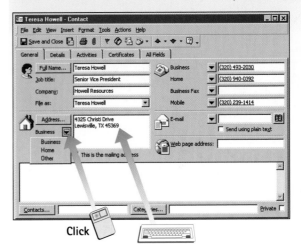

Click

6 Save the Contact

After filling out all of the pertinent information (don't forget to enter an email address), click the **Save and Close** button to add the contact to your database. To enter another contact, click the **Save and New** button to open another Contact form.

Save and New button

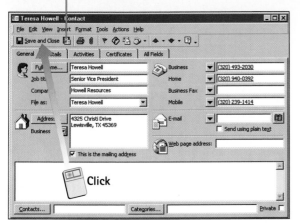

Click

End

How-To Hints

Adding Email and Web Pages

The Contact form has places for adding a contact's email address and Web page address. You can use this information to send an email or visit a Web page directly from the contact form.

More Details

Use the **Details** tab in the Contact form to enter information such as spouse's name, birthdays, anniversary, and other details.

Editing Contacts

To edit a contact, double-click the contact's name in the Contacts folder. This reopens the Contact form, where you can make changes to the data.

How to Import Contact Data

If you already have a contacts database in another program, whether it's an Office program such as Excel or Access or a non-Microsoft program such as Lotus Organizer, you can import the database into Outlook. Use Outlook's Import and Export Wizard to walk you through the steps.

TASK *8*

Begin

1 Open the Import and Export

Open the **File** menu and select **Import and Export**.

Click

2 Choose an Action

In the first wizard dialog box, choose an import or export action. Because you are importing addresses, choose **Import Internet Mail and Addresses** and then click **Next** to continue.

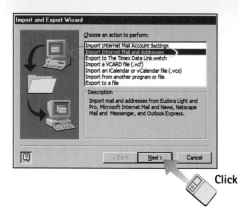

Click

3 Choose a File Type

In the next wizard dialog box, choose the type of address file you want to import. Scroll through the list, make your selection, and then click **Next**.

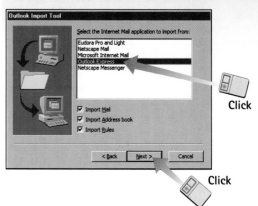

Click

Click

274

4 Choose a Destination Folder

Depending on the type of import you're performing, the remaining steps might differ. (For example, you might need to create a destination folder for the import.) Select a destination folder to hold the imported data. If you're importing addresses, consider placing them in the Contacts folder. If a prompt box appears asking you to enter the path of the file you want to import, type the path into the text box or use the **Browse** button to locate the exact file to import.

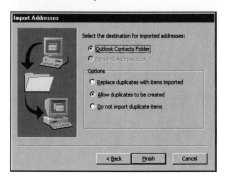

5 Click Finish

You can also choose to replace duplicate items. Select an option and click **Finish** to start the import.

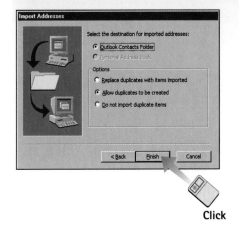

Click

6 Read the Import Summary

When the import is finished, a summary box appears, telling you how successful the import was; click **OK**. (If you want to save a copy of the summary, click the **Save in Inbox** button.)

Click

End

How-To Hints

Copying and Pasting Outlook Items

Not only can you import and export with Outlook, you can also copy and paste Outlook items between the Office programs by using the Copy and Paste commands. To learn more about sharing data between programs, see Chapter 17, "How to Integrate Office Applications."

How to Phone a Contact

If your computer has a modem, you can use it to dial the phone numbers of contacts in your Contacts list. Of course, after the number is dialed, you will have to pick up the receiver to start talking. However, rather than waste time trying to find a phone number or memorizing it yourself, let Outlook take care of it.

Begin

1 Select the Contact

From the Contacts folder, select the contact you want to call.

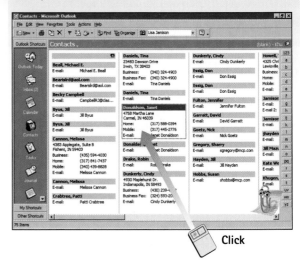

Click

2 Use AutoDialer

Click the **Dial** button on the Outlook toolbar to open the New Call dialog box.

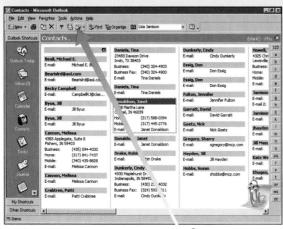

 Click

3 Choose the Number

Click the **Number** drop-down arrow and select the number you want to dial (such as business, home, or mobile).

Click

4 Dial the Number

Click the **Start Call** button to have your modem dial the number.

Click

5 Pick Up

When the Call Status changes to Connected, pick up the receiver to talk. When your conversation is finished, click the **End Call** button.

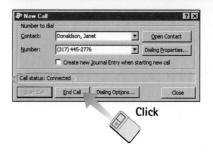

Click

6 Close the Box

Click the **Close** button to close the dialog box.

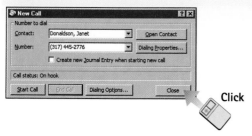

Click

End

How-To Hints

Create a Journal Entry

To help you track your calls, use Outlook's Journal feature to create a journal entry that documents the call. Before dialing the number, click the **Create New Journal Entry When Starting New Call** check box.

How to Create a New Folder

Outlook saves items you create in folders and subfolders. Email messages are saved in the Inbox folder, notes are saved in the Notes folder, and so forth. When managing the many items you create, you might want to organize them into different folders. For example, you might want to store all of the Outlook items related to a particular project into one folder. You can easily create new folders and move Outlook items into them as needed.

Begin

1 Open the Folder List

To see all of the folders that come with Outlook, open the Folder List. Click the **Folder Name** drop-down arrow and click the **Pushpin** icon in the upper right corner of the list to keep the list open onscreen.

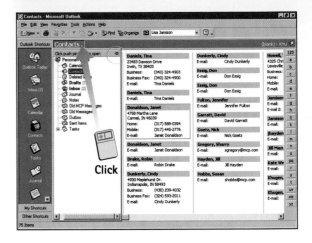

2 Choose a Parent Folder

To create a new subfolder, first select the parent folder (the folder to hold the subfolder). Suppose you want a Sales Project folder to be stored in the Tasks folder. First, select the **Tasks** folder.

Click

3 Open the Create New Folder Box

Right-click the folder to display a shortcut menu and then select **New Folder**. This opens the Create New Folder dialog box.

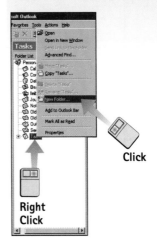

Click

Right Click

4 Enter a Folder Name

Enter a name for the new folder in the **Name** box.

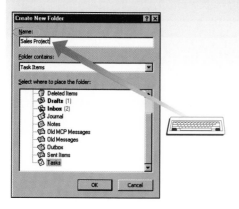

5 Select Items

Use the **Folder Contains** drop-down list to choose which items you want to store in the folder. Click **OK** to exit the dialog box and create the folder.

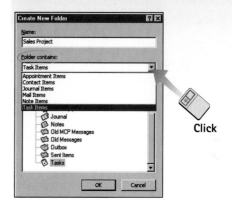

Click

6 The Folder Is Saved

A prompt box asks if you want to save the folder as an icon on the Outlook Bar. Click **No**. The folder name is now added to the Folder List.

How-To Hints

How Do I Put Items in the New Folder?

Check out Task 11, "How to Move Items to Folders," to learn how to move items between folders.

Subfolders in Subfolders

You can create subfolders within subfolders. For example, you might have a subfolder in the Inbox folder named **Vendor Mail**, and additional folders within that folder named **Suppliers** and **Printers**.

End

How to Move Items to Folders

After you create your own folders, you will want to move Outlook items into the folders. You might want to keep all of your email correspondence from a particular client in one folder so you can easily retrieve old messages, or you might want to keep personal messages separate from business messages. With Outlook, moving items from one folder to another is easy.

Begin

1 Open the Folder List

To see your folders, open the Folder List. Click the **Folder Name** drop-down arrow, or open the **View** menu and choose **Folder List**.

Click

2 Select the Item

Open the folder containing the item you want to move and select the item.

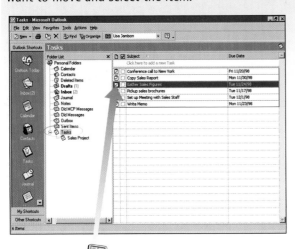

Click

3 Use the Move Command

Open the **Edit** menu and select the **Move to Folder** command. This opens the Move Items dialog box.

Click

4 Choose a Folder...

Choose the folder to which you want to move the selected item and click **OK**.

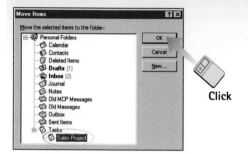

Click

5 ...Or Use Drag and Drop

Another method for moving items between folders is to drag and drop them. Select the item you want to move and then hold down the left mouse button and drag the item to the new folder name. Drop it in place.

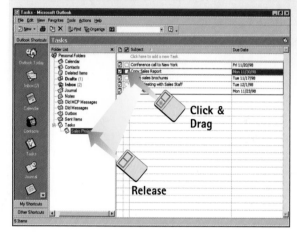

Click & Drag

Release

End

How-To Hints

Drag and Drop

You can also drag and drop items from open folders into any folder on the Outlook Bar. Select the item and drag and drop it into the appropriate folder.

How to Delete Items

Items you delete in Outlook don't disappear entirely; instead, they're held in Outlook's Deleted Items folder. To truly delete them, you must empty the folder. This works just like the Windows Recycle Bin. (Items you delete from your Windows desktop are held in the Recycle Bin until you remove them.)

A good idea is to clear your Deleted Items folder before you exit Outlook. If you forget, the items tend to stack up and take up space on your hard drive.

Begin

1 Open the Deleted Items Folder

To empty your deleted items, first open the **Deleted Items** folder by clicking its icon on the Outlook Bar. Use the **Scroll** arrow button to locate the icon.

Click

2 Choose the Items to Delete

To permanently erase an Outlook item from your system, select the item from the **Deleted Items** folder. To select more than one item, hold down the **Ctrl** key while clicking items.

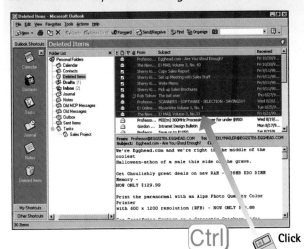

Ctrl **Click**

3 Click the Delete Button

Click the **Delete** button on the Outlook toolbar.

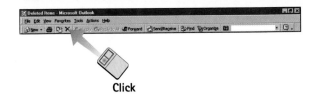

Click

4 Confirm the Deletion

A confirmation box appears, asking if you really want to delete the item. Click **Yes**.

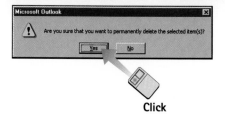

Click

5 Undelete Items

If you have sent Outlook items to the Deleted Items folder but change your mind about deleting them, you can retrieve them. Select the item and drag it to any folder in the Outlook Bar.

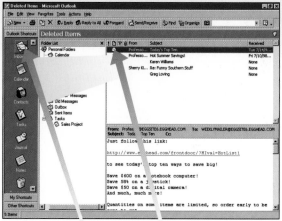

 Release   **Click & Drag**

End

How-To Hints

Automatic Delete

You can set up Outlook so it automatically deletes items from the Deleted Items folder whenever you exit the program. Open the **Tools** menu and select **Options**. Display the **Other** tab, select the **Empty the Deleted Items Folder Upon Exiting** option, and click **OK**.

Task

CHAPTER 13

How to Use Outlook's Email Features

*O*utlook's desktop management applications wouldn't be complete without messaging capabilities. Outlook is designed to be your personal message center, whether you're sending email to colleagues on a corporate intranet or users on the global Internet. Outlook can monitor multiple mail sources and email accounts. You can collect email messages from commercial services (such as America Online, CompuServe, and your local Internet service provider) or internal post offices (such as Lotus Notes or cc:Mail).

Outlook's email features include composing and sending messages, forwarding messages, and attaching files. Messages you send or receive are saved in folders, and you can easily organize email items into specific folders. You can keep all your business correspondence, for example, in a separate folder from your personal correspondence. The email features are also integrated with the other Outlook components. You can record your email messages, for instance, as Journal entries or turn a message into a contact in your Contacts database.

In this chapter, you'll learn how to work with the basic email features. ●

TASK *1*

How to Compose and Send a Message

Providing that you have the correct email address, you can use Outlook to send a message to anyone with an email account. Like the other Outlook components, the email portion features a message form you can fill out. If you know that the recipient uses Outlook, too, you can even add formatting to your message.

Before you can use Outlook's email options, however, you must have a modem and an email account, whether through a service provider, a network connection, or a commercial service. The easiest way to track and send messages is through the Inbox folder. Click the **Inbox** icon on the Outlook Bar to open the folder.

Begin

1 Open a New Message Form

From the Outlook Inbox folder, open the **Actions** menu and select **New Mail Message**, or click the **New Mail Message** button on the toolbar. This opens the Message window.

New Mail Message button

Click

2 Enter a Recipient Address

The Message window resembles a form. Fill out the form, using the **Tab** key to move from field to field. To begin, click inside the **To** text box and type in the email address of the recipient. To send the message to multiple recipients, enter a semicolon between each email address.

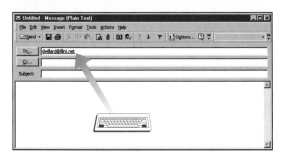

3 Carbon Copy

To carbon copy the message to someone else, enter another address in the **Cc** text box. To carbon copy multiple people, use a semicolon to separate each recipient's address from the others listed.

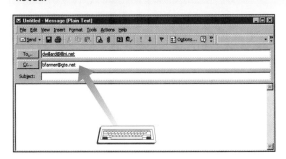

4 Enter the Subject

Click inside the **Subject** text box and enter a title or phrase to identify the content or purpose of your message.

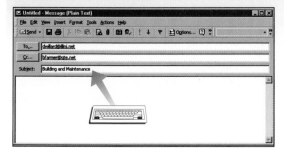

5 Type Your Message

Click inside the message box and type in your message text. Outlook automatically wraps the text for you. Use the **Delete** and **Backspace** keys to fix mistakes, just as you would in a Word document.

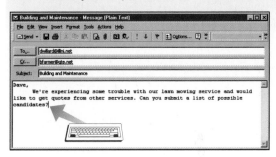

6 Send the Message

To send the message, click the **Send** button. If you're offline (not connected to the Internet or network), the message waits in the Outbox until the next time you go online to collect your mail.

Click

End

How-To Hints

Setting Up for Email

If you haven't set up Outlook to work with your Internet account, stop and do so now. Open the **Tools** menu and select **Accounts**. Click the **Add** button and select **Mail**. A wizard walks you through the necessary steps. Follow each prompt as directed.

Message Options

Use Outlook's **Options** button on the message form's Standard toolbar to assign options such as priority levels or tracking options.

View Toolbars

The message form's toolbars share one row, by default. You can choose to view both the Standard and Formatting toolbars in full; open the **Tools** menu, choose **Customize**, click the **Options** tab, and deselect the **Standard and Formatting Toolbars Share One Row** check box. Click **Close**.

Use the Address Book

In addition to typing an email address directly, you can also click the **To** button in the message form and select the recipient from your list of addresses. Learn more about this feature in the next task.

How to Add an Address to Your Personal Address Book

The Personal Address Book is one of two address sources you have in Outlook. The other address book is your Contacts list, which you can learn how to use in Chapter 12, "How to Use Outlook," Task 7, "How to Create a New Contact." Unlike the Contacts list, the Personal Address Book enables you to create Personal Distribution Lists, which are address groups that enable you to send a message to a large group of recipients without accidentally forgetting to include a name.

Begin

1 Open the Personal Address Book

From the Inbox folder, open the **Tools** menu and select **Address Book**, or click the **Address Book** button on the toolbar to open the Address Book window.

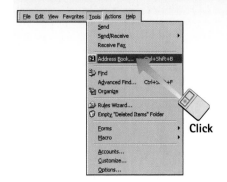

Click

2 Click New Entry

Click the **New** button on the Address Book toolbar and click **New Contact**.

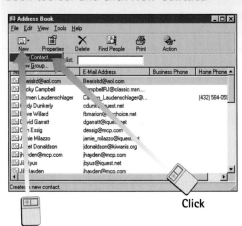

Click

Click

3 Enter a Name

From the **Personal** tab, enter the person's name, pressing **Tab** to move from field to field.

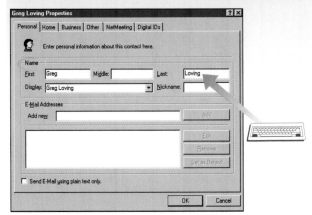

4 Fill in the Information

Enter the email address in the **Add New** text box and click **Add**.

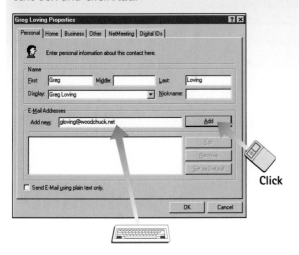

Click

5 Close the Properties Box

Use the other tabs in the Properties dialog box to enter additional information about the person. When you're finished, click **OK**.

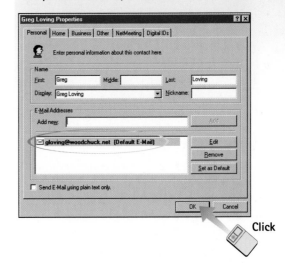

Click

6 Close the Address Book

When finished adding new entries, exit the Address Book window. Click the **Close** button or select **File, Close**.

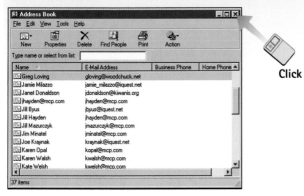

Click

End

How-To Hints

Create a Personal Distribution List

In the Address Book window, choose **File, New Group**. Type a **Name** for the list and click **Select Members**. Double-click each name you want to add, choose **OK** twice, and choose **File, Close** to exit.

Microsoft Exchange User?

If you've used Microsoft Exchange for email, all of your addresses are stored in the Exchange Personal Address Book. Outlook and Exchange share the same Personal Address Book, so all those addresses are available in Outlook, too.

Plain Text Only

If you plan on sending email to the contact and you know their email account has difficulty receiving formatted email messages, consider selecting the **Send E-Mail Using Plain Text Only** check box in the Properties dialog box.

How to Read an Incoming Message

Use the Inbox to see messages you receive in Outlook. The Inbox displays each message as a single line with a From field that tells you who sent it, a Subject field that gives you a clue as to what's in the message, and a Date field that tells you when it was received. The symbol columns at the left of the Inbox provide important information about each message, such as priority level or whether it has a file attachment.

Use the Preview pane below the list of messages to view message text. You can also open each message in its own window. To hide the Preview pane, choose **View**, **Preview Pane**. You can then use the AutoPreview feature to see the first three lines of a message in the list box before you open it. To turn AutoPreview on, choose **View**, **AutoPreview**.

Begin

1 Check for New Mail

To check for new messages from the Inbox folder, click the **Send and Receive** button on the Outlook toolbar to go online to pick up mail. Your new messages appear in your Inbox.

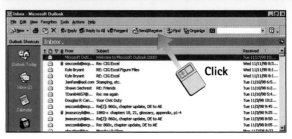

Click

2 Open a Message

To open a message in its own message window, double-click the message you want to open and read.

Double Click

3 Read a Message

The message opens for you to read. If it's a long message, use the scroll bars to scroll through the message. If you want to print the message, click the **Print** button on the message toolbar.

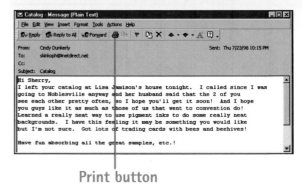

Print button

4 Read the Next Message

To continue reading new mail messages without returning to the Inbox, click the **Next Item** button on the message toolbar. To return to the previous message, click the **Previous Item** button.

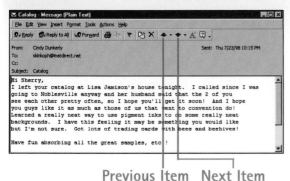

Previous Item   Next Item

5 Delete a Message

If you don't need to keep a message, click the **Delete** button in the message toolbar.

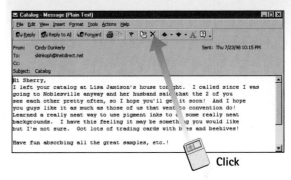

Click

6 Close a Message

When you're finished reading a message and you want to keep it, click the **Close** button in the top right corner of the message. If you want to reply to the message or forward it to someone else, see Task 4, "How to Reply to or Forward a Message." (Don't close the message; replying and forwarding close it automatically.)

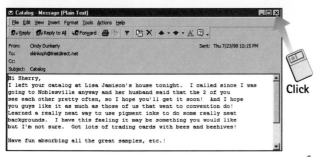

Click

End

How-To Hints

Read and Unread

You can mark messages in the Inbox as read or unread. By default, Outlook marks messages as read after you open them. If you want to remember to read the message again later, close it, right-click the message line in Inbox, and click **Mark as Unread**. The message returns to unread-mail status.

Delete Messages

If you're cleaning out your Inbox, delete old messages by selecting the message and clicking the **Delete** button on the Outlook toolbar. The messages are moved to the Deleted Items folder. To remove them completely, open the folder, select the messages (press the **Shift** key as you click each one), and click the **Delete** button.

Turn a Message into an Address Book Entry

When you receive a message, the sender's name and address are always included is the **From** line of the message form. To transfer the name and address directly into your Personal Address Book, right-click the sender name and click **Add to Contacts**.

How to Reply to or Forward a Message

You can quickly reply to or forward any message immediately after opening and reading the message. A *reply*, of course, is an answer to a message sent to you, and a *forward* is a message you have received that you send on to others. Outlook creates a reply or forward message that includes all the original text. When you reply or forward a message, the action and the date are recorded in the original message (and copies of your replies and forwards are kept in the Sent Items folder).

Begin

1 Click Reply

To reply to an open message, click the **Reply** button to open the Reply Message window. If the message you received contains names in the **Cc** box, you can send your reply to all recipients by clicking **Reply to All** instead.

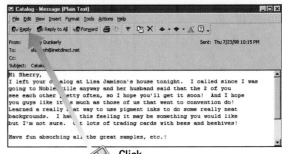

 Click

2 Enter Your Reply

The Reply Message window includes the original text with the sender's name in the **To** text box. Select and delete any text you don't need to include. Type your response to the message.

3 Send Your Reply

When your reply is ready, click the **Send** button on the message window's toolbar.

 Click

4 Or Forward the Message

To forward an open message to others, click **Forward** in the original message window. This opens a new copy of the message.

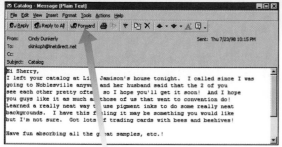

 Click

5 Enter the Forwardee's Address

Fill in the **To** box with the address of the person to whom you're forwarding the message. Add a note to the top of the message and select and delete any text you don't want to include in the forwarded message.

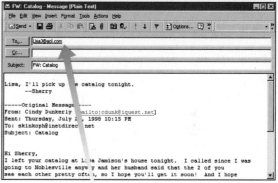

6 Send It Forward

When the message is ready to be forwarded, click the **Send** button on the message window's toolbar.

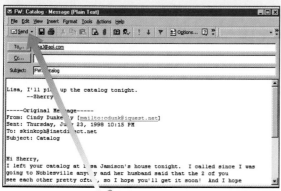

 Click

End

How-To Hints

What About Attachments?

When you forward a message, the attachments are also forwarded. If you want to delete the attachments, click each one and press **Delete**. When you reply to a message, the attachments automatically disappear. To keep the attachments in place, you must either forward the message instead of just replying to it, or you must reattach the attachment. Learn more about attaching files in the next task.

Oops!

If you send a message and then realize you left out a recipient, you don't have to retype another message. Instead, open the My Shortcuts folder group in the Outlook Bar and open the Sent Items folder. Select the message and click the **Forward** button and address the message. Click **Send** to email it.

How to Attach a File to a Message

You can attach files of any type to Outlook messages. You can send your boss the latest sales figures from your Excel worksheet, for example, or pass along your Word report to your colleague on the Internet. You can also attach other Outlook items, such as a contact or note.

When you attach a file to a message, it appears as an icon on the message. The recipient can open the file from within the message or save the file to open later. Keep in mind, however, that the recipient *must* have the appropriate program to view the file. If you send a PowerPoint presentation to a coworker, for example, he or she must have PowerPoint installed in order to view the file.

Begin

1 Click Insert File

After you compose the message, click the **Insert File** button on the message toolbar. This opens the Insert File dialog box.

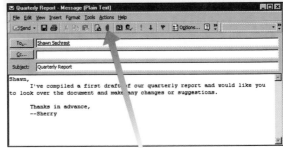

 Click

2 Locate the File

Use the **Look In** drop-down list to locate the folder or drive where the file is stored.

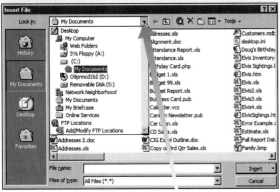

 Click

3 Select the File

From the list box, select the file you want to attach and click **OK**.

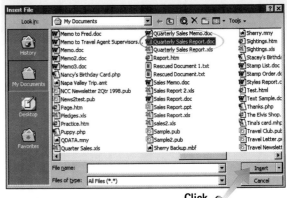

Click

4 The File Is Attached

The file appears as an icon in your message text. You can now send the message.

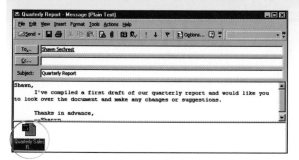

5 Attach Outlook Items

To attach an Outlook item to a message, open the **Insert** menu and select **Item**. This opens the Insert Item dialog box.

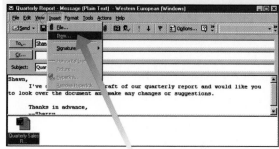

Click

6 Locate the Item

Open the folder in which the item is stored and select the item. In the **Insert As** area, choose **Attachment**. Click **OK** and send the message.

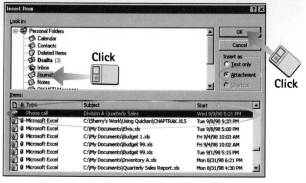

Click

Click

End

How-To Hints

Receiving Attachments

If you receive a message that contains an attached file, you will notice a paper-clip symbol in the Attachments field in your Inbox. Open the message, and you will see an icon in it that represents the attached file. To view the file, double-click the attachment icon. To save the file, right-click on the attachment icon and choose **Save As**. Select a folder to save the file in and click **Save**.

TASK 6

How to Archive an Email Message

Use Outlook's AutoArchive feature to archive old email messages as well as other Outlook items automatically. If unchecked, your Outlook Inbox will continue to grow as more and more email messages are added to the folder. To help remove clutter and restore disk space, archive items you no longer need to access.

You can archive old items manually or use AutoArchive to do it for you. When you archive items, they are removed from their current folder and copied to an archive file.

Begin

1 Open the Options Dialog Box

Open the **Tools** menu and select **Options**. This opens the Options dialog box.

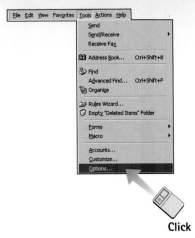

Click

2 Display the Other Tab

Next, click the **Other** tab and click the **AutoArchive** button. This opens the AutoArchive dialog box.

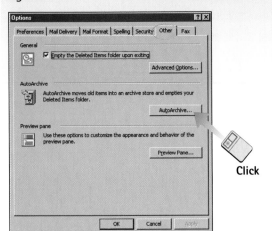

Click

3 Turn AutoArchive On

Select the **AutoArchive Every** check box. You can now specify the number of days between archives, or you can set up each folder's properties to archive differently (proceed to step 4 to learn how). Click **OK** twice to exit the dialog boxes.

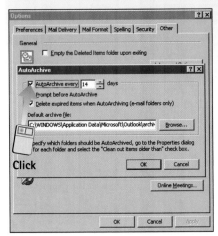

Click

4 Open the Properties Dialog Box

You can set the AutoArchive properties for each Outlook 98 folder, including the Inbox. To display the Properties dialog box for a folder, right-click the folder in the Outlook Bar and select **Properties** from the shortcut menu.

Right Click

Click

5 Set Archive Options

Click the **AutoArchive** tab and select the **Clean Out Items Older Than** check box. Designate the value in months when items will be automatically archived.

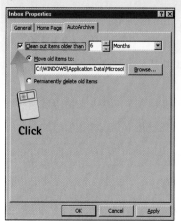

Click

6 Set an Archive Folder

Outlook stores the archived items in a default archive folder, but you can choose another folder, if needed. Click the **Browse** button and select another archive folder. Click **OK** to exit the dialog box and the AutoArchive properties are set.

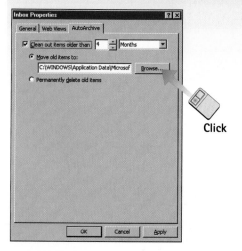

Click

How-To Hints

Manual Archive

To archive an Outlook item manually, such as an email message, open the **File** menu and choose **Archive**. To archive all the folders, choose **Archive All Folders According to Their AutoArchive Settings**. To archive one folder, choose **Archive This Folder and All Subfolders** and select the folder. Use the **Archive Items Older Than** option to set a limit to the archive items. Items dated before the date specified will be automatically archived. Click **OK** to exit.

End

Task

CHAPTER 14

How to Use Publisher

Microsoft Publisher 2000 is a desktop publishing tool designed to help you create polished, professional publications. It comes with a vast assortment of publications for every occasion; all you have to do is choose a design and fill in your own text. For example, you can produce quality newsletters, brochures, business cards, letterhead and matching envelopes, flyers and advertisements, even Web pages—and that's just the tip of the iceberg. Forget about agonizing over designs and layouts; let Publisher do all the hard work for you. It's like having a professional printing service inside your computer.

Half the battle of creating any publication is figuring out what the design and layout should be; but with Publisher's premade publications and wizards that walk you through each step of the process, the battle is already fought. The only thing that remains is entering your own text, and Publisher is even willing to help you with that. Click Publisher's Show Help button for instant assistance with any aspect of your publication. If premade publications aren't for you, you can also design your own from scratch. Use what you learn about inserting and manipulating frames in this part of the book to whip up your own standout publications. ●

How to Use the Catalog

Files you create in Publisher are called *publications*. When you first open Publisher, the Catalog box appears with a variety of publication choices, much like a directory. The three tabs you see offer you three different ways to start a publication. You can create a new publication and use a wizard to help build it, choose to create a publication based on a particular design, or build your own publication from scratch. In addition, you can also open an existing publication that you previously created and saved. This task explains the various ways to use the Catalog.

Begin

1 View the Publications by Wizard Tab

From the Catalog box, click the **Publications by Wizard** tab if it's not already showing. The Wizards list on the left shows the available publication types or categories. The Quick Publications list on the right shows various styles for the selected publication.

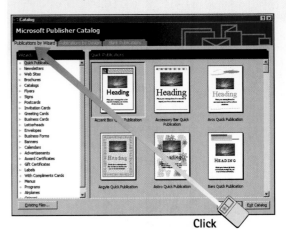

Click

2 View Subcategories

Publications with arrow icons next to them have additional subcategories to choose from. Click the publication to view the sub-list; for example, if you click **Brochures**, a list of different brochure types appears.

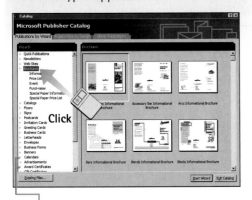

Arrow icons

3 View the Publications by Design Tab

Click the **Publications by Design** tab. This tab features publications that go together using the same design elements. For example, you can create a business card that matches your letterhead.

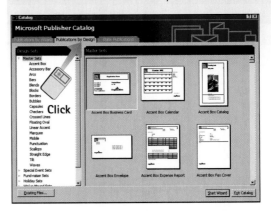

Click

4 View Design Categories

Like the **Publications by Wizard** tab, the **Publications by Design** tab lists the various types of publications on the left and examples of each on the right. Arrow icons next to the design set name indicate that more categories are available to view. For example, click the **Fund-raiser Sets** design set to reveal a list of styles.

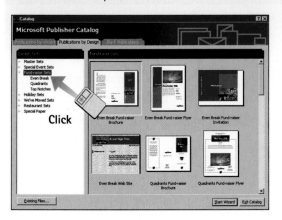

5 View the Blank Publications Tab

You can also create blank publications; click the **Blank Publications** tab. A list of publication types appears on the left, and samples appear on the right.

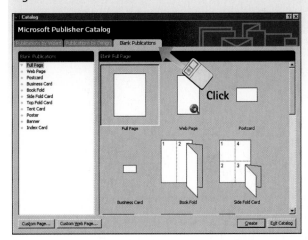

6 Open an Existing Publication

If you've already created and saved a publication, you can open it again; click the **Existing Files** button in the bottom-left corner of the **Publications by Wizard** or **Publications by Design** tab. This opens the Open Publication dialog box. Locate the folder containing the file you want to open, then double-click the filename to open the publication.

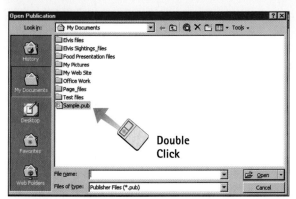

End

How-To Hints

Use the Scroll Arrows

Depending on the type of publication you select in the list box on the left, the examples you see in the right list box will vary. Some publications have only a few styles; others have dozens. Use the scroll arrows to view the available styles in the list.

Open and Close the Catalog

To exit the Catalog box without choosing a publication, click the **Exit Catalog** button. To start a new file from the Publisher program window, open the **File** menu and select **New**. This displays the Catalog box and you can choose a publication wizard to use.

One File at a Time

Unlike other Windows programs, you can open only one file at a time in Publisher. Multiple document windows do not exist in Publisher.

How to Create a Publication with a Wizard

The easiest way to create a publication is to use one of Publisher's wizards. A wizard takes you through each step in building your publication by asking questions. You supply your answers regarding the options available for the type of publication you selected. At the end of the steps, you end up with a layout ready to be filled in with text. The wizard remains open onscreen in case you want to change any of the options.

In this task, I'm creating a newsletter. Depending on the publication you choose, your steps may vary.

Begin

1 Choose a Wizard

From the Catalog dialog box, click the **Publications by Wizard** tab, then select the wizard for the type of publication you want to create from the list on the left.

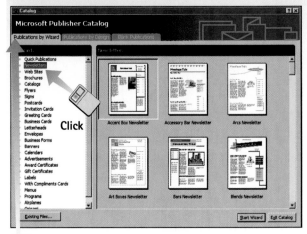

Click

2 Choose a Publication Style

From the list of available publication styles on the right, click the publication you want to make, then click the **Start Wizard** button.

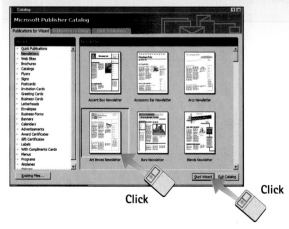

Click

Click

3 A Prompt Box Appears

Publisher displays a prompt box that tells you the wizard will fill in personal information about you for the publication you selected. Click **OK** to continue.

Click

4 The Personal Information Dialog

The Personal Information dialog box opens for you to enter information about you and your business, including address and phone number. If you plan on creating publications that use this kind of information, it's a good idea to enter it in now. Start by selecting a personal information set, such as **Primary Business**.

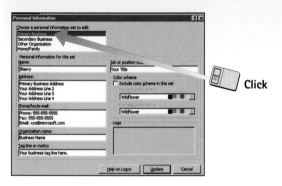

Click

5 Fill Out the Form

Click inside each text box and enter the appropriate information, if applicable. When you're finished, click the **Update** button to continue working with the wizard. If you prefer not to enter such information at this time, click the **Cancel** button.

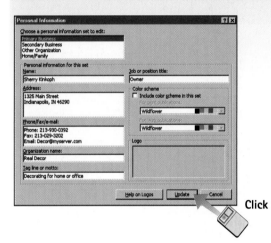

Click

6 The Wizard Starts

The first wizard box introduces you to the wizard. Wizard questions appear in the pane on the left and the area on the right displays the publication you're creating. Click the **Next** button to continue.

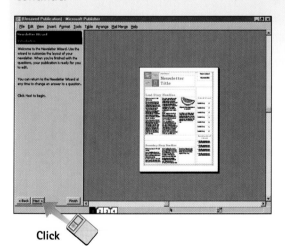

Click

7 Choose a Color Scheme

The wizard presents a series of questions, each requiring a specific type of answer. For example, you may be asked to select a color scheme to use for the publication; click the color scheme, then click the **Next** button to continue.

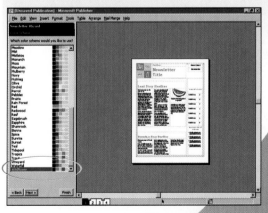

Continues

8 Choose the Number of Columns

Depending on your publication, you may be asked to select the number of columns to use. Click the option you want, such as **2 Columns**, then click **Next** to continue. Notice that the publication on the right changes to reflect the choices you make.

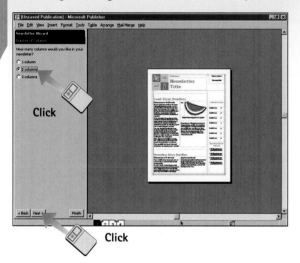

Click

Click

9 Add the Customer's Address

If building a newsletter, the next wizard question asks you if you want to include a place-holder on the publication for the customer's address. Choose **Yes** or **No**, then click **Next**.

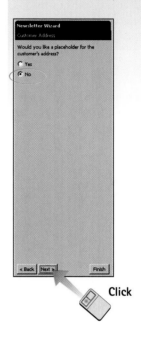

Click

10 Single- or Double-Sided Printing

Again, depending on the publication, you might be asked if you want to use single- or double-sided printing. Make your selection and click **Next**.

Click

11 Click Finish

The last wizard question shows the **Next** button grayed out. Answer the final question by selecting the appropriate option, then click the **Finish** button.

Click

12 The Publication Is Created

Publisher creates the publication and keeps the Wizard pane open. Now you're ready to start filling in the publication with your own text.

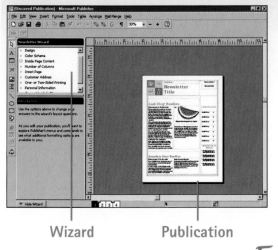

Wizard   Publication

End

How-To Hints

Must I Include Personal Information?

You don't have to fill out the Personal Information form at this time; click the **Cancel** button to bypass it (the wizard steps may vary slightly if you don't include personal information for your project). You can always enter new information or update the existing information at a later time. Click the **Personal Information** option in the **Wizard** list box, then click **Update** to reopen the form.

Go Back a Step

During the course of answering the wizard's questions, you can return to a previous question at any time by clicking the **Back** button. You can also choose to exit the wizard and jump right into the publication without answering all the wizard's questions. Just click the **Finish** button.

Change Publication Options

You can go back and change any of the answers you supplied to the wizard by clicking the option from the Wizard list box.

Save Your Work

Unlike other Office programs, Publisher prompts you to save your work every 15 minutes. A prompt box suddenly appears asking you to save the file; click **Yes** to save (give the file a name if you haven't already).

How to Navigate the Publisher Window

The Publisher 2000 program window looks a bit different from the other Office 2000 programs. For starters, you don't see the program window until you select a publication to create or open an existing publication. After you display a publication, the file (or document) you're working with appears in the middle and the Wizard pane remains open on the left side of the window. Also on the left side is a vertically displayed Objects toolbar.

Take a few moments and familiarize yourself with the onscreen elements found in the Publisher window.

Begin

1 Title Bar and Menu Bar

The top of the window features the familiar title bar (which indicates the name of the program and the current file you're working on), and the menu bar (which houses all the commands for using the program). Use the program window controls to minimize, maximize, or close the window.

Title bar   Menu bar   Program window controls

2 The Default Toolbars

Like the other Office programs, Publisher has two default toolbars with shortcuts to commonly used commands that appear directly below the menu bar: the Standard toolbar and the Formatting toolbar. The buttons on the Formatting toolbar change based on the publication item you're working with.

Standard toolbar

Formatting toolbar

3 The Objects Toolbar

Anchored on the far-left side of the program window is the Objects toolbar. It has buttons for working with objects, such as graphics or shapes, that you can add to the publication.

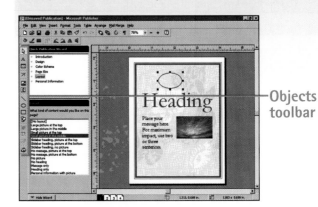

Objects toolbar

4 The Wizard Pane

The Wizard pane remains open on your screen regardless of what kind of publication you create. When open, you can easily make changes to the various elements of your publication. To free up work space, you can close the wizard by clicking the **Hide Wizard** button.

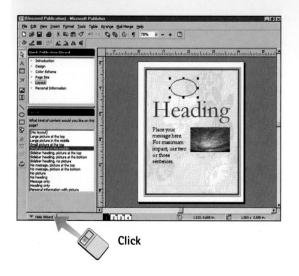

Click

5 Redisplay the Wizard

To open the wizard again at any time, click the **Show Wizard** button.

Click

6 Move Around the Page

Use the vertical and horizontal scrollbars to move around the publication page. Click the scroll arrows or drag the scroll box. To move to another page, click the page number icon at the bottom of the window.

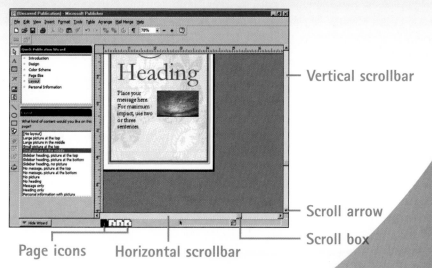

Vertical scrollbar

Scroll arrow

Scroll box

Page icons   Horizontal scrollbar

End

How to Zoom In and Out

By default, Publisher opens your publication in a zoomed-out view so that you can keep an eye on the overall picture. However, it's difficult to view headings and text at this zoom level, particularly when you start typing in text. You can quickly zoom in and out using the F9 key on the keyboard.

Begin

1 Click Inside a Text Box

When you click a text box that has body text and begin entering your own words, you're typing blind because you can't see what you're typing.

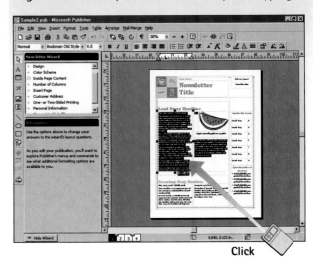

Click

2 Press F9

Press **F9** on the keyboard to zoom in up close and personal. Now you can see what you started typing in step 1.

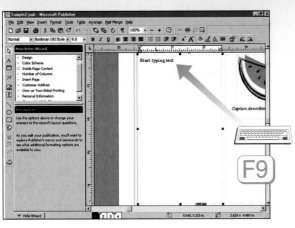

3 Scroll Over

Use the scrollbars and scroll arrows to move to the appropriate position on the page.

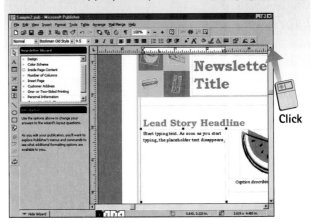

Click

4 Zoom Out

When you finish typing or working with the publication item you zoomed in to see, press **F9** again.

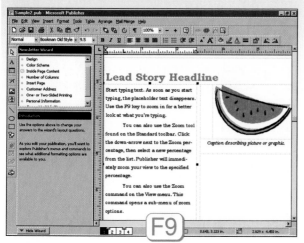

5 View the Publication

This zooms you back to see the overall effect.

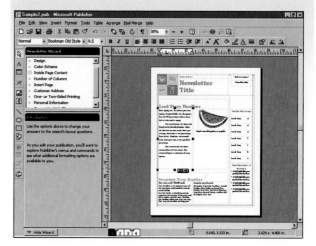

End

How-To Hints

Other Zoom Tools

If you prefer a tailor-made zoom, open the **View** menu, select **Zoom**, and choose a zoom percentage to use from the submenu that appears. You can also use the **Zoom** drop-down list on the Standard toolbar to select a zoom percentage. For a quick zoom, you can also click the plus (Zoom In) or minus (Zoom Out) button next to the Zoom control on the toolbar.

A Word About Menus

Publisher's menus can be personalized to show only the commands you use the most, just like the other Office programs. To turn this feature on, open the **Tools** menu and choose **Options**. Click the **General** tab and click the **Menus Show Recently Used Commands First**. Click **OK** to exit the dialog box and apply the feature.

How to Enter and Edit Text

Your publication layout emerges from the wizard steps with headlines and body copy already inserted. This is placeholder text. You must enter your own text to begin filling in your publication. All the text is enclosed in text boxes called *frames*. You must select each text frame to enter or edit text.

Begin

1 Click a Frame

Click anywhere in a text frame to highlight the placeholder text, whether it's a single line of text or several columns' worth of text.

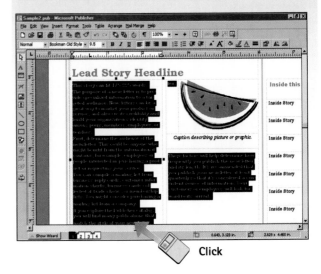

Click

2 Enter Your Text

Enter the text you want for this text frame. As soon as you enter the first character, the highlighted text disappears.

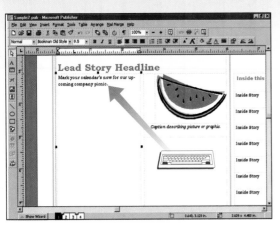

3 Edit Your Text

To correct any mistakes as you type, use the **Backspace** key. To correct existing text, click inside the text and use the **Delete** or **Backspace** key to make your corrections.

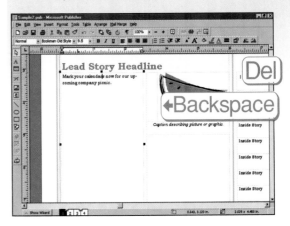

4 Select Text

You can select text in Publisher just like you do in Word. Click in front of the word or sentence you want to select, then drag to highlight the text.

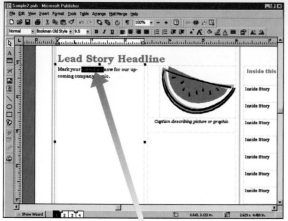

Click & Drag

5 Deselect the Frame

Click anywhere outside the publication page to deselect the text frame you're working with.

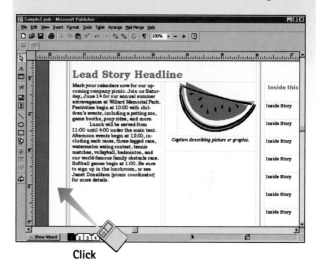

Click

6 Use the Undo Command

If you make corrections to your text and then change your mind, or type in text and decide you don't want it, you can quickly undo your actions with the Undo command. Click the **Undo** button on the Standard toolbar.

Click

End

How-To Hints

Use F9 to Zoom

Don't forget that you can quickly zoom in to see a text box by pressing F9 on the keyboard.

Cut, Copy, and Paste

You can use the Cut, Copy, and Paste commands in Publisher the same way you do in the other Office programs. You'll find buttons representing these commands on the Standard toolbar as well as on the Edit menu. To learn more about these commands, turn to Task 1, "How to Cut, Copy, and Paste Data Among Programs," in Chapter 17, "How to Integrate Office Applications."

How to Add a New Text Frame

You can't just start typing on the page to begin entering text in Publisher. Every element in your publication, including text, must have a *frame*. A frame is a box designated for text or graphics. All the wizard publications have premade text frames ready to go, but you might need to add your own sometimes as well, particularly if you create a blank publication.

Begin

1 Select the Text Frame Tool

Click the **Text Frame Tool** on the Objects toolbar. As soon as you select the tool, the mouse pointer takes the shape of a crosshair icon.

Click

2 Click in Place

Position the crosshair icon in the place where you want the upper-left corner of the text frame to sit.

Click

3 Drag the Frame

Then hold down the left mouse button and drag down and right until the frame is the size you want it.

Click & Drag

4 Release

Release the mouse button and the frame is set. Notice that the frame is selected and the cursor flashes inside the frame ready for you to start entering text.

Release

5 Enter Text

To enter text into the new text frame, just start typing (if the frame isn't selected, click it).

6 Format the Text

After entering the text, you can format it; select the text and then use the buttons on the Formatting toolbar to change the text's font, size, position, and so on.

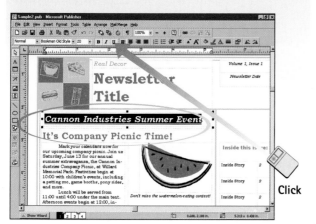

Click

End

How-To Hints

Delete Frames

If you don't like the text frame you created and want to start over, right-click over the frame and select **Delete Object** from the shortcut menu.

Use the Objects Toolbar

The Objects toolbar works like any other toolbar; it's just vertical instead of horizontal. To learn what each button is, hover your mouse pointer over the button and read the ScreenTip.

How to Move and Resize Text Frames

You can easily move and resize your text frames as needed using your mouse. This is true of picture frames (frames that hold graphics), too. When you select a frame, it's surrounded by tiny black boxes called *selection handles*. You can drag any of the handles to resize the frame. When you move a frame, you're literally moving it from one location in your publication to another.

Begin

1 Select a Frame

Click anywhere in the text frame to select it. A border with selection handles appears around the frame.

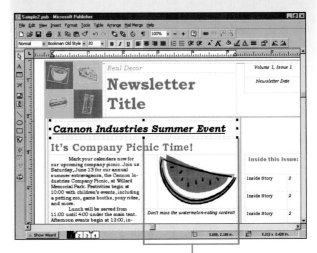

Selection handles

2 Resize a Frame

To change the size of the frame, move your pointer to any sizing handle; the pointer changes to a Resize pointer.

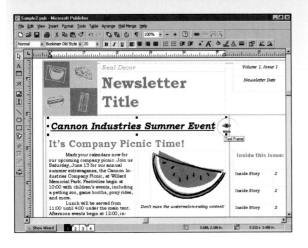

3 Drag to Resize

Drag the sizing handle in the appropriate direction. An outline of the new size appears as you drag.

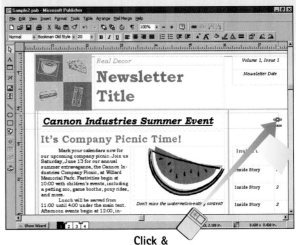

Click & Drag

4 Release the Button

Release the mouse button and the frame is resized.

Release

5 Move a Frame

To move the frame, position your pointer on a border between sizing handles until the pointer turns into a moving van.

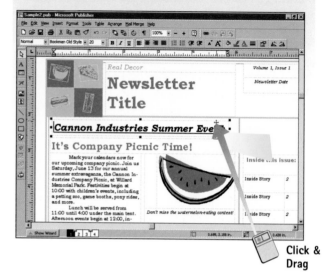

Click & Drag

6 Drag to Move

Drag the frame to a new location. Release the mouse button and the frame is moved.

Release

End

How-To Hints

Keep Proportions

When you resize a text frame, you can keep the proportions intact by holding down **Shift** as you drag a corner handle. Release the mouse button before you let go of the **Shift** key.

Resize a Tip

Use a corner handle if you want to change two sides of the frame at once while you drag.

How to Drag

To drag a frame, either resizing or moving, hold down the left mouse button, move the mouse until the frame reaches the desired size or location, and then release the mouse button.

How to Handle Overflow Text

When you have more text than can fit in a frame, it's called overflow text. It's still there; you just can't see it. Publisher holds the extra text in an overflow area and lets you know it's there with the Text in Overflow indicator button at the bottom of the text frame. Use the Connecting tools to connect frames and place the overflow text.

Begin

1 Recognize Overflow Text

When you have more text than can fit in the frame, Publisher displays the frame's connect button so that it displays three dots.

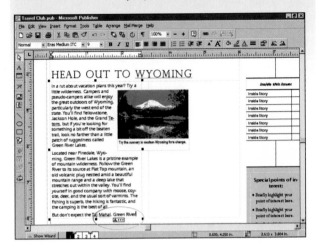

2 Use the Connect Frames Toolbar

As soon as you encounter overflow text, the Text Frame Connecting toolbar appears next to the Standard toolbar.

Text Frame Connecting toolbar

3 Use the Connect Text Frames Button

Click the **Connect Text Frames** button on the Text Frame Connecting toolbar.

Click

4 The Pitcher Icon

As soon as you click the toolbar button, your pointer turns into a pitcher icon that looks like it's holding the extra text. Move to (or create) another text frame, either on the same page or another page and position your pointer in the text frame to see the pitcher.

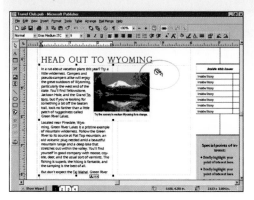

5 Pour the Text

Click to pour the overflow text into the frame. The connect button indicates that this is continuation text.

Go to Previous Frame button

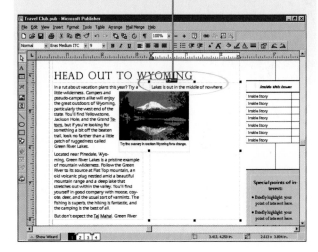

6 Move Between Frames

To return to the previous text frame, click the **Go to Previous Frame** button at the top of the frame. To go back to the overflow text frame again, click the **Go to Next Frame** button at the bottom of the current text frame.

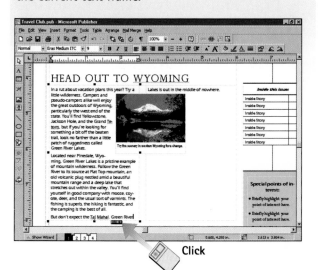

Click

End

How-To Hints

Just a Little Too Much?

If your overflow text is only a word or sentence, try reducing the font size or resizing the frame.

Unconnect Frames

To unconnect frames, select the first frame, then click the **Disconnect Text Frames** button on the Text Frame Connecting toolbar.

How to Add Pictures to Your Publication

Publisher provides thousands of clip art pictures, all thoughtfully arranged by category. You'll certainly find exactly the artwork you need to make a point, draw attention, or illustrate your text. You can quickly insert clip art into any picture frame in your publication.

Begin

1 Use the Clip Gallery Tool

Click the **Clip Gallery Tool** button on the Objects toolbar.

Click

2 Position the Pointer

Position your pointer where you want the upper-left corner of the frame.

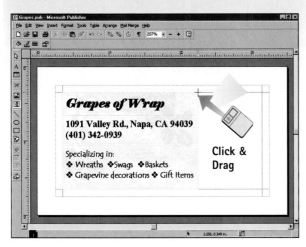

Click & Drag

3 Drag and Release

Drag down and right to create the frame and release the mouse button when the frame is just the right size.

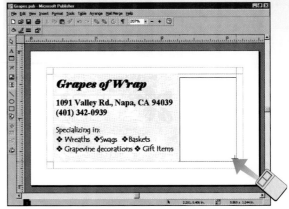

Release

4 Choose a Category

The Insert Clip Art dialog box appears. Scroll through the category list and select a category. Use the **Back** and **Forward** buttons to move back and forth between categories you've viewed.

5 Select a Picture

When you find a piece of clip art you want to use, click it and then click the **Insert Clip** button. Click the **Close** button to exit the dialog box.

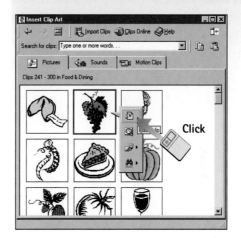

6 The Picture Is Inserted

The clip art now appears on your publication in the picture frame you drew. You can resize and move the frame as needed (see Task 7, "How to Move and Resize Text Frames").

clip art

End

How-To Hints

Fill in Existing Picture Frames

If you chose a publication design that has preset picture frames, you can easily change the default picture. Double-click the picture frame to open the Insert Clip Art dialog box and choose another graphic or photo.

Use the CD

Be sure your Office CD-ROM is in the CD-ROM drive, because the majority of clip art files aren't transferred to your hard drive during installation. Instead, they remain on the CD-ROM.

Check It Out

Use the other tabs in the Insert Clip Art dialog box to insert sound clips or even video clips. Of course, these media types aren't useful with printed publications, but if you send the publication electronically via email, others can hear or view the sound or video files.

How to Wrap Text Around a Frame

To illustrate an article in your publication, you might place a picture frame inside a text frame. When you move a picture frame into a text frame, the text wraps around the frame itself, not the actual artwork. If it's done properly, this can look very professional. If you prefer, you can also wrap text around the artwork itself. Use Publisher's wrap controls on the Formatting toolbar to create the effect you want.

Begin

1 Select the Frame

Select the picture frame you want to wrap text around (click the frame to select it).

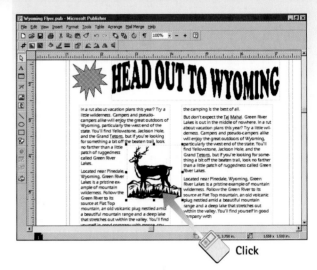

Click

2 Wrap Text to Picture

Click the **Wrap Text to Picture** button on the Formatting toolbar to wrap text around the image.

Click

3 The Text Wraps

The text wraps around the artwork. Depending on the artwork, you may have some text cut off from the rest. You can easily fix this.

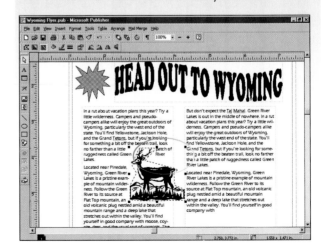

4 Wrap Irregular Text

Click the **Edit Irregular Wrap** button.

Click

5 Drag a Handle

The art is surrounded by many handles. Drag a handle to move the wrap frame outward to push back any text in the wrong spot, or drag a handle inward to create a better wrap. As you drag, the pointer becomes an Adjust icon.

In a rut about vacation plans this year? Try a little wilderness. Campers and pseudo-campers alike will enjoy the great outdoors of Wyoming, particularly the west end of the state. You'll find Yellowstone, Jackson Hole, and the Grand Tetons, but if you're looking for something a bit off the beaten trail, look no farther than a little ruggedness called Green River Lakes.

Located near Pinedale, Wyoming, Green River Lakes is a pristine example of mountain wilderness. Follow the Green River to its source at Flat Top mountain, an old volcanic plug nestled amid a beautiful mountain range and a deep lake that stretches out within the valley. You'll find yourself in good company with moose, coyote, deer, and the usual sort of varmints. The

But don't expect the Taj Mahal. Green River Lakes is out in the middle of nowhere. In a rut about vacation plans this year? Try a little wilderness. Campers and pseudo-campers alike will enjoy the great outdoors of Wyoming, particularly the west end of the state. You'll find Yellowstone, Jackson Hole, and the Grand Tetons, but if you're looking for something off the beaten trail, look no farther the patch of ruggedness called Green

Located near Pinedale, Wyoming, Green River Lakes is a pristine example of mountain wilderness. Follow the Green River to its source at Flat Top mountain, an old volcanic plug nestled amid a beautiful mountain range and a deep lake that stretches out within the valley. You'll find yourself in good company with

Click & Drag

6 Release the Handle

When you release the handle, the irregular text readjusts around the artwork. Move as many handles as needed to create the effect you want.

In a rut about vacation plans this year? Try a little wilderness. Campers and pseudo-campers alike will enjoy the great outdoors of Wyoming, particularly the west end of the state. You'll find Yellowstone, Jackson Hole, and the Grand Tetons, but if you're looking for something a bit off the beaten trail, look no farther than a little patch of ruggedness called Green River Lakes.

Located near Pinedale, Wyoming, Green River Lakes is a pristine example of mountain wilderness. Follow the Green River to its source at Flat Top mountain, an old volcanic plug nestled amid a beautiful mountain range and a deep lake that stretches out within the valley. You'll find yourself in good company with moose, coyote, deer, and the usual sort of varmints. The

But don't expect the Taj Mahal. Green River Lakes is out in the middle of nowhere. In a rut about vacation plans this year? Try a little wilderness. Campers and pseudo-campers alike will enjoy the great outdoors of Wyoming, particularly the west end of the state. You'll find Yellowstone, Jackson Hole, and the Grand Tetons, but if you're looking for something a bit off the beaten trail, look no farther than a little patch of ruggedness called Green River Lakes.

Located near Pinedale, Wyoming, Green River Lakes is a pristine example of mountain wilderness. Follow the Green River to its source at Flat Top mountain, an old volcanic plug nestled amid a beautiful mountain range and a deep lake that stretches out within the valley. You'll find yourself in good company with

Release

End

How-To Hints

The Ever-Changing Formatting Toolbar

Remember, the buttons on the Formatting toolbar change according to the type of frame you select. If you select a text frame, you see buttons for formatting text. If you select a picture frame, you see buttons for working with the graphic or clip art image.

Oops!

If you make a mistake while using any of the text wrap tools, click the **Undo** button to undo your last action and try again.

Transparent Text Frames

When placing text frames on top of picture frames or graphic objects, sometimes you want the text frame to be transparent so that you can see what's behind it. To make the text frame transparent, press **Ctrl+T**.

How to Add a Border

When you hang pictures on the wall, the frame you choose can enhance the picture, the wall, and the room. The same thing is true of the elements in your publication. Frame your text and graphic elements to make your publication more interesting and professional. Use the Border tool to add borders that set off headlines and important text, or make graphics more distinguished.

Begin

1 Select a Frame

Select the frame to which you want to add a border.

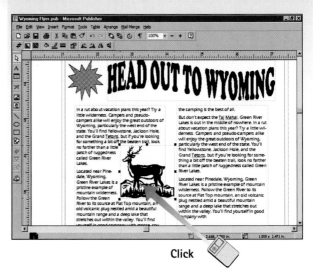

Click

2 Use the Line/Border Button

Click the **Line/Border Style** button on the Formatting toolbar, then click **More Styles**.

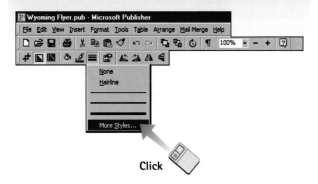

Click

3 Choose a Line Thickness

In the **Line Border** tab of the Border Style dialog box, choose a line thickness from the available styles. The preview area on the right shows what the line thickness will look like.

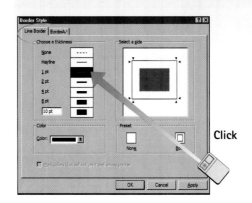

Click

4 Choose a Color

If you like, you can also change the color of the border. Click the **Color** drop-down arrow and choose another color from the palette.

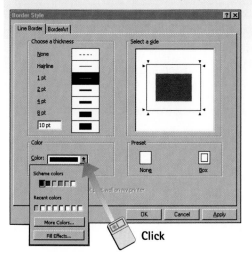

Click

5 Or Use Border Art

If you're looking for a more stylistic border, click the **BorderArt** tab and scroll through the list of premade border art. To select a border, click it; the preview area shows a sample of the border. Use the other tab options to specify size and color.

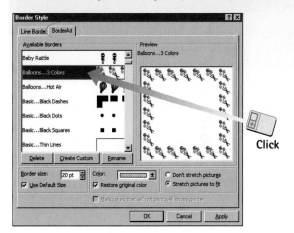

Click

6 Apply the Border

Click **OK** to exit the dialog box and apply the border you selected in the Line Border or BorderArt tab.

End

How-To Hints

Quick Border

To create a line border quickly, click the **Line/Border Style** button on the Formatting toolbar and select one of the borders on the Border palette.

How to Work with the Background Page

Every publication has a background, which sits underneath the pages you create. If you place elements on the background, you can see those elements on every page in your publication. This makes the background an ideal container for page numbers, or a corporate logo. One of the most common things to place on a background is text.

Begin

1 Move to the Background

To move to the background of your publication, press **Ctrl+M**.

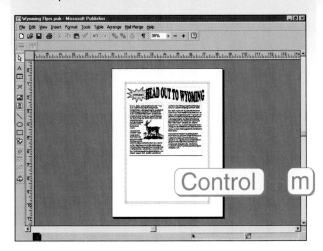

2 Background Mode

The background displays in the Publisher window (it looks like a blank page).

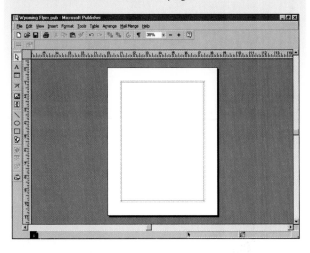

3 Add a Text Frame

Create a text frame on the background to hold your text and enter the text (press **F9** to zoom in, if necessary) you want to see on every page of your publication. (Flip back to Task 6, "How to Add a New Text Frame," earlier in this chapter to learn how to add frames.)

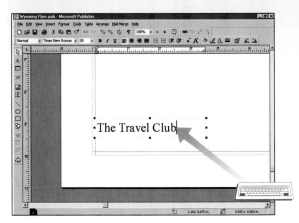

4 Format the Text

Apply any formatting to the text using the tools available on the Formatting toolbar.

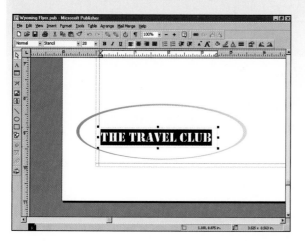

5 Add a Picture Frame

You can also add picture frames to your background page. Use the **Picture Frame Tool** or **Clip Gallery Tool** on the Objects toolbar to insert artwork or a graphic onto the background.

Clip Gallery tool   Picture Frame tool

6 Return to the Foreground

To return to the foreground again, press Ctrl+M.

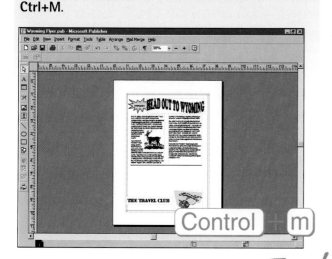

Control +m

End

How-To Hints

Background Tip

Remember that your foreground pages are usually full of text and graphics. Keep your background text short and near the top or bottom edge of the page or it won't be seen clearly.

Insert Page Numbers

While in background mode, draw a text frame where you want the page number to appear. Then open the **Insert** menu and choose **Page Numbers**. Publisher automatically inserts a page number code in the text box. The code looks like a pound sign on the background; it becomes the page number on the foreground.

How to Use the Design Gallery

Need a calendar for the company newsletter? How about a coupon for a customer mailing you're preparing? Maybe you just need a decorative element to draw attention to a headline or make a bland page look lively. You'll find plenty of special elements to add to your publications in Publisher's Design Gallery.

Begin

1 Click Design Gallery Object

Click the **Design Gallery Object** button on the Objects toolbar.

Click

2 Choose a Design Category

The Microsoft Publisher Design Gallery dialog box opens. Use the **Objects by Category** tab to select a design category. In this example, the **Mastheads** category is selected and the list on the right displays a variety of mastheads you can add to your publication.

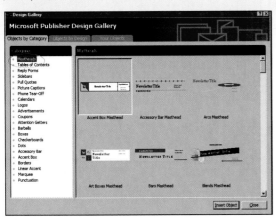

3 Or Choose an Object

Click the **Objects by Design** tab to view available design sets and choose a specific design object to use in your publication. For example, clicking the **Blocks** design set reveals several different uses of the block design, including a calendar.

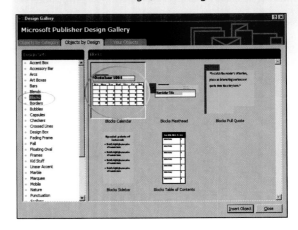

4 Choose a Design

When you locate an item you want to insert into your publication, select it and click the **Insert Object** button.

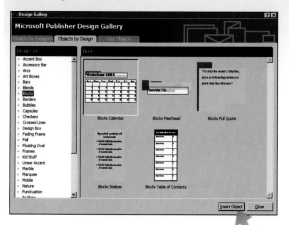

Click

5 The Object Appears

The object appears in your publication.

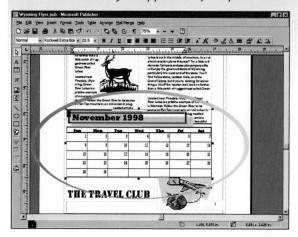

6 Resize or Edit

You can now resize and place the object as needed and make any edits to text just as with any other frame. (Click the **Wizard** button at the bottom of the object to change any options.)

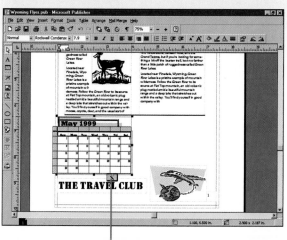

Wizard button

End

Task

15

How to Use the
Office Internet Tools

Microsoft specifically designed the Office suite of programs to utilize the Internet and the World Wide Web. You will find plenty of Web browsing features in each Office program. You can access information from the Web without leaving an application. You can also create Web documents by using Web publishing features found in each Office program. Just about every file you create can be converted to an HTML file to publish on the Web or a corporate intranet.

In addition to Web-related features, you can also use Microsoft's Web browser, Internet Explorer, to view and access Web content. Internet Explorer 5 comes with Office 2000, or you can download the latest copy of the program from Microsoft's Web site.

In this chapter, you learn about Internet Explorer's basic features, and how to use the Office 2000 program's Web tools. ●

TASK *1*

How to Navigate the Web with Internet Explorer

Internet Explorer, or IE for short, is a Web browser you can use to view Web pages on the Internet. Not only can you view Web content, but you also can search for information, download files, view multimedia clips, and more. This book can't cover all the Internet Explorer features, but you will learn the basics needed to begin using the browser.

Begin

1 Log On

Internet Explorer starts in the same way as any other Office program. If the desktop has a shortcut icon, you can double-click it to open Internet Explorer. Before the program opens, however, you are prompted to log on to your Internet connection (unless you have already done that).

Click

2 View the Onscreen Elements

When you open Internet Explorer, the browser window displays the default start page (the home page your browser is configured to load whenever you open the program). The program window consists of the familiar title bar, menu bar, and toolbar, along with scrollbars and a status bar. These features work in the same way they do in the other Office programs.

Title bar   Menu bar   Toolbar

Status bar   Scrollbar

3 View Other Toolbars

Internet Explorer has two more toolbars: The Address toolbar enables you to enter Web page addresses, and the Links toolbar enables you to quickly access popular Web sites with a click of a button. Depending on your monitor's display mode, the Address and Links toolbars might share space in your program window. To make it easy to see the toolbars, I've displayed them as two separate bars in this figure. Your screen will differ.

Address toolbar   Links toolbar

4 Visit a Web Page

Each page on the Web has a specific address, called a URL (Uniform Resource Locator). You can visit specific pages on the Web by typing their URLs. To practice, click inside the **Address** text box and type **www.mcp.com** and press **Enter**. You don't need to enter the prefix **http://**—Internet Explorer inserts this prefix for you.

Address text box

5 The Page Loads

Internet Explorer displays the Web page. The time it takes to display a page varies based on your modem speed, how busy Internet traffic is, or how many graphics are on the page. When the page appears, you can read its information. Depending on the size of the page, you can use the scrollbars to view different parts of the page.

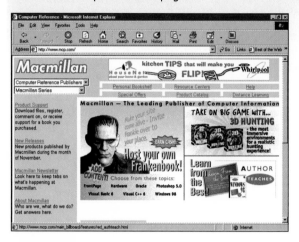

6 Use Links

Another way to view Web pages is to follow links. Links take you to other pages, whether on the same Web site or on a completely different site, the same as entering URLs. Links commonly are underlined words on a Web page, but you will also find graphic images, buttons, or icons used as links on Web pages.

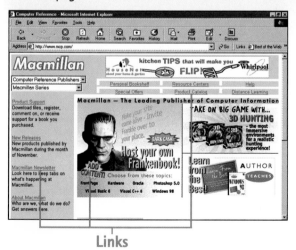

Links

7 Follow a Link

When the mouse pointer hovers over a link, the pointer takes the shape of a hand. Click a link to display its Web page. When you click a link, the corresponding Web page loads. Some pages take longer than others do to display; the status bar keeps you posted on the progress, both in contacting the Web site and when the page is fully loaded.

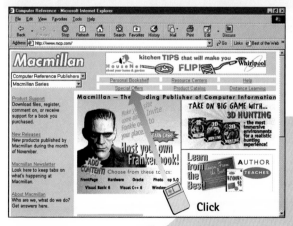

Click

Continues

8 Use the Navigation Buttons

After you begin viewing pages, you might want to return to a previous page. Use the **Back** button on the Internet Explorer toolbar to return to the previous page. Use the **Forward** button to move to the page you were viewing before using the Back button.

Click

9 Use the Stop Button

If a page is taking a particularly long time to display, you can cease and desist by clicking the **Stop** button on the toolbar.

Click

10 Use the Refresh Button

If for some reason a page doesn't display properly—perhaps it's missing some text or graphics—try clicking the **Refresh** button to reload the page.

Click

11 Return to Your Home Page

To return to your start page—the page that opens automatically whenever you open Internet Explorer—click the **Home** button.

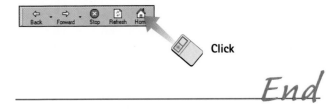

Click

End

How-To Hints

Take a Tour

The first page Internet Explorer displays when you open the program is a welcome page, shown in step 2. You can launch a tour of the program from this page by clicking the **Click Here to Take the Tour Now** link. If you don't want to take a tour, click the other link to open the Internet Explorer home page.

Define a New Home Page

When you first install Internet Explorer, it uses a Microsoft Web page as the default home page. However, you can define another page as your home page. Open the **View** menu, select **Internet Options**, and then click the **General** tab. Under the **Home Page** options, click inside the **Address** text box and enter the URL of the Web page you want to use as your home page. Click **OK**. The next time you start Internet Explorer, the new home page appears automatically.

How to Mark Your Favorite Web Pages

As you come across Web pages you like and want to revisit, take time to mark them as favorites. When you save a Web page as a favorite, you can quickly access it again later. By default, favorite Web pages are stored in the Favorites folder, but you can easily create new folders and keep your favorite Web sites organized.

Begin

1 Add a Favorite

When you find a Web page you want to mark, open the **Favorites** menu and choose **Add to Favorites**. This opens the Add Favorite dialog box.

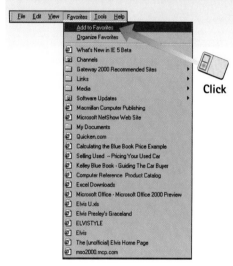

Click

2 Give the Page a Name

Click inside the **Name** text box and give the page a name you will recognize. Internet Explorer attempts to assign a default name, but you can enter another name if you like.

3 Exit the Dialog Box

Click **OK** and the page is added to your Favorites list.

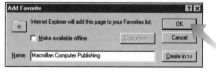

Click

4 Open the Favorites List

To display the Favorites list, click the **Favorites** button on the Internet Explorer toolbar. This opens the Favorites list as a separate pane in the Internet Explorer window.

Click

5 Select a Favorite

To revisit a favorite during another session, click the page name in the **Favorites** pane. If you have organized the pages into other folders, open the folder with a double-click and then select the name.

Favorites pane

Click

6 Close the List

To close the Favorites list pane, click the **Favorites** button again on the toolbar.

Click

End

How-To Hints

Organizing Favorites

Internet Explorer saves the pages you mark as favorites in folders. To create new folders or organize the URLs into different folders, open the **Favorites** menu and select **Organize Favorites**. This opens the Organize Favorites dialog box, where you can create new folders, move URLs between folders, or rename folders.

Passing On Your Favorites

You can pass along the name and address of your favorite Web page to a friend or colleague. Right-click a favorite page listed in the **Favorites** pane and choose **Send To, Mail Recipient**. Now you can send an email address with the Web page address embedded in the message. (To learn more about email, turn to Chapter 13, "How to Use Outlook's Email Features.")

How to Perform a Web Search

One of the most frustrating aspects of using the Web is searching for information. When following links won't take you to the information you're looking for, you need to use a search engine to help narrow your search. Search engines are specially designed to frequently catalog and index World Wide Web pages. When you enter a key word or phrase, the search engine looks through its catalog and returns a list of related matches.

Internet Explorer's Search button accesses several of the most popular search engines available. The default search engine varies each time you use Internet Explorer, but you can perform comparable searches by using each search engine. The following examples were created with Infoseek. Other search engines work in a similar fashion and provide many of the same features; however, because each search engine has its own design, the specifics might vary somewhat.

Begin

1 Click the Search Button

From the Internet Explorer window, click the **Search** button on the toolbar.

Click

2 The Search Pane Opens

The Search pane opens and displays a default search engine. In this figure, the MSN search tool is displayed.

Search pane

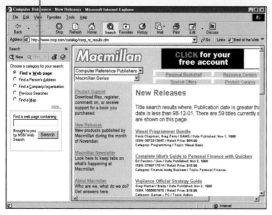

3 Enter Search Text

Enter a word or phrase in the text box, and click **Search** to start the engine hunting (the button's name might be different in other search engines). In this figure, I'm searching for the word *roses*. (A prompt box might appear, warning you that you're about to send information over the Internet; click **Yes** to continue.)

Click

4 View the Results

The result of the search is a list of links to Web pages that contain your word or phrase; the list might be very long, or it might have no links at all. Scroll through the list to see various links you can follow. A search of the word *roses* produced more than 88,660 sites.

5 Click a Link in the Results List

In the results list, click a likely hyperlink to jump to that Web page. The Web page pane displays the page. (To maximize your screen space, click the **Search** button on the Internet Explorer toolbar to close the Search pane.)

Click

6 Get Search Help

If you have a problem finding what you want, get help with your search from the search engine. Most engines provide a **Search Tips** or **Help** link on their home page that can help you with your choice of search words or phrases. In the case of MSN, click the **Use Advanced Search** link to open detailed fields you can fill in to help narrow your search.

End

How-To Hints

Use Another Search Engine

To select a search engine other than the default, click the **Next** button at the top of the Search pane and choose another search engine from the drop-down list.

Search Tips

To search for two or more words that appear together, enclose the words in quotation marks. To search for occurrences of both words in a document, but not necessarily together, use a plus sign in front of each word.

Try, Try Again

If the search results aren't narrow enough for you or don't produce the type of links you were hoping for, try again. Be sure to apply search tips or other search options offered by the search engine's Web site to help you find the results you want.

How to Download Files from the Web

Web pages aren't the only thing you will find on the Web. You will also encounter all kinds of files: text files, graphic files, program files, multimedia files, and more. After you find a file you want (perhaps an interesting shareware program or clip art for your newsletter), the next step is to transfer a copy of the file from the Internet site where it's stored to your computer. This is called *downloading*. (File transfer is called *downloading* when you receive the file, and *uploading* when you send the file.)

Before you download, be sure you have enough room on your hard drive to accommodate the file, and keep in mind that downloads of large files can keep your computer occupied for a considerable length of time (large files—5MB and larger—can take hours). Even with a fast modem, the time required to download depends on the speed of the modem's connection and how many other people are downloading from the same Web site at the same time.

Begin

1 Find a File

When you come across a file you want to download, select the file or follow its download link.

Click

2 Start the Download

Click the file's download link to start the download process. If the file must be purchased, follow the directions given by the Web site.

Click

3 Save the File on Your Hard Drive

In the File Download dialog box, click the **Save This File to Disk** option, and then click **OK**.

Click

4 Choose a Hard Drive Location

When downloading is ready to begin, the Save As dialog box appears. Navigate to the folder in which you want to save the file, just as you would with any document, and then click **Save**.

Click

5 Wait for the Download

As the download begins, a dialog box appears that gives you as many details as Windows can find out about the file size, the time remaining, and so forth. If you decide you can't spend six hours waiting for the download, click **Cancel** to stop the download, and try it again later.

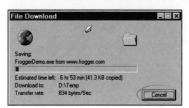

End

How-To Hints

Virus Alert

Be aware that any file you obtain from the Internet can contain a computer virus. To keep your computer protected against viruses, consider purchasing an antivirus program. Programs such as McAfee VirusScan and Norton Anti-Virus can check for viruses while you are downloading the file, to ensure that a tainted file doesn't get into your hard drive.

Plan Your Download Times

If you have to download large files, try to do it during a time when most other users won't be using the Internet. For example, if you live in the United States on the East Coast, download early in the morning before the rest of the country has had a chance to wake up; if you're on the West Coast, download late at night when everyone else is asleep.

Use Zipped Files

Some of the larger files you download from the Internet are compacted into a zip file format, which simply means the files are compressed to take up less storage space. When you download such a file onto your computer, you'll need to "unpack" it to return it to its full size again. Some compressed files unpack themselves; others might require a special program, like WinZip, to unpack the files. (You can find a copy of WinZip at **www.tucows.com**.)

How to Open a Web Document from an Office Program

If an Office file has a link or URL, you can open the corresponding Web page without leaving your Office program window or opening your Web browser. Microsoft's programmers have designed each Office program to access the Web on its own. Using the Web toolbar, you can navigate pages, perform a search, and follow links. You can type the URLs for pages you want to view, or follow links from page to page.

Begin

1 Follow a Link

If you're currently viewing a document that has a link you want to follow, click the link.

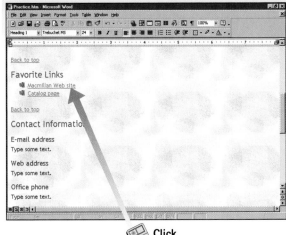

Click

2 Log On

If you're not logged on to your Internet connection, a Dial-up Connection dialog box appears. Click **Connect**.

 Click

3 Document Is Displayed

After you have established your connection, your Office program window displays the Web page.

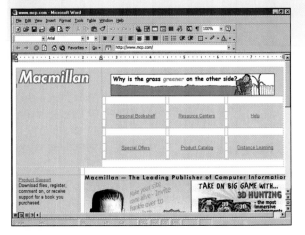

4 Display the Web Toolbar

If the Web toolbar isn't displayed, right-click a toolbar area and select **Web** (or open the **View** menu and choose **Toolbars**, **Web**).

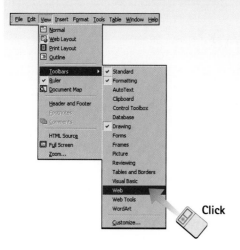

Click

5 Navigate Pages

You can use the Web toolbar to navigate the Web from within the program window. Use the **Back** and **Forward** buttons to view pages you have loaded. You can enter new URLs or click links to see other pages.

Forward

Back

End

How-To Hints

Save Pages

You can save Web pages by using the Save As dialog box. Open the **File** menu and select **Save As**. You can assign the page a name and choose to save it as an HTML document or another file type.

How to Convert Office Files to HTML

You can easily save any Office file as an HTML document to be posted on the Web. If you have a Word document you want to post on the Internet or add to your Web site, for example, save the file in HTML format. This converts the formatting into codes that Web browsers can interpret.

Begin

1 Open the File

Open the file you want to save as an HTML document.

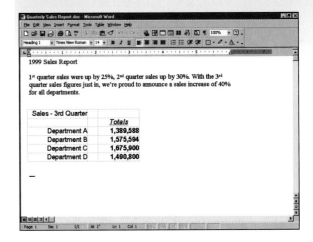

2 Open the Save As Dialog Box

Display the **File** menu and select **Save as Web Page**. This opens the Save As dialog box.

Click

3 Enter a Filename

Designate a folder to save the file to, and assign a name to the file if needed. Notice that the **Save as Type** box lists the file type as a Web page.

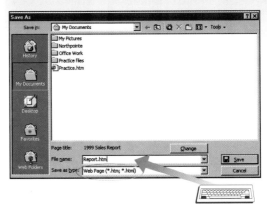

4 Click Save

Click the **Save** button.

Click

5 File Is Converted

The file is converted to HTML format, and the file's name on the title bar now reflects a Web page format.

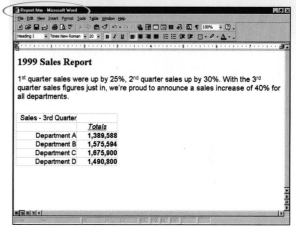

End

How-To Hints

Formatting Warning

Keep in mind that not all formatting you apply with Word's formatting features will translate to HTML code. When you save the file as an HTML document, some formatting might be lost. For that reason, it's best to keep your Web page formatting simple.

How to Use Word's Web Page Wizard

Word comes with an excellent wizard for helping you create professional-looking Web pages. Web pages are formatted in *HTML code*, which stands for Hypertext Markup Language—coding that Web browser programs can interpret. You can save any Word document you create as an HTML file, but the Web Page Wizard offers you preformatted layouts in various styles. All you have to do is fill in your own text. With the Web Page Wizard, you can create several pages that make up your own Web site.

Begin

1 Open the New Dialog Box

From the Word program window, open the **File** menu and select **New**. This opens the New dialog box.

Click

2 Choose the Web Page Wizard

From the Web Pages tab, double-click the **Web Page Wizard**. This opens the wizard and also displays a sample Web page in the background.

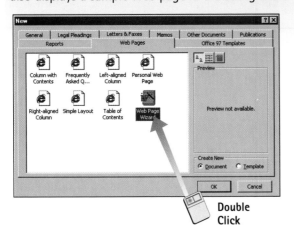

Double Click

3 Start the Wizard

In the first wizard dialog box that appears, click **Next** to get started.

Click

4 Name Your Web Site

Click inside the **Web Site Title** text box and enter a name for your Web site. To save the pages in the default location, click **Next** to continue. To save the pages in another location besides the default location, click the **Browse** button and locate the folder where you want to save the pages.

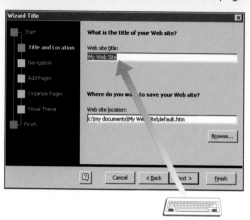

5 Choose a Navigation

Most Web pages use frames for navigation so that you can see parts of the site from one page. Choose the type of frame navigation you prefer to use for your site, and click **Next** to continue.

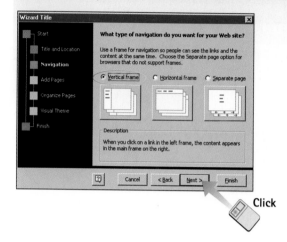

Click

6 Choose Pages

Use the next wizard box to designate how many pages you want to create for your Web site. You can use one page or many pages, depending on how much information you want to present. By default, the wizard starts with three pages. To add another page, click the **Add New Blank Page** button. To remove a page, select it in the list box and click **Remove Page**. Click **Next** to continue.

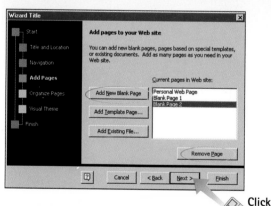

Click

7 Order the Pages

Use the next box to organize how you want the pages to appear. To rearrange the order, select a page in the list box and click the **Move Up** or **Move Down** button. Use the **Rename** button to rename a page. Click **Next** to continue.

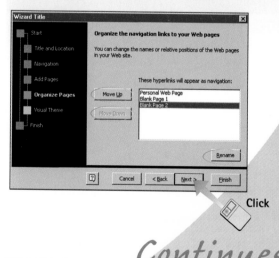

Click

Continues

How to Use Word's Web Page Wizard Continued

8 Set a Theme

To add some pizzazz to your Web pages, consider adding a theme—a preset background format. Click the **Add a Visual Theme** option, and then click the **Browse Themes** button.

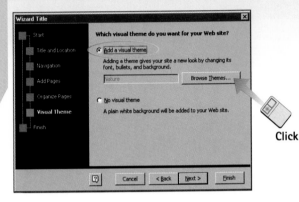

Click

9 Choose a Theme

From the Theme dialog box, select a theme, and the sample area shows you what it looks like. When you find a theme you like, select it and click **OK**.

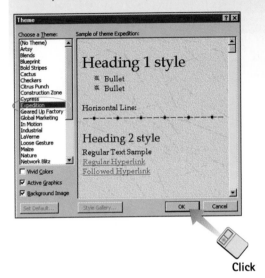

Click

10 Continue

You're returned to the wizard dialog box. Click **Next** to continue.

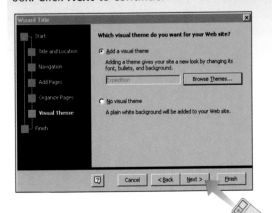

Click

11 Finish

At the final wizard dialog box, click **Finish**.

Click

12 The Web Page Opens

The Web page (or pages) opens in Word, along with the floating Frames toolbar. From here you can start replacing the placeholder text with your own. Select the text and type your own text. You don't have to worry about formatting because the template has already assigned compatible formatting throughout.

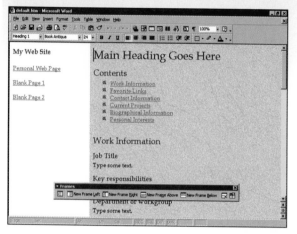

How-To Hints

Not Installed?

Some of the themes you can select in the Theme dialog box aren't installed. Insert your Office CD and click the **Install** button to install the theme to your hard disk drive.

Publish to the Web

Use Microsoft's Web Publishing Wizard to help you post your Web page to a server. If you're posting to a network server in your company, you need to check with the system administrator for assistance. If you're posting the Web page to your Internet service provider's server, be sure to check the guidelines. When you're ready to post, click the **Start** menu and choose **Programs, Accessories, Internet Tools, Web Publishing Wizard**.

Save Your Work

Don't forget to save your work when you're finished. Word saves your Web page or pages as an HTML document when you click the **Save** button on the toolbar.

More Web Tips

In the tasks to come, you can learn how to change the theme background, insert hyperlinks into your Web page, and even add graphics.

How to Create a Web Page in Word from Scratch

If you prefer to design your own Web page without help from Word's Web Page Wizard, you can use Word's formatting tools to assign styles and create headings and body text for your page. You can easily add lists and graphics. When you're finished, save your page to post on the Web.

Begin

1 Open the New Dialog Box

Display the **File** menu and select **New**. This opens the New dialog box.

Click

2 Select the Blank Web Page

From the **General** tab, double-click the **Web Page** icon.

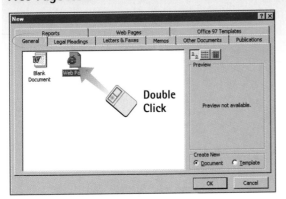

Double Click

3 It's Blank

Word opens a blank Web page in your program window.

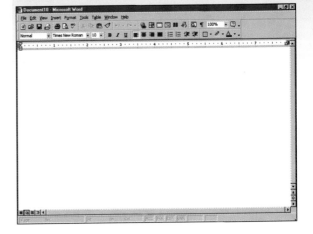

4 Select a Heading Style

To enter a heading for the Web page, click the **Style** drop-down list on the Formatting toolbar and choose a heading style, such as **Heading 1**. Heading styles range in sizes from large to small.

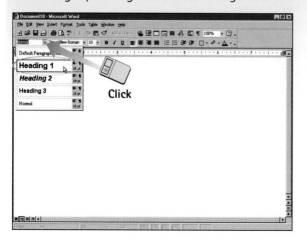

Click

5 Type the Heading Text

Type the heading text. If you're creating a personal Web page, for example, you might type **Welcome to Ralph's Page**. If you're creating a company Web page, type the company name.

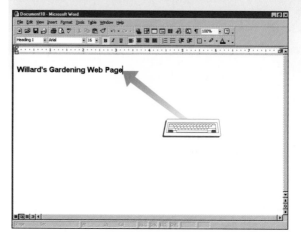

6 Keep Adding Text

Continue selecting styles to use and typing your own text. You can format the text any way you like, changing fonts, increasing fonts sizes, and more. When you're finished, be sure to save your work. Check out Tasks 9 through 11 to learn how to add links, backgrounds, and other effects to your Web page.

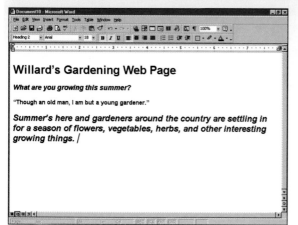

End

How-To Hints

Use the Web Tools Box

To help you format and build your Web page, display the floating Web Tools toolbar. Right-click over any toolbar and select **Web Tools**. To learn what a button does, hover your mouse pointer over the button to reveal a ScreenTip.

Web Page Preview

You can preview how your Web page will look in a Web browser. Open the **File** menu and select **Web Page Preview**. This opens Internet Explorer and enables you to see how the page looks. Close the browser window to return to Word.

Make a Web Page with Publisher

If your version of Office 2000 came with Publisher, you can easily create Web pages by using Publisher's wizards and tools. Use the Web Page Wizard to help you create just the right Web page. For more information about using Publisher, check out Chapter 14, "How to Use Publisher."

How to Insert Hyperlinks

You can quickly insert a hyperlink into your file, whether it's a Word document, an Excel worksheet, or any other Office file. The Office programs recognize URLs as links when you type them. However, you must be careful to spell the URL correctly.

When you're creating Web pages, you can turn any text into a link by using the Insert Hyperlink dialog box. The dialog box enables you to create links to other Web pages or other Office files. If your Web page is exceptionally long, you can even link to other areas on the page. You learn how to insert hyperlinks in this task.

Begin

1 Select the Text

Start by entering the text you want to use as a link. If you created a Web page by using the Web Page Wizard, for example, you can select a pre-underlined link and type your own text. If you created a Web page from scratch, you can select any word or phrase to turn into a link.

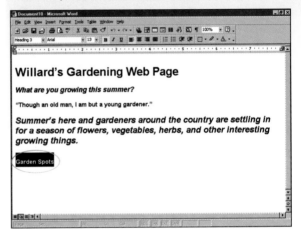

2 Open Insert Hyperlink Dialog Box

Click the **Create Hyperlink** button on the Standard toolbar. This opens the Insert Hyperlink dialog box.

Click

3 Enter the URL

Click inside the **Type the File or Web Page Name** text box, and enter the URL of the Web page to which you want to link. If the URL you want to use is listed in the list box, you can select it instead of typing it.

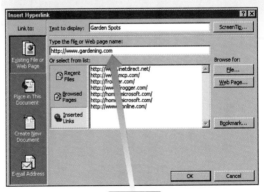

4 Exit the Dialog Box

Click **OK** to close the dialog box.

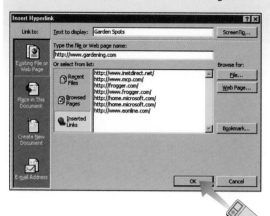

Click

5 Examine the Link

The text you worked with appears in blue and has an underline to indicate it's a hyperlink. You can repeat these steps to add as many links as you like to the page.

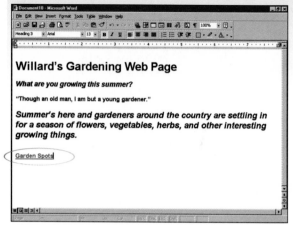

End

How-To Hints

Check Them Out

Be sure to check your URLs to make sure they're correct. It's frustrating to a Web surfer to encounter URLs that aren't up-to-date or that take the user to the wrong information.

Add Graphics

Learn how to add graphics to your Web page in Task 12. Graphic elements can add interest to your Web page.

How to Use Word's Themes

If you created a Web page with the Web Page Wizard, you briefly saw how to add a theme to your page. Themes are preformatted backgrounds, fonts, and sizes you can apply to your Web page, similar to styles. You can change the theme of your Web document at any time to create new looks or make your Web page seem more up-to-date.

Begin

1 Open the Web Page

Start by opening the Web page you want to use in Word.

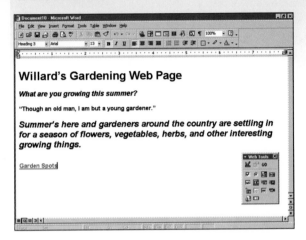

2 Select the Theme Command

Open the **Format** menu and select **Theme**. This opens the Theme dialog box.

3 Preview a Theme

Select a theme from the list box. A sample of the theme then appears in the sample box. Use the scrollbar to scroll through the list of available themes, and preview each one.

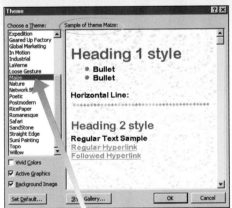

Click

4 Select a Theme

When you find a theme you like, select it and click **OK** to close the dialog box.

Click

5 Theme Applied

Word applies the theme to your Web page. If you decide you don't like it after all, click the **Undo** button, or return to the Theme dialog box and choose another.

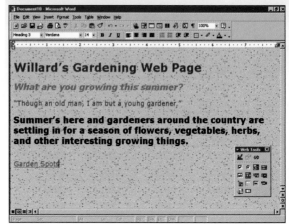

End

How-To Hints

Not Installed?

Some of the themes you can select in the Theme dialog box aren't installed. Insert your Office CD and click the **Install** button to install the theme to your hard disk drive.

Check It Out

It's a good idea to check how your page appears in the Web browser after choosing a theme. Open the **File** menu and select **Web Page Preview**. This opens the page in your browser. Now you can see if the background is too busy, or if the text is legible.

11

How to Add Backgrounds and Frames

If you're creating a Web page from scratch, or fine-tuning one created with the Web Page Wizard, you might want to change the background. This is particularly true if you don't like the current background, or if you can't find a theme background that looks right. Instead, try a simple color background, or choose from the many effects available in the Fill Effects dialog box.

Frames can help the Web user navigate a site or page. You can apply frames to your current page to make the site contents more manageable. In this task, you learn how to change the background and add frames.

Begin

1 Open the Background Dialog Box

Start by opening the Web page you want to use in Word. Open the **Format** menu and select **Background**. This opens a submenu that includes a palette of colors you can apply. To assign a plain color background, select a color from the palette.

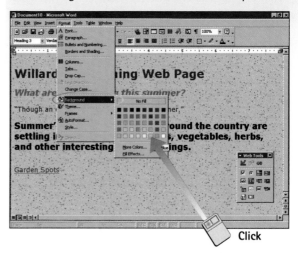

Click

2 More Colors

For more color choices, click the **More Colors** option in the Background submenu to open the Colors dialog box. Click a color from the palette and click **OK** to apply it to your Web page.

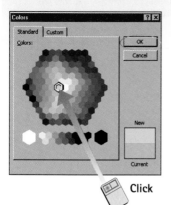

Click

3 Try a Fill Effect

Click the **Fill Effects** option on the **Background** submenu to open the Fill Effects dialog box. This dialog box has tabs for selecting a gradient effect, a pattern, or a texture. Explore each tab to see the various effects you can create. For example, click the **Texture** tab and select a texture; click **OK** to exit the dialog box and apply the effect.

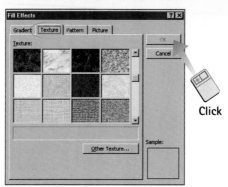

Click

4 Add a Frame

To add a frame to your Web page, open the **Format** menu and select **Frames**, and then choose the type of frame. For example, select the **Table of Contents in Frame** to create a frame that holds a table of contents for your Web site. To create a blank frame, select **New Frames Page**.

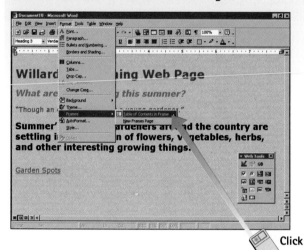

Click

5 Use the Frames Toolbar

If you selected the Table of Contents, Word opens a table of contents frame to the left, and a floating Frames toolbar appears; edit the contents frame to suit your needs. If you selected a blank frame, the floating Frames toolbar appears, and you can begin adding as many frames as you need.

Table of contents frame

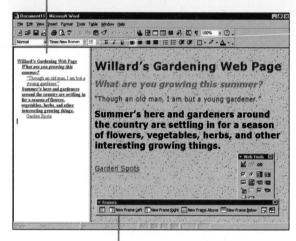

Floating toolbar

6 Add Frames

Click at the bottom of the Web page, and then click the **New Frame Below** button on the Frames toolbar. This adds an empty frame below, as shown in this figure. You can add text to a frame and edit that text, assign a background to the frame, or add links inside the frame, treating it just like another Web page.

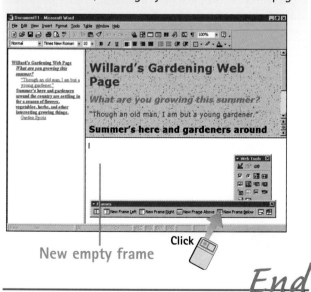

New empty frame

Click

How-To Hints

Delete a Frame

To remove a frame from your Web page, click inside the frame, and then click the **Delete Frame** button on the Frames toolbar.

Working with Frames

Each frame is a separate document, so you can add and edit text, and add any other item to the document, including graphics, backgrounds, and more. You must also save the document as part of your Web site.

End

How to Collaborate Online

If you're using Internet Explorer 5 (which comes with Office 2000), you can conduct online discussions about a Web page with your colleagues. For example, you might share comments about a résumé or report. When you use the Web Discussion feature, you can add comments to a Web document that the other users can see and add to, as well.

This feature works only with Web documents stored on a site running Microsoft's Internet Information Server Web server and using Office 2000 features. In most instances, you won't find such sites on the Internet at large, but the Web Discussion feature is especially useful with intranets (corporate Internets). Check with your system administrator to find out if your intranet is set up for the Web Discussions feature. If so, you can follow the steps in this task.

Begin

1 Open the Web Page to Discuss

Navigate to the Web page you are going to discuss by using any of the methods described in the first task of this chapter. You might be required to log on to the Web site if this is a private corporate site. If so, enter the username and password supplied by your site administrator.

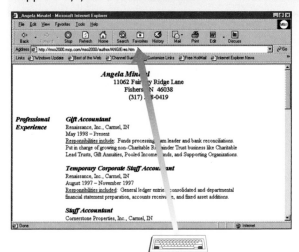

2 Change to Discussion View

Open the **View** menu, choose **Explorer Bar**, and then choose **Discuss**.

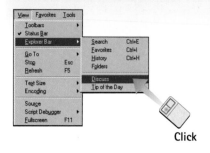

Click

3 Log On to the Discussion Server

The first time you use the Web Discussion feature, a dialog box appears into which you can enter the server's address and name. Type the full Web address of the server in the top text box, type a name you can remember for the server in the bottom text box, and then click **OK**. If required, you are asked to log on here, too. If so, supply the correct username and password.

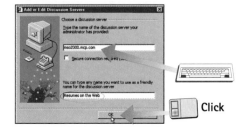

Click

4 Start a Comment

After you log on to the server, a new Discussion toolbar appears at the bottom of the Internet Explorer window. To make a comment in the document, click the **Insert Discussion in the Document** button on the toolbar. Small page icons appear in the document. Click any of the page icons to insert a discussion comment at that point.

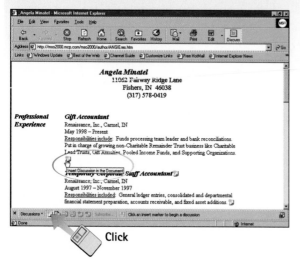

Click

5 Type Your Comment Text

In the dialog box that appears, type a subject and the message of your comment. Then click **OK**. Comments from you appear with your name beside them. Internet Explorer inserts the username you entered when you set up Office or the name you specified in the Options dialog box of Word, Excel, or the other Office applications.

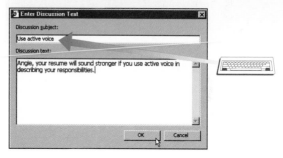

6 View Your Comment

After a moment, Internet Explorer displays your comment. You can see it and so can other users. You can click the icon at the end of your comment and choose the option to **Edit** or **Delete** the comment if needed. If you are reading a comment inserted by someone else, you can select **Reply** and add your own comment to the discussion.

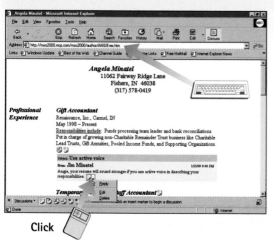

Click

How-To Hints

Hide Discussion Comments

At the beginning of the discussion comment, you'll see a page icon with a minus. To hide this comment from view, click the icon. To redisplay a hidden comment, click its page icon.

Close the Discussion

Click the **Close** button on the Discussion toolbar to exit the Web Discussion feature.

Discussing with Word or Excel

You can also use the Web Discussion feature from Word or Excel. Open the **Tools** menu and select **Online Collaboration, Web Discussions**. You can now log on to the Web server and display the Web page you want to discuss. The Discussion toolbar appears at the bottom of the window for you to use to insert comments.

End

Task

16

How to Work with Office Graphics Tools

*T*he Office programs share a lot of common features, but many users aren't aware of the common graphics tools available in all the programs. Each application enables you to add objects to your files, such as clip art, shapes, WordArt, and more. You can dress up a Word document with a piece of clip art from the Microsoft Clip Gallery, for example, or insert an image file from another program into your Outlook email message. You can draw your own shapes to include on Excel charts or PowerPoint slides.

In this chapter, you'll learn how to utilize the Office graphics tools to enhance your documents, worksheets, database tables and forms, slides, and more. You'll also learn how to draw basic shapes, insert pictures and clip art, create a WordArt image, and manipulate and format graphics objects. Don't be intimidated by the thought of creating and adding visual objects to your files. The Office 2000 graphics tools make it easy to illustrate any Office item you create. ●

How to Draw Basic Shapes

One of the easiest ways to add visual appeal to a document, worksheet, or slide is to add a shape, such as a rectangle or oval. A shape can draw attention to parts of your text or other data, create a nice background effect, or function as a design element. You can also add lines, arcs, and freeform shapes using the drawing tools.

The Office drawing tools are accessible in Word, Excel, and PowerPoint. To view them, open the Drawing toolbar, right-click over any toolbar, and select **Drawing** or click the **Drawing** button (Word and Excel). By default, the Drawing toolbar appears automatically in PowerPoint.

Begin

1 Select a Tool

Click the shape tool you want to draw: choose from **Rectangle** or **Oval**. To draw a rectangle, for example, click the **Rectangle** tool on the Drawing toolbar. Your mouse pointer takes the shape of a crosshair.

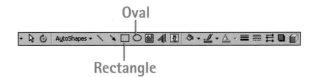

Oval

Rectangle

2 Drag the Shape

Move the mouse pointer to the location on the document, worksheet, or slide where you want the shape to appear. Click and drag the mouse to draw the shape. When the shape reaches the desired shape and size, click the mouse button again. You can now resize, move, or format the shape object.

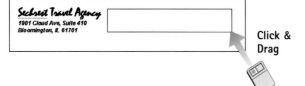

Click & Drag

3 Draw a Line

Drawing lines or arrows is a lot like drawing shapes. Click the tool you want to draw: choose from **Line** or **Arrow**. To draw a line, for example, click the **Line** tool on the Drawing toolbar. Your mouse pointer takes the shape of a crosshair.

Arrow

Line

4 Drag the Line

Move the mouse pointer to the location on the document, worksheet, or slide where you want the line to appear. Click and drag the mouse to draw the line. When the line is the size you want, click the mouse button again.

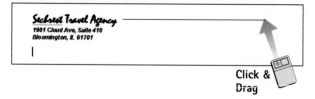

Click & Drag

5 Draw a Freeform Shape

Use the Freeform tool to draw a polygon or freeform shape. To open the Freeform tool, click the **AutoShapes** button on the Drawing toolbar, select the **Lines** category, and choose the **Freeform** tool.

Click

6 Drag or Anchor

To draw a polygon shape, click where you want the shape to start and keep clicking each *anchor point* (also called a *vertex*) in place until the shape is finished. To draw a freeform shape, drag the mouse instead of clicking (the mouse pointer takes the shape of a pencil icon) and click in place when finished. The figure below shows the two types of techniques applied.

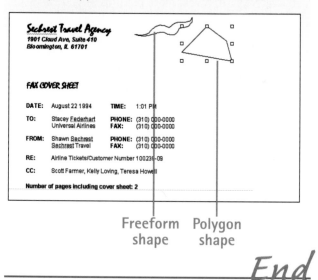

Freeform shape   Polygon shape

End

How-To Hints

Use AutoShapes

If you're not too keen on drawing your own shapes, use the available predrawn shapes. Click the **AutoShapes** tool on the Drawing toolbar to display a list of categories. Click the category you want to use; a palette of custom shapes appears. Click a shape. You can now click and drag the mouse pointer on the document until the shape reaches the size you want. Release the mouse button, and the complete shape appears.

Draw Perfect Shapes

To draw a perfect shape every time, hold down the **Shift** key while you drag. This keeps the proportions intact as you drag.

Switch Views

When you draw a shape in Word, you're automatically switched to Print Layout view where you can see graphics objects onscreen.

How to Insert Clip Art

Another way to add visual impact to your Office files is to insert clip art. Clip art images are ready-made drawings covering a wide range of topics and categories. You can insert clip art into any Office item you create, such as a letter, a worksheet, a database form, an Outlook note, or a slide.

In the Microsoft Clip Gallery dialog box, you can choose from clip art and photographs, as well as sounds and videos. In addition to the clip art available in the Gallery, you can also find clip art on the Web.

Begin

1 Open the Clip Gallery Dialog Box

Click the mouse pointer where you want the clip art inserted, open the **Insert** menu, and choose **Picture**, **Clip Art**. This opens the Insert ClipArt dialog box.

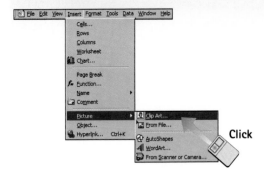

Click

2 View Categories

From the **Pictures** tab, peruse the categories of clip art. Use the scroll box arrows to help you see all the available categories. To choose a category, click it.

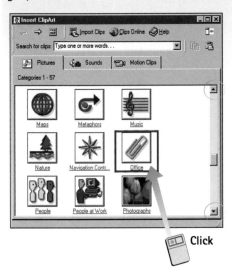

Click

3 View Pictures

Scroll through the available pictures. Some categories may include a Keep Looking link you can click to reveal more pictures. If you can't find the picture you want, click the **Back** button to return to the Category list and try another category.

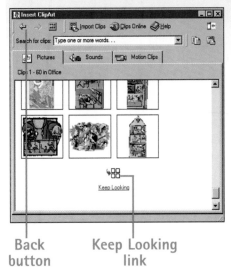

Back button   Keep Looking link

4 Select a Picture

When you find a clip art piece you want to use, click it to reveal a balloon menu, as shown in the figure below. Click the **Insert Clip** button on the menu and click the **Close** button to exit the dialog box. To preview the picture before adding it to your file, click the **Preview Clip** button.

Close button

Click

5 The Picture Appears

The clip art appears in your file along with the Picture toolbar. You can now resize or move the image as needed (see Task 5, "How to Move and Size an Image").

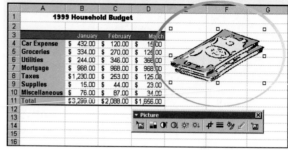

End

How-To Hints

Use Photos, Sounds, and Videos

In addition to the vast collection of clip art, the Insert ClipArt dialog box also contains sound clips and video clips that you can add to your file. Be sure to check out the other tabs in the Insert ClipArt dialog box to see what's available.

Find Clip Art on the Web

You can import clip art images from Microsoft's Web site. Click the **Clips Online** button in the bottom right corner of the Clip Gallery dialog box and click **OK**. This opens your Web browser to the Microsoft site where you can choose more clip art. (You must first connect to your Internet account.)

Look Up Clip Art

To search for a specific type of clip art, click inside the **Search for Clips** text box in the Insert ClipArt dialog box and enter key words to search for, such as **money** or **elephant**. Press **Enter** and the list box displays any matches.

Insert Other Graphics

You can also use graphics created in other programs. For example, you might have a picture file created with Microsoft Paint. You can use the picture file in your Office documents. Task 3, "How to Insert an Object," explains how to insert other graphic objects.

How to Insert an Object

If you have a picture file from another program, you can insert it into your Office document, worksheet, database form, email message, or slide. You can also insert objects such as scanned images, Word tables, Excel worksheets, and other types of visual objects.

You can insert visual objects in different ways, depending on the program you're using. One way is to use the Insert, Object command. This opens the Object dialog box where you can access a variety of visual objects.

Begin

1 Open the Object Dialog Box

Display the **Insert** menu and select **Object**. This opens the Insert Object dialog box.

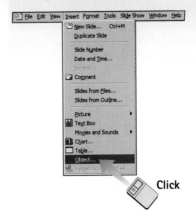

Click

2 Click Create from File

To insert an existing object file in PowerPoint, click the **Create from File** option. If you're using Word or Excel, click the **Create from File** tab.

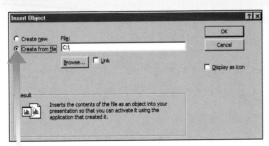

Click

3 Open the Browse Dialog Box

To find the object file you want to insert, click the **Browse** button to open the Browse dialog box.

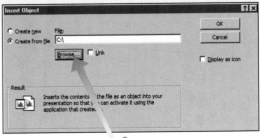

Click

4 Locate the Object File

Locate the picture file or other visual object file you want to use. When you find the file, select it and click **OK** (in PowerPoint) or click **Insert** (Word and Excel) to return to the Insert Object dialog box.

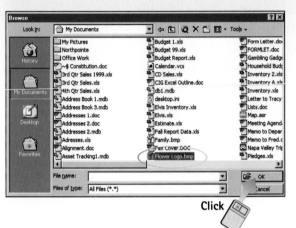

Click

5 Click OK

When you're ready to insert the object file, click **OK**.

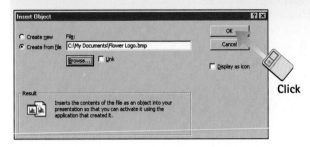

Click

6 The Object Is Inserted

The object appears in your file. You can now resize or move it as needed.

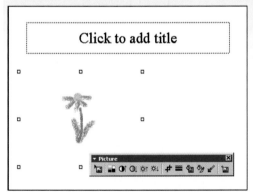

End

How-To Hints

Resizing and Moving

After you insert the picture, you can resize it or move it around. Learn how in Task 5 later in this chapter.

Insert Trick

If you find that you need to add the same picture file repeatedly to Word documents, add the picture file to Word's AutoCorrect collection. First, insert the picture file into a document and select the graphic. Open the **Tools** menu and choose **AutoCorrect**. In the AutoCorrect dialog box, enter the picture's file name in the **With** box and type a text entry for the picture in the **Replace** box. If it's a company logo, for example, you might type **mylogo**. Click **Add** to add the entry to the list and click **OK**. Next time you type **mylogo**, the picture will replace the text.

How to Insert a WordArt Image

One of the more popular features of the Office graphics tools is the WordArt application. WordArt enables you to turn text into graphic objects that bend, twist, rotate, and assume a variety of special effects. You can turn ordinary words into works of art.

WordArt is especially helpful when you need to create a company logo, a banner for a newsletter or flyer, or draw attention to important words, such as *sale* or *urgent*. After you design a WordArt object, you can move and resize it as needed.

Begin

1 Open the WordArt Gallery

Open the **Insert** menu and select **Picture**, **WordArt**. This opens the WordArt Gallery dialog box. If the Drawing toolbar is displayed, you can also click on the WordArt button.

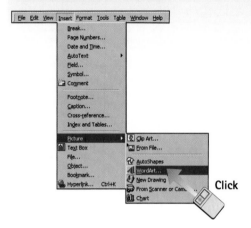

Click

2 Choose an Effect

Select a WordArt style that best suits your needs. The samples show the shape and effect of the style. Click **OK** to continue.

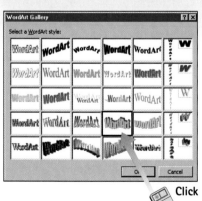

Click

3 Enter Your Own Text

In the Edit WordArt Text dialog box, enter the text you want to use as your WordArt object.

4 Format the Text

Use the **Font** drop-down box to select another font style, if necessary. You can also change the formatting attributes for size, bold, or italic. When you have finished with your selections, click **OK**.

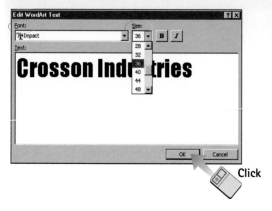

Click

5 WordArt Is Created

The WordArt object appears in your Office file along with the WordArt toolbar. Use the toolbar buttons to fine-tune your WordArt object. You may have to move or resize the WordArt object. To learn more about moving and resizing objects, see Task 5.

End

How-To Hints

Edit WordArt

Any time you need to edit your WordArt object, double-click it to reopen the text box where you can edit the text. You can use the tools on the WordArt toolbar to format the object.

Try Them All!

To change your WordArt's shape or style, select the WordArt object and click the **WordArt Gallery** button on the WordArt toolbar. This opens the WordArt Gallery dialog box again, and you can choose a new style to apply. You may need to experiment with several kinds before you find one you like.

I Changed My Mind!

If you open the WordArt Gallery and change your mind about using the feature, click **Cancel**. If you have already started creating an image and then change your mind, click outside the picture. To remove a WordArt image you have already created, select it and press the **Delete** key.

Endless Selections

By changing the text effects, fonts, sizes, and formatting attributes, you can create different WordArt shapes and designs. To reverse any of the changes you make, click **Undo**.

How to Move and Size an Image

You can resize and move any visual object that you add to your Office file. This includes graphic images, clip art, WordArt, and any other drawing or shape you create. After you select an object, selection handles surround it. You can drag these handles in any direction to resize the object. You can also drag the object to a new location. The tricky part is knowing exactly where to click to perform either action. In this task, you will learn how to move and resize any object.

Begin

1 Select the Object

Select the object you want to move or resize. Notice that as soon as you select it, tiny boxes called *selection handles* surround it.

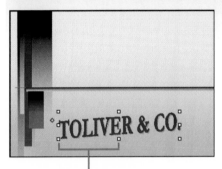

Selection handles

2 Drag to Move

Hover your mouse pointer over the selected object until you see a four-headed arrow. Drag the object to a new location and release. Notice the black dotted lines that show you exactly where you're moving the object.

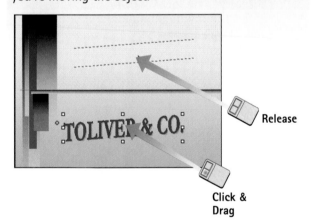

Release

Click & Drag

3 Resize in One Dimension

To resize a selected object in one dimension—that is, to stretch or shrink the object—use only the resizing handles along the sides of the object. To stretch the object, for example, hover your mouse pointer over the handle on the right side and drag the handle. Release when the object is stretched the way you want it.

Click & Drag

Release

4 Resize in Two Dimensions

To resize the object in two dimensions, use any of the corner handles. This will enable you to resize both the object's height and width at the same time. Hover your mouse pointer over a corner handle and drag.

Click & Drag

Release

5 Use the Shift Key

To maintain the object's height-to-width ratio while resizing, hold down the **Shift** key while you drag a corner selection handle. Release the mouse button and **Shift** key when the object is sized the way you want it.

↑Shift

Click & Drag

Release

6 Use the Ctrl Key

To resize in two dimensions at once, from the center of the object outward, hold down the **Ctrl** key and drag any corner selection handle. Release the mouse button and **Ctrl** key when the object is sized the way you want it.

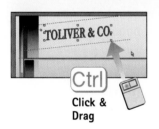

Ctrl

Click & Drag

Release

End

How-To Hints

Copy and Paste

You can easily copy and paste objects that you draw or insert with the Office graphics tools. Select the object and use the **Cut**, **Copy**, and **Paste** commands to move the object to a new location. You can also copy the object and place it in a new location. Use the **Cut**, **Copy**, and **Paste** buttons on the toolbar, or use these options on the **Edit** menu.

Rotate Your WordArt

Use the **Free Rotate** button on the WordArt toolbar to rotate your WordArt object. To rotate, drag any rotation handle, and the WordArt object is rotated in the direction you drag.

How to Change Image Formatting

Many of the visual objects you add can be enhanced with formatting tools. You can format the shapes you draw, for example, by changing the fill color or line style. Adjusting your image's formatting can completely change the look of the object. You can tone down an object's loud primary colors by using pastel colors instead. You can also change the importance of the line you have drawn by making its line weight thicker.

Begin

1 Select the Object

First, select the object whose formatting you want to change.

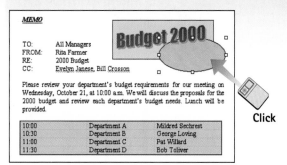

Click

2 Choose the Format Command

Right-click the object to display the shortcut menu and select the **Format** command at the bottom of the menu. Depending on the type of visual object you select, the name of the command will vary. If you right-click a shape, for example, it appears as **Format AutoShape**. If you right-click a text box, it says **Format Text Box**.

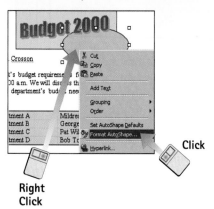

Click

Right Click

3 The Format Dialog Box

The Format dialog box appears, based on the type of visual object you selected. Click the **Colors and Lines** tab to find options for changing the color or line style of the object.

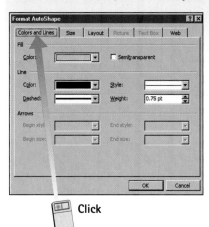

Click

4 Change the Fill Color

To change the fill color, click the **Fill Color** drop-down list and choose another color from the palette.

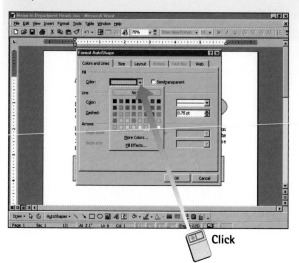

Click

5 Change the Line Weight

If your object contains an outline or border, or if it is a line or arc, use the **Line** options in the **Colors and Lines** tab to change the line's color, style, or weight (set an exact thickness). Click the **Style** drop-down arrow, for example, to display a list of line styles.

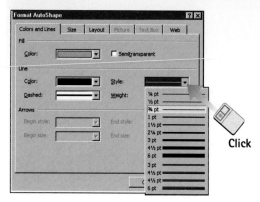

Click

6 Wrap Text Around Objects

If you want the visual object to sit in the middle of text, you can apply wrapping commands to designate how the text flows around (or through) the object. Click the **Layout** tab and choose a wrapping style to apply. Click **OK** to exit the dialog box and apply any new formatting settings.

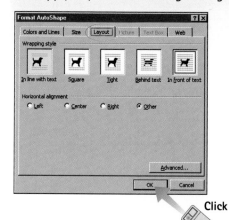

Click

End

How-To Hints

Other Formatting Options

Be sure to check out the other tabs in the Format dialog box. You can apply numerous other options, depending on the visual object you selected.

Or Use the Drawing Toolbar

The Drawing toolbar contains formatting tools that you can apply directly to the objects you select. To fill an object with a color, for example, click the **Fill Color** button. To choose another line style to use, click the **Line Style** button.

Task

17

How to Integrate Office Applications

*A*lthough each Office application is a powerful tool in itself, the combined programs offer even more versatility. Integrating the Office programs expands the type of tasks you can perform, and sharing data between programs can save you valuable time.

You can share data among programs in several ways. You can use the standard Cut, Copy, and Paste commands to move or copy data quickly from one program to the next by way of the Windows Clipboard (a temporary storage area). The cut or copied data does not retain a relationship with the original program however. Use linking and embedding, or *OLE* (stands for *object linking and embedding*), to retain a connection to the data's source of origin. For example, you can link an Excel range to a Word report. Any time the information changes in the Excel range, the linked data in the Word report reflects the changes, too. You can link entire files or specific data. You can embed objects you have already created or embed new objects you create from scratch.

In this chapter, you will learn how to use the various methods for sharing data across programs and learn how to integrate information from one Office program into another. ●

How to Cut, Copy, and Paste Data Among Programs

The easiest way to share data among programs is to use the Cut, Copy, and Paste commands. Use the Cut command to move data from one program to the next. Use the Copy command to duplicate the data in one program and place it in another. When you cut or copy data, it's placed in the Windows Clipboard, a temporary storage area, until it's pasted into a new location.

You can use the Cut, Copy, and Paste commands to move or duplicate text, pictures, formulas, or any type of data you place in a file. You can also use these commands to share data between non-Microsoft programs, too.

Begin

1 Select the Data

Select the data you want to cut or copy.

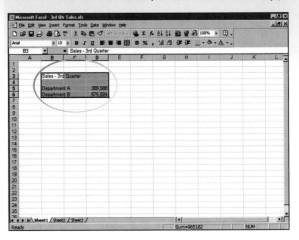

2 Move with the Cut Command...

To move the data from one file to another, click the **Cut** button on the toolbar, or open the **Edit** menu and select **Cut**. This removes the data from the file and places it in the Windows Clipboard.

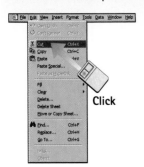

Click

3 ...or Copy with the Copy Command

To copy the data from one file to another, click the **Copy** button on the toolbar, or open the **Edit** menu and choose **Copy**. This places a duplicate of the data in the Windows Clipboard.

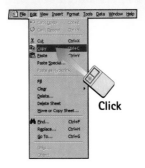

Click

4 Open the File to Cut or Copy To

Next, open the file where you want to place the cut or copied data. Click the cursor where you want to insert the data.

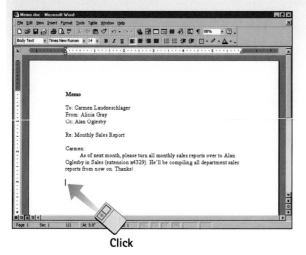

Click

5 Use the Paste Command

Click the **Paste** button on the toolbar or open the **Edit** menu and select **Paste**.

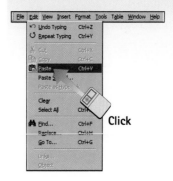

Click

6 The Transfer Is Complete

The cut or copied data now appears in the new file.

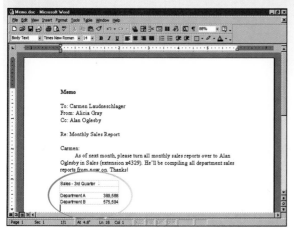

End

Shortcut Menu

You can also right-click the data to find the Cut, Copy, and Paste commands on the short-cut menu.

Working with Multiple Files

To learn more about working with two or more open program files, turn to Task 9, "How to Work with Multiple Files," in Chapter 1, "How to Use Common Office Features."

Drag and Drop

You can also drag and drop data between programs. If both the source file and destination files are open, use the Windows taskbar to switch between open program windows, or resize the windows so you can view both onscreen at the same time. Then you can drag the data from one program window to another and drop it in place. To copy data with the drag and drop method, hold down the **Ctrl** key while you drag.

TASK 2

How to Paste with the Clipboard Toolbar

A new feature added to Office 2000 is the Clipboard toolbar. It allows you to paste multiple items you cut or copy in your documents. For example, you might cut two or three different paragraphs, then paste them back into your file, whether it's an Excel worksheet or a Word document, in a different order. The Clipboard toolbar lets you pick exactly which item to paste, and you can choose to cut or copy up to 12 items.

Begin

1 Cut or Copy Text

Use the skills you learned in the previous task to cut or copy text. You can cut or copy up to 12 different items. When you cut or copy more than one item, the Clipboard toolbar automatically appears.

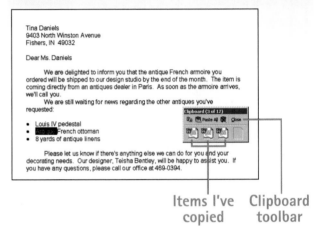

Items I've copied   Clipboard toolbar

2 Place the Insertion Point

Click in the place where you want to paste an item you cut or copied.

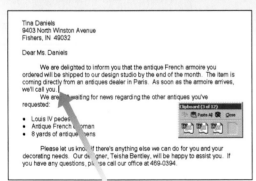

Click

3 Select an Item to Paste

From the Clipboard toolbar, choose the item you want to paste. If you're not too sure which item is which, hover your mouse pointer over an icon and a ScreenTip appears describing the cut or copied text.

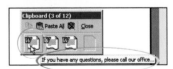

4 Click to Paste

Click the icon representing the text you want to paste.

Click

5 The Item Is Pasted

The text is immediately pasted into your document. To paste another Clipboard item, repeat steps 3-4.

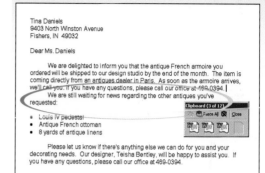

6 Close the Clipboard Toolbar

To close the Clipboard toolbar when you're finished pasting, click the **Close** button.

Click

End

How-To Hints

Using Other Clipboard Buttons

To clear the Clipboard's contents, click the **Clear Clipboard** button to the left of the Close button. To paste all the cut or copied items at once, click the **Paste All** button.

Where's My Clipboard Toolbar?

If you can't see your Clipboard toolbar, or you've accidentally closed it before you could use it, you can open it by displaying the **View** menu, selecting **Toolbars**, **Clipboard**.

It's in the Way!

If the Clipboard toolbar is blocking your view of the area you want to paste to, you can drag it out of the way. Drag the toolbar's title bar to move the toolbar to a new location on-screen.

How to Link and Embed Data

Object linking and embedding, called *OLE* for short, enables Windows programs to share data transparently. The data maintains a relationship with the original program. When you link data, any changes made to the data in the source program (the program you originally used to create the data) are reflected in the destination file (the program receiving the shared data).

When you embed data, the data, when changed, isn't updated in the destination file, but it does retain a relationship with the source file. Any time you want to edit the data in the destination file, double-click it to reopen the source file where you can make your changes. With embedding, you can access the source file directly and bypass opening the source program and file, make the changes, and copy and paste data into the destination file.

Begin

1 Copy to the Clipboard

The first step in linking or embedding is to copy the data to the Windows Clipboard. Open the source file containing the data you want to link or embed, select the data, and then choose **Edit**, **Copy** or click the **Copy** button.

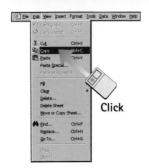

Click

2 Open the Destination File

Next, open the file where you want to link or embed the data and click where you want the data to appear.

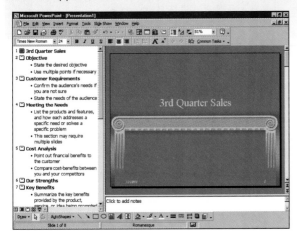

3 Open the Paste Special Dialog Box

Display the **Edit** menu and select **Paste Special**. This opens the Paste Special dialog box, where you can link or embed data.

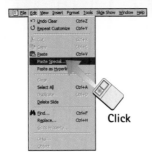

Click

4 Link the Data

To link the data, choose the **Paste Link** option and select a format to use from the **As** list box. The formats listed will vary depending on the type of data you select to link. When you select a format, the Result area at the bottom of the dialog box displays notes about what will happen.

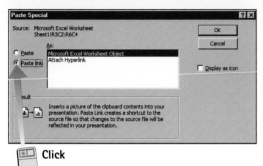

Click

5 Embed the Data

To embed the data, choose the **Paste** option and select a format from the **As** list box. Notice the Result area describes what will happen.

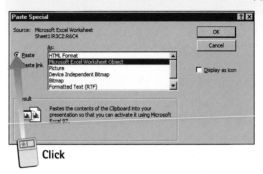

Click

6 Click OK

Click **OK** to exit the dialog box and link or embed the data.

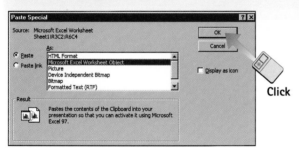

Click

End

How-To Hints

Linking Options

Use the **Display as Icon** check box in the Paste Special dialog box to display the pasted object as an icon instead of the data itself. If you're linking sound clips to an Office file, for example, display the link as an icon. To play the sound clip, double-click the icon.

Editing Links

If you rename, delete, or move the source file, the link between the source and the destination file is broken and you will see an error message in the destination file. To edit your links, use the **Edit**, **Links** command. This command opens the Links dialog box where you can break the link, change the link's source, or apply other options.

Editing an Embedded Object

To edit data you have embedded, double-click the data to open the original program in which the data was created. Make your changes and then choose **File**, **Exit**, or click anywhere outside the selected object.

HOW TO LINK AND EMBED DATA **379**

How to Manage Links

After you link data to a file, you must maintain the source file's name and keep the file in the same location. If you move or rename the file, the link is broken, and an error message appears in the destination file. Microsoft Office makes it easy to manage links and make changes using the Links dialog box, as explained in this task.

Begin

1 Open the Links Dialog Box

To change a link, open the **Edit** menu and select **Links**. This opens the Links dialog box.

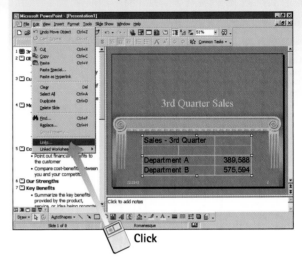

Click

2 Select the File

From the Links dialog box, select the source file from the list box.

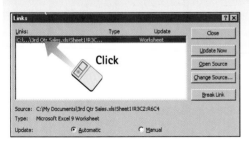

Click

3 Automatically Update the Link

If you want the link updated automatically any time the data changes, choose the **Automatic** option.

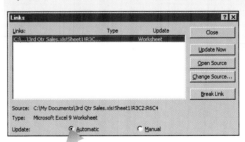

 Click

4 Manually Update the Link

If you prefer to update the link only when you want it updated (thus avoiding minor changes in data, for example), select the **Manual** option. The next time you need to update the link, open the Links dialog box, choose the link, and click the **Update Now** button.

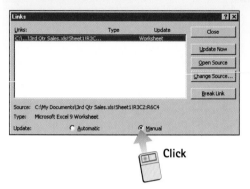

Click

5 Change the Source

If you need to change the source file that the link uses, click the **Change Source** button. This opens the Change Source dialog box where you can enter the new file name or location.

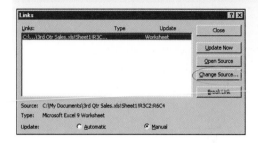

6 Break the Link

To discontinue an associated link, click the **Break Link** button. A message box asks you to confirm the break. Click **OK** and the link is broken: The data is no longer associated with the source file.

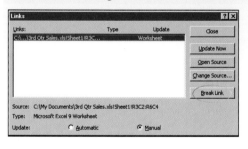

End

How-To Hints

Exiting

To close the Links dialog box after editing your links, click **Close** to exit the dialog box and return to the program window.

Opening the Source Program

Use the **Open Source** button in the Links dialog box to open the source program. You can then check the source data and make changes to the data in the source program.

Glossary

absolute reference   A cell reference that specifies the exact address of a cell. An absolute reference takes the form A1, B3, and so on.

Access   A database program designed to organize and sort large quantities of data.

active cell   The selected cell (it's surrounded by a dark border). You can enter or edit data in the active cell.

active document   The document that is currently selected in your software window.

active window   In a multiple-window environment, the window that you are currently using, or that is currently selected. Only one window can be active at a time, and keystrokes and commands affect the active window.

active worksheet   The Excel worksheet on which you are currently working. When a sheet is active, the name on the sheet tab is bold.

add-in   A small program that can be installed to add commands and functions to a main program.

alignment   The way text lines up against the margins of a page, within the width of a column, against tab stops, or in a worksheet cell.

archiving   The process of moving Outlook items out of Outlook and into storage files, where they are saved for future reference.

argument   Information you supply to a function for calculation. An argument can be a value, a reference, a name, a formula, or another function.

attachment   A complete file or item that is sent with an email message or stored with an Outlook item, such as a task or journal entry.

AutoCalculate   An Excel feature that automatically calculates any selected cells.

AutoContent Wizard   A PowerPoint feature that walks you through the process of creating a slide show presentation.

AutoCorrect   A Word feature that corrects text or changes a string of characters to a word or phrase automatically.

AutoFill   An Excel feature that enables you to create a series of incremental or fixed values on a worksheet by dragging the fill handle with the mouse.

AutoFit   An Excel feature that helps you fit data into columns and rows.

AutoFormat   A feature found in Word and Excel that helps you quickly format your data based on preset formats.

AutoText   A formatted block of boilerplate text that you can insert wherever you need it.

axes   Borders on the chart plot area that provide a frame of reference for measurement or comparison. On column charts, data values are plotted along the Y axis and categories are plotted along the X axis.

Bcc   Blind carbon copy. A copy of an email message that you send without the primary recipient's knowledge.

browser   A program for surfing the Internet (such as Netscape or Internet Explorer).

build   A special effect in a PowerPoint slide show that presents one slide item at a time.

C

Cc   Carbon copy; when you send an email message, you can send Cc (copies) to other recipients.

cell   The intersection of a column and a row.

cell address   The location of a cell on a sheet; this consists of a row address and a column address, such as F12, which indicates the intersection of column F and row 12. Also referred to as cell reference.

cell reference   The set of row and column coordinates that identifies a cell location on a worksheet. Also referred to as the cell address.

chart   A graphical representation of worksheet data. Charts are linked to the data from which they were created and are automatically updated when the source data changes.

chart area   The entire region surrounding the chart, just outside the plot area. When the chart area is selected, uniform font characteristics can be applied to all text in the chart.

chart sheet   A sheet in a workbook that's designed to contain only a chart.

chart type   The way chart data is displayed; column, bar, and pie are common chart types.

Chart Wizard   A wizard that guides you through the steps required to create a new chart or to modify settings for an existing chart.

client   A program that receives data that is linked, copied, or embedded from another program. (Also called a destination program or document.)

clip art   A predrawn illustration or graphics object you can insert into an Office file. Microsoft Office comes with a collection of clip art files you can use to illustrate your documents.

Clipboard   See Windows Clipboard.

close box   A small box with an X in it that's located in the upper-right corner of every Windows 95 window; click it to close the program or file or item in the window.

column   A vertical range of cells. Each column is identified by a unique letter or letter combination (such as A, Z, CF).

column heading   The label at the top of a column in a table view (also called the field name).

command   An instruction that tells the computer to carry out a task or perform an action.

comment   Extra information provided for an Excel cell or Word text. The comment remains hidden until you point to the Comment indicator symbol.

constant   A cell value that does not start with an equal sign. For example, the date, the value 345, and text are all constants.

criteria   Information in a specific field that identifies items you want to find, such as a last name of Smith or the category Business; criteria are used to filter a view to find only those items containing the criteria.

cursor   The flashing vertical line that shows where text is entered (for example, in a cell during in-cell editing). Also referred to as the insertion point.

D

data marker   A bar, area, dot, slice, or other symbol in a chart that represents a single data point or value originating from a worksheet cell. Related data markers in a chart comprise a data series.

data point   An individual value, plotted in a chart, that originates from a single cell in a worksheet. Data points are represented by bars, columns, lines, pie or doughnut slices, dots, and various other shapes called data markers.

data series   A group of related data points in a chart that originate from a single worksheet row or column. Each data series in a chart is distinguished by a unique color or pattern.

data source   The underlying worksheet data that's displayed in a chart or PivotTable.

database   A computer program that specializes in organizing, storing, and retrieving data. The term also describes a collection of data.

datasheet   A view in Access that lets you see your data as a table.

delimiter   A character (such as a tab, space, or comma) that separates fields of data in a text file.

destination document   The document or file containing the data you link or embed from the source document.

document   A file you create with a program such as Word. A document can be saved with a unique filename by which it can be retrieved.

document window   A rectangular portion of the screen in which you view and edit a document. A document window is typically located inside a program window.

download   To transfer a file from the Internet to your computer through telephone lines and a modem.

drag and drop   A technique for moving or copying data from one location to another. Select the item to move or copy, hold down the left mouse button, drag the item to a new location, and release the mouse button to drop it in place.

E

email   Electronic mail; a system that uses the Internet to send messages electronically over telephone wires instead of on paper.

embed   To insert an object from a source program into a destination document. When you double-click the object in the destination document, the source program opens and you can edit the object. See also link.

embedded chart   A chart that's located on a worksheet instead of on a separate chart sheet.

Excel   A popular spreadsheet program designed for organizing and working with numbers, performing calculations, and other mathematical operations.

export   The process of converting and saving a file to be used in a another program. See also import.

F

favorites   In Internet Explorer, you can add your favorite Web sites to the Favorites folder so you can easily access them again.

field   In a list or database, a column of data that contains a particular type of information, such as Last Name or Phone Number or Quantity.

field name   The name of the field, also commonly called a column heading.

fill handle   The small black square in the lower-right corner of the selected cell or range. When you position the mouse pointer over the fill handle, the pointer changes to a black cross and the contents can be AutoFilled.

fill series   In Excel, a fill series is a series of related information you can fill across cells, such as days of the week or month, or a series of numbers or labels.

filter   A set of criteria you can apply to show specific items and hide all others.

flag   A visual symbol indicating that some sort of follow-up to an email message is requested; flags appear in the Flag Status column in table views.

floating palette   A palette that can be dragged away from its toolbar.

floating toolbar   A toolbar that is not docked at the edges of the application window. A floating toolbar stays on top of other windows within the application window.

font   A typeface, such as Arial or Tahoma.

font formatting   Characteristics you can apply to text to change the way it looks; these include bold, italic, color, and font size.

footer   Text that appears at the bottom of every printed page. See also header.

form   In Access, a form is a special feature you can use to enter data into a database in an organized manner, one record at a time.

formatting   Commands you apply to data to change the way it looks or appears in a file. Formatting controls range from text formatting to formatting for objects such as graphics.

formula   A sequence of values, cell references, names, functions, or mathematical operators that produces a new value from existing values. A formula always begins with an equal sign (=).

Formula bar   A bar near the top of the Excel window that you use to enter or edit values and formulas in cells or charts. This bar displays the formula or constant value from the active cell or object.

function   A built-in formula that uses a series of values (arguments) to perform an operation and then returns the result of the operation. You can use the Function Wizard to select a function and enter it in a cell.

G

grammar checker   An Office tool you can use to check your document for grammatical errors.

graphics object   A line or shape (button, text box, ellipse, rectangle, arc, picture) you draw using the tools on the toolbar, or a picture you paste into a file.

gridlines   Lines that visually separate columns and rows.

gridlines (chart) Lines you can add to your chart that extend from the tickmarks on an axis across the plot area. Gridlines come in various forms: horizontal, vertical, major, minor, and various combinations. They make it easier to view and evaluate data in a chart.

group To combine one or more objects to act as a single object, which you can then move or resize.

H

handles Small black squares located around the perimeter of selected graphics objects, chart items, or chart text. By dragging the handles, you can move, copy, or size the selected object, chart item, or chart text.

handouts A PowerPoint feature that lets you create paper handouts to go along with the slide presentation.

header Text that appears at the top of every printed page. See also footer.

home page In Internet Explorer, the home page is the default page that always opens whenever you start the browser.

HTML Stands for Hypertext Markup Language, a special file format for Web pages.

hyperlink Colored, underlined text that you can click to open another file or go to a Web address.

I

import The process of converting and opening a file that was stored or created in another program. See also export.

insertion point A flashing vertical line that shows the text entry point. Also referred to as the cursor.

Internet The worldwide network of networks, in which everyone is connected to everyone else.

Internet Explorer A popular Web browser program included with Microsoft Office.

Internet service provider (ISP) A private enterprise that provides a server through which you can connect to the Internet, usually for a small fee (also called Local service provider and mail service).

intranet A miniature Internet that operates within a company or organization.

J–L

key The criteria by which a list is sorted.

label Text you provide to identify data, such as column headings.

Landscape The horizontal orientation of a page; opposite of Portrait, or vertical, orientation.

legend A chart element you can add to Excel charts that tell what each data series on the chart represents.

link To copy an object, such as a graphic or text, from one file or program to another so that a dependent relationship exists between the object and its source file. The dependent object is updated whenever the data changes in the source object.

list A range of cells containing data that is related to a particular subject or purpose. In Excel, the terms list and database are used interchangeably.

Local service provider See Internet service provider.

M

mail merge The process of creating several identical documents (such as form letters or mailing labels) that each pull a different set of information (such as addresses) out of a database.

mail service See Internet service provider.

mathematical operators Characters that tell Excel which calculations to perform, such as * (multiply), + (add), - (subtract), and / (divide).

maximize To enlarge the program window to its maximum screen size.

merge fields The placeholder text in a mail merge document where database information is inserted in each finished, or merged, copy of the document.

message An email message, or any text typed into the large message box in an item dialog box.

minimize To reduce the program window to a button on the taskbar.

mixed reference A combination of a relative reference and an absolute reference. A mixed reference takes the form $A1 or A$1, where A is the column cell address and 1 is the row cell address. The $ indicates the fixed, or absolute, part of the reference.

N–O

name   A unique identifier you create to refer to one or more cells. When you use names in a formula, the formula is easier to read and maintain than a formula containing cell references.

object   A table, chart, graphic, equation, or other form of information you create and edit. An object can be inserted, pasted, or copied into any file.

Office Assistant   Animated Office help system that provides interactive help, tips, and other online assistance.

OLE   Short for object linking and embedding, the technology that allows different programs to share data.

order of precedence   In Excel formulas, Excel calculates the values based on the order of operator precedence, performing calculations on all values and operators in parentheses first, then exponential equations, then multiplication and division, and finally addition and subtraction.

Outlook Bar   The vertical bar on the left side of the Outlook window; the Outlook Bar contains icons for Outlook features and folders.

Outlook Bar group   A group of icons displayed in the Outlook Bar, such as the Mail group, the Outlook group, and the Other group; display a group by clicking the button for that group.

P

palette   A box containing choices for color and other special effects that you use when designing a form, report, or other object. A palette appears when you click a toolbar button, such as Border or Fill Color. See also floating palette.

Personal Address Book   An address book that is separate from Contacts, although it stores similar information (name, address, phone numbers, email address, and so on). In a Personal Address Book you can create Personal Distribution Lists (which cannot be created in Contacts).

Personal Distribution List   A group of names and email addresses; when you send mail to a personal distribution list, the email goes to everyone on the list.

PivotTable   A special Excel table that analyzes data from other lists and tables.

plot area   The area of a chart in which data is plotted. In 2D charts, it is bounded by the axes and encompasses the data markers and gridlines. In 3D charts, the plot area includes the chart's walls, axes, and tick-mark labels.

Portrait   The vertical orientation of a page; opposite of Landscape, or horizontal, orientation.

PowerPoint   A presentation program designed to create and view slide show programs and other types of visual presentations.

precision   The number of digits Excel uses when calculating values. By default, Excel calculates with a maximum of 15 digits of a value (full precision).

Preview   A view that displays your document as it will appear when you print it. Items such as text and graphics appear in their actual positions.

primary key   A field in an Access table that supplies entries to a corresponding field in another Access table. For example, a table containing information about customers might supply customer names to a table containing order information.

print area   An area of a worksheet that is specified to be printed.

Q–R

query   A set of criteria that tells Access to extract data from a database, sort the data, and arrange it for a report.

range   Two or more cells on a sheet. Ranges can be contiguous or discontiguous.

record   A single row in a database or list. The first row of a database usually contains field names, and each additional row in the database is a record.

reference   The location of a cell or range of cells on a worksheet, indicated by column letter and row number.

reference type   The type of reference: absolute, relative, or mixed.

relative reference   Specifies the location of a referenced cell in relation to the cell containing the reference. A relative reference takes the form A4, C12, and so on.

report   A tool in Access that lets you extract data and create a report you can print and view.

row   A horizontal set of cells. Each row is identified by a unique number.

S

scenario   A named set of input values that you can substitute in a worksheet model to perform a what-if analysis.

ScreenTips   Helpful notes that appear on your screen to explain a function or feature.

server   A computer used on the Internet or a network environment that stores email messages, Web pages, and other data.

shareware   Software programs, created by individuals or smaller software firms, that are usually available for a reasonable cost after you try them out.

sheet tab   The name tab at the bottom of a worksheet that identifies the worksheet.

shortcut keys   Keyboard keys you can press to operate commonly used commands instead of using the mouse.

slide show   A visual presentation you can create with PowerPoint which uses text, graphics, and other effects. Use slideshows for business presentations, training presentations, and other tasks that require visual presentations.

sort   A method of organizing items so that you can find the items you want easily.

sort key   The field name or criteria by which you want to sort data.

source   The document or program in which the data was originally created.

split bar   The horizontal or vertical line dividing a split worksheet or document. You can change the position of the split bar by dragging it, or you can remove the split bar by double-clicking it.

style   A collection of formatting settings you can apply to text.

T

tab, sheet   The name at the bottom of a worksheet that identifies and selects the worksheet.

table   Data about a specific topic that is stored in records (rows) and fields (columns).

taskbar   The horizontal bar across the bottom of the Windows desktop; it includes the Start button and buttons for any programs, documents, or items that are open.

template   Available in Word, Excel, and Publisher, templates provide predesigned patterns on which Office documents can be based.

toolbar   A collection of frequently used commands that appear as icon buttons you can click to activate.

U–Z

URL (uniform resource locator)   A Web site address.

value   A numeric entry in a spreadsheet or database program.

Web   See World Wide Web.

Windows Clipboard   A temporary holding area in computer memory that stores the last set of information that was cut or copied (such as text or graphics). You transfer data from the Clipboard by using the Paste command. The Windows Clipboard can hold up to twelve cut or copied items.

wizards   A set of dialog boxes that ask you questions to walk you through processes such as creating a file or an object based on your answers.

Word   A popular word processing program used to create text-based documents.

workbook   An Excel document that contains one or more worksheets or chart sheets.

worksheet   A set of rows, columns, and cells in which you store and manipulate data. Several worksheets can appear in one workbook, and you can switch among them easily by clicking their tabs with the mouse.

World Wide Web (WWW)   The part of the Internet where Web sites are posted and available to Web browsers.

X axis   On most charts, categories are plotted along the X axis. On a typical column chart, the X axis is the horizontal axis.

Y axis   On most charts, data values are plotted along the Y axis. On a typical column chart, the Y axis is the vertical axis. When a secondary axis is added, it is a secondary Y axis.

Index

A

F

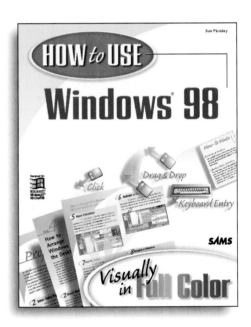